T0330409

Management and Industry in Russia

Management and Industry in Russia

Formal and Informal Relations in the Period of Transition

Edited by Simon Clarke

Professor of Sociology
Centre for Comparative Labour Studies
University of Warwick
Coventry, UK

MANAGEMENT AND INDUSTRY IN RUSSIA SERIES

Centre for Comparative Labour Studies, Warwick
Institute for Comparative Labour Relations Research, Moscow

Edward Elgar

Published by
Edward Elgar Publishing Limited
Gower House
Croft Road
Aldershot
Hants GU11 3HR
England

Edward Elgar Publishing Company
Old Post Road
Brookfield
Vermont 05036
USA

British Library Cataloguing in Publication Data

Clarke, Simon
Management and Industry in Russia: Formal and Informal Relations in the Period of Transition.
    I. Clarke, Simon
    338.0947

Library of Congress Cataloguing in Publication Data

Management and industry in Russia : formal and informal relations in the
  period of transition / edited by Simon Clarke.
    256p. 22cm.
    Includes bibliographical references and index.
    1. Industrial relations—Russia (Federation) 2. Management—Russia
(Federation) 3. Russia (Federation)—Economic conditions—1991–
I. Clarke, Simon, 1946–
HD8530.2.M36 1995
331'.0947—dc20

95–4048
CIP

ISBN 1 85898 062 3

Printed in Great Britain at the University Press, Cambridge

Contents

Preface

The papers collected in this volume have all been written within the framework of a collaborative research project on the restructuring of management and industrial relations in Russia directed by Simon Clarke and Peter Fairbrother of the Centre for Comparative Labour Studies, University of Warwick.[1] The research has been conducted since 1991 by teams of Russian researchers in four contrasting regions of Russia: Moscow, Samara, Kuzbass and the Komi Republic.[2] In 1994 this research collaboration was institutionalised with the establishment of a new inter-regional Centre for Comparative Labour Studies, based in Moscow.

The core of the research is a series of intensive longitudinal case studies of between two and four enterprises in each region which have been studied continuously since the beginning of the period of reform at the end of 1991. In general two researchers work in each enterprise, one focusing on management, down to the level of shop chief, and the other focusing on shop floor relations. The research uses a wide range of qualitative and ethnographic research methods which are well established in Western sociology, but which were and remain largely unfamiliar in Russia. The research on which these papers are based was therefore path-breaking in being the first to be able to use qualitative and ethnographic research methods to explore the reality of production relations in the Soviet enterprise.[3]

Alongside the case studies, each research team has been monitoring the economic, social and political development of their region, including developments in other enterprises, following up local press and documentary sources with interviews and attendance at meetings. Interview transcripts and field notes are regularly written up and circulated to all the research groups, with enterprise reports being updated every three months. The progress of the research is discussed at regular weekly meetings of each of the research teams, at which the materials circulated by the other groups are also discussed. All the researchers meet together for residential seminars of between three and five days every six months.

On the basis of the initial fieldwork the individual researchers identified separate research themes around which to develop their own research, individually or in groups, within the broader framework of the project as a whole. This volume brings together papers which address different aspects of the relation between formal and informal relations in production. A companion volume will be published shortly, comprising a set of papers around the theme of conflict and change in the post-Soviet enterprise, and a further volume will bring together case study reports of the enterprises which have been the focus of the research.[*]

The research themes addressed in this volume were initially identified and discussed at a seminar in Moscow in April 1993, and the first draft of each paper was written on the basis of fieldwork in the author's own enterprise, with additional material drawn from interview transcripts and research reports generated by the other case study enterprises. These drafts were discussed extensively at the weekly meetings of the relevant local research groups before being circulated to the other groups over the summer of 1993. The revised papers were then presented to a seminar held in Samara in September 1993, and were further revised and developed over the following six months. Thus, although each paper is individually authored and emerges from research in one particular enterprise, each has been through a long process of collective discussion and elaboration on the basis of comparative data.

The papers have been translated from the Russian by Simon Clarke, in consultation with the authors and with help and advice from Vadim Borisov and Marina Kiblitskaya. Our original intention had been to rewrite the papers for a Western readership. However once the papers were completed we decided that this would be to distort an analysis which derives from a Russian context. We have therefore tried to keep the translations true to the style and analysis of the originals, so that they convey something not only of the object of the research, but also of the way in which the researchers think of that object. This means that we have not attempted to translate the original Russian into a non-sexist English, or to remove forms of expression which to Western readers may smack of political incorrectness, although we have discussed the substantive issues extensively with our collaborators.

The introduction to the book has been written by Simon Clarke on the basis of material which has similarly been prepared, circulated and discussed among the research teams. Although the book was prepared by Simon Clarke, Peter Fairbrother has been a full and close collaborator at all stages of its preparation.

Our research project is continuing for as long as we can secure the funding to sustain it (and any offers would be most welcome). In addition to the forthcoming publications already referred to, other results of our research can be found in the following publications:

PROJECT PUBLICATIONS

Simon Clarke, 'Pochemu Krizis porazil sovietskuyu sistemu?', *Ezhegodnik Sotsiologicheskie Ocherki*, 2, Moscow, 1992.

Simon Clarke and Peter Fairbrother, 'The Workers' Movement in Russia', *Capital and Class*, 49, London, 1992, pp. 7–17.

Vadim Borisov, 'The Fall of Russia's Exchange and Mart', *Guardian*, London, June, London, 1992.

Simon Clarke, 'Privatisation and the Development of Capitalism in Russia', *New Left Review*, 196, November/December, London, 1992, pp. 3–27.

Simon Clarke and Petr Bizyukov, 'Privatisation in Russia: The Road to a People's Capitalism?', *Monthly Review*, 44, 6, New York, 1992, pp. 38–45.

Simon Clarke, Peter Fairbrother, Michael Burawoy and Pavel Krotov, *What about the Workers? Workers and the Transition to Capitalism in Russia*, Verso, London, 1993.

Simon Clarke, 'Popular attitudes to the transition to a market economy in the Soviet Union on the eve of Reform', *Sociological Review*, 41, 4, Keele, 1993, pp. 619–52.

Vadim Borisov, 'The Name Game', *New Statesman*, 19 March, London, 1993.

Veronika Kabalina and Alla Nazimova, 'Privatisation through Labour Conflicts the Case of Russia', *Economic and Industrial Democracy*, 14, Stockholm, 1993, pp. 9–28.

Galina Monousova and Veronika Kabalina, 'A Record of Labour Action Starting from 12 June, 1991', *Economics and Industrial Democracy*, 14, Stockholm, 1993, pp. 133–41.

Simon Clarke, 'Trade Unions, Industrial Relations and Politics in Russia', *Journal of Communist Studies*, 9, 4, London, 1993, pp. 133–160.

Leonid Gordon, Veronika Kabalina and Alla Nazimova, 'Sotsial'no-
trudovye konflicty pri perekhode k rynochnoi ekonomike',
Obshchestvo i Ekonomika, 2, Moscow, 1993, pp. 3–19.

Simon Clarke and Peter Fairbrother, 'The Emergence of Industrial
Relations in the Workplace', Richard Hyman and Anthony Ferner
(eds), *New Frontiers in European Industrial Relations*, Blackwell,
Oxford, 1994, pp. 368–397.

Simon Clarke, 'Trade Unions, Industrial Relations and Politics in
Russia', Martin Myint and Michael Waller (eds): *Parties, Trade
Unions and Society in East-Central Europe*, Frank Cass, London,
1994, pp. 133–60.

Vadim Borisov, Peter Fairbrother and Simon Clarke, 'Is There Room
for an Independent Trade Unionism in Russia? The Case of the
Federation of Air Traffic Controllers' Unions', *British Journal of
Industrial Relations*, 32, 3, London, 1994, pp. 359–378.

Vadim Borisov, Simon Clarke and Peter Fairbrother, 'Does Trade
Unionism have a Future in Russia?', *Industrial Relations Journal*,
25, 1, Glasgow, 1994, pp. 15–25.

Simon Clarke, Peter Fairbrother and Vadim Borisov, 'The New
Workers' Movement in Russia', *Critique*, 26, Glasgow, 1994, pp.
55–68.

Simon Clarke, Peter Fairbrother Vadim Borisov and Petr Bizyukov,
'The Privatisation of Industrial Enterprises in Russia: Four Case
Studies', *Europe-Asia Studies*, 46, 2, Glasgow, 1994, pp. 179–214.

Simon Clarke and Vadim Borisov, 'Reform and Revolution in the
Communist National Park', *Capital and Class*, 53, London, 1994,
pp. 9–14.

Simon Clarke, 'The Politics of Labour and Capital', S. White, A.
Pravda and Z. Gitelman (eds): *Developments in Russian and Post-
Soviet Politics*, Macmillan, Harmondsworth, 1994.

Veronika Kabalina and Tanya Metalina, 'Mozhno li izbezhat'
Bezrabotnitsy', *Novoe Rabochee i Profsoyuznoe Dvizhenie*, 2,
Moscow, 1994, pp. 65–77.

Vadim Borisov, 'Komu Plachem?', *EKO*, 11, Novosibirsk, 1994, pp.
85–103.

Galina Monousova, 'Attitude a l'égard des syndicats dans les
entreprises de l'industrie: les réalités de la transition', *Les Syndicats
en Russie: Problèmes politiques et sociaux*, serie Russie, 724, 25
mars, Paris, 1994, pp. 33–4.

Valentina Vedeneeva, 'Promyshlenye predpriyatiya v perexodnyi period – case study', *Working Papers of Stockholm Institute of East European Economics*, Stockholm, 1994.

Veronika Kabalina and Tanya Metalina, 'Sotsial'nye mekhanismy politiki zanyatosti na rossiskix prepriyatiyax v 1992–gg', *Mirovaya Ekonomika i Mezhdunarodnye Otnosheniya*, 7, Moscow, 1994.

Galina Monousova, 'Profsoyuzy na promyshlennyx predpriyatiyax: realii perekhodnogo perioda', *Profsoyuzy v Rossii*, June–July, Moscow, 1994.

Vadim Borisov, 'A Very Soviet Privatisation', *Labour Focus on Eastern Europe*, 47, 1994, pp. 37–41.

Petr Bizyukov, 'The Social and Political Situation in the Kuzbass', *Labour Focus on Eastern Europe*, 47, 1994, pp. 31–36.

NOTES

1   The research was funded by the University of Warwick Research and Innovations Fund, and subsequently by the East-West Programme of the British Economic and Social Research Council, Grant Y309253049.

2   In addition to the authors credited in this volume the following have participated in the collective elaboration of the papers: Peter Fairbrother, Irina Kozina, Tanya Metalina, Igor Mansurov, Veronika Bizyukova, Lena Varshavskaya, Inna Donova, Olga Pulyaeva, Kostya Burnishev, Vladimir Ilyin, Pasha Krotov, Marina Ilyina, Veronika Kabalina, Galya Monoussova, Vadim Borisov, Elain Bowers.

     The papers by Pasha Romanov and Lena Lapshova and Irina Tartakovskaya were presented to the International Labour Process Conference, Aston University, Birmingham and the BASEES Conference, University of Cambridge, in March 1994. Marina Kiblitskaya's paper was also presented to the International Labour Process Conference.

3   We continue to refer to the system of production as Soviet, despite the collapse of the wider Soviet system, because the fundamental relations of the enterprise have changed little, despite the dramatic changes in the external environment.

4   These volumes are to be published by Edward Elgar as *Conflict and Change in the Restructuring of the Russian Enterprise*, and as *The Russian Enterprise in Transition: Case Studies*. All names in this volume have been changed to preserve the anonymity of enterprises and informants.

The Authors

Sergei Alasheev is a researcher in the Sociology Laboratory of Samara State Pedagogical University. Sergei was born in 1959, and worked as an electrician on leaving middle school in 1977, and then as a fourth grade tester of electronic components in an instrument-making factory in Samara. He became an enthusiastic amateur archaeologist and ethnographer. In 1987 he graduated from Samara State University and joined the Sociology Laboratory of the Pedagogical Institute. This work was close to his youthful interests and allowed him to continue to join archaeological and ethnographic expeditions in his free time. His main responsibility was for the computer analysis of sociological data. However his participation in this research project has allowed him to combine his interests and to develop the use of case-study methods in industrial enterprises.

Petr Bizyukov was born in Magadan in 1959, and now lives in Kemerovo in Western Siberia. He graduated from the Economics Faculty of Kemerovo State University in 1983, immediately moving into research on the economics and sociology of labour, joining Boris Proshkin's team of radical young researchers who were very active in the early years of perestroika. Since 1992 Petr has been scientific director of his Sociology Laboratory in the Economics Faculty of Kemerovo State University. He has carried out a wide range of research, mostly in the coal industry, and acts as a consultant to the regional organisation of the Independent Miners' Union. Petr not only studies paternalism, but aspires to be a paternalist himself. His wife and children humour his ambition.

Lena Lapshova was born in 1965. After graduation from the Samara Pedagogical Institute she worked as a schoolteacher, but with perestroika she joined the independent sociological centre Sotsio, which became the Sociology Laboratory of the Pedagogical Institute. She has participated in a series of sociological research projects dealing with industrial relations and with different aspects of cultural and political life. She is married with a beautiful little daughter, and has just returned to the Sociology Laboratory from maternity leave.

Irina Tartakovskaya was born in 1964. She graduated with distinction from the Historical Faculty of Samara University and was unemployed. Her scientific interests, apart from industrial sociology, include political sociology and the sociology of culture. She has just completed her candidate's dissertation in the sociology of literature. Her hobbies are journalism and literary criticism, and she is interested in the ideas of feminism. She has a husband and a dog.

Pavel Romanov was born in 1964 into a family of office workers in the metallurgical complex. He is married and bringing up a daughter. Before he became a sociologist he was involved in a range of very different activities. He worked as an unskilled labourer and as a fitter in a factory and worked in a Siberian national park. After a five year break to study for a degree in biology at Samara University, he was one of the founders of the independent sociological centre Sotsio, where he worked on various political and socio-economic themes, and finally worked in the Laboratory of the Samara Pedagogical University. His interests include management of industrial enterprises and the specific socio-cultural features of Russian industry.

Marina Kiblitskaya was born in Moscow in 1962. She graduated in philosophy from Moscow university in 1987 and was awarded her candidate's degree in sociology in 1993. Marina attended the summer school for Soviet sociologists in Manchester in 1992, and is now studying for a doctorate with a Soros scholarship at the University of Warwick. She has been studying industrial conflict in various enterprises for several years, and is now conducting a comparative study of her Russian enterprise with its British equivalent. Marina recently divorced, and combines her research with caring for her son Sasha.

Valentina Vedeneeva was born in Rostov in 1951. She graduated in history from Moscow University in 1975, and was awarded her candidate's decree for a dissertation on the history of the Polish workers' movement in 1986. She has worked as a scientific researcher since 1975, initially in the Gorki House Museum, then in the Institute for the International Labour Movement, the Institute of Employment, and now in the Centre for Comparative Social and Economic Research of the Institute of World Economy and International Relations.

1. Formal and Informal Relations in Soviet Industrial Production

Simon Clarke

INFORMAL RELATIONS IN SOVIET AND SOVIETOLOGICAL RESEARCH

The Soviet ideology of production has always been very strongly technologistic, with the organisation and management of production based on the concept of the 'scientific organisation of labour', according to which the social organisation of labour is largely determined by technological characteristics of the production process. The scientific organisation of labour was embodied in reams of technical and normative documents which defined the labour and production process in minute detail, in a managerial hierarchy that was dominated by engineers, and in a formal system of accreditation of employees according to their level of technical education and training. The formal system was developed in various research and technical institutes which drew up and revised the normative documents on the basis of technical specifications of equipment and production processes and a conception of the social organisation of production as a reflection of its technical characteristics, based on the non-antagonistic co-operation of individuals and social groups within a collective production effort.[1]

The formalism of the 'scientific organisation of labour' could not possibly be adequate to the everyday reality of production, marked by shortages of labour, equipment and supplies, by regular breakdowns and disruptions, and by its necessary reliance on the initiative of real human beings. In practice production was only possible because the formal norms were regularly violated and ignored, production at every level being dominated by informal norms and relationships in which the personal qualities of individual workers and managers could play a decisive role. However the formalism of the normative documents could not be dispensed with, as it was dictated by the need for a framework within which to assert a rigidly hierarchical and centralised control over the use and allocation of resources and the achievement of plan targets. Although everybody knew that the technical and normative documents were rarely read, let alone adhered to, they provided a basis on which sanctions could be legitimated against the formalistic rationality of bureaucratic norms, even though such sanctions were in practice largely discretionary and often arbitrary.

The role of informal relations in the Soviet system of production is something with which everybody in Russia has always been very familiar, and which has long featured, at least in the background, in Soviet fiction. Nevertheless it is something which was barely researched or even discussed by sociologists before the period of perestroika, despite the fact that industrial sociology and the sociology of labour occupied a leading place in the work of Soviet sociologists from the middle of the 1970s.[2]

We can crudely distinguish two levels at which this sociological work was carried out. At a general level was work which was not so much to establish the reality of everyday production relations in industrial enterprises as to define the specific features of 'socialist' methods of production and the specifically non-antagonistic character of social relations in the production process in 'socialist enterprises', emphasising the importance of such factors as the identification of the individual with the collective, the elevation of the 'cultural' and educational level of the labour force, the reduction of absenteeism and labour turnover, or the constructive use of free as well as working time. This work was conducted primarily in research institutes, mostly at an abstract level, and rested on a restricted empirical base, primarily of quantitative survey data. Its practical purpose was to provide guidelines for the formation of the social development plans of enterprises, which were given an increasingly important role through the 1970s as the 'human factor' came to be seen as an important contributor to labour productivity. The best of such research, primarily that of the 'Krushchev generation', contained a subversive element in its repeated stress on the importance of job control, the integration of mental and manual labour, and the positive virtues of increased worker participation.[3]

Soviet sociology certainly recognised problems of labour discipline and labour motivation under socialism, and one of its primary purposes was to identify the causes of such anti-social behaviour in order to provide remedies. This more concrete kind of research was carried out primarily at the local level, particularly through the hundreds of sociology departments attached to large industrial enterprises and to regional Party and Komsomol Schools, and the vast majority of it was unpublished. However this research had a predominantly social-psychological character, the defects of the system of production being attributed to the psychological and moral characteristics of individual workers and managers and specific deficiencies of their educational formation and social environment. This research produced innumerable indices and correlations of satisfaction, of social cohesion, of labour motivation, of the moral-psychological climate and of leadership qualities, and was used primarily in the attempt to improve the training and social organisation of labour, as well as to identify candidates for recruitment to leadership positions.

Perestroika and glasnost created new conditions for sociological research, but most of the leading industrial sociologists turned to political questions and to the development of sociological education, while many enterprise sociology departments were cut back or closed, so that there was a massive decline in research and publication in the field.' This was not just a matter of the decline in research funding and of changing research priorities, but also of the fact that the existing sociological tradition did not provide the theoretical and methodological resources to take advantage of the situation and to develop new research questions.' Thus, to the best of our knowledge, there has not been a single book or article published by a Russian researcher in the past five years that contains detailed description or analysis, or is based on a detailed description of the real life of a Russian industrial enterprise. The majority of publications contain either abstract theoretical analysis or are devoted to macro-economic processes in the country, using federal, and more rarely departmental, statistics, the results of public opinion surveys touching on industrial issues, and occasionally interviews with enterprise directors. The few books and articles published in the last five years which have been based on enterprise level research have largely remained within the traditional framework, although there is a small amount of work which contains interesting material.'

Western Sovietologists have been able to guess at the significance of informal relations, but have never been able to get more than a glimpse of their reality. The foundations of the Western understanding of the Soviet enterprise were laid by the classic studies of Granick, based primarily on press reports, and Berliner, based primarily on interviews with émigrés, which focused on the management structures that developed in the 1930s.[7] More recent studies have built on these classics, using the same type of sources, without modifying their essential features.[8]

The main focus of the classic studies was the horizontal and vertical connections of enterprises with other supplier and customer enterprises, state bodies and Party organisations. In these relations the importance of informal and personal connections in the negotiation of plan targets and in the acquisition of scarce resources was emphasised,[9] but analysis of the internal functioning of the enterprise was necessarily sketchy.[10]

Studies of the organisation of the labour process in Soviet enterprises have been few and far between, and have been severely constrained and conditioned by the sources on which they have been forced to rely.[11] Until recently the most valuable sources remained the memoirs of those Western specialists who worked in Russia, usually as engineers, during the 1930s.[12] As noted above, the two interview projects on which most US research was based were dominated by a political concern with senior management and political structures and barely touched on the internal relations of the enterprise. Mary McAuley's study of labour disputes uses a range of materials to provide a unique insight into shop-floor relations.[13] Don Filtzer's work has used an extensive range of newspaper sources, official reports and research data to document Ticktin's argument that labour shortage gave Soviet workers an unprecedented degree of control over the labour process, at least in the negative sense of being able to resist the imposition of work and production discipline, expressed in high levels of inefficiency, lack of co-ordination and waste.[14] While Filtzer's work has been pioneering in establishing the barriers that confront central control of management and managerial control of the labour process, his interpretation is strongly influenced by the sources on which he has relied, which have primarily been those which report disciplinary violations and the negative features of worker behaviour, bemoaning low levels of discipline as part of orchestrated campaigns (the other side of the reports extolling worker heroism and commitment on which apologists for the Soviet Union have relied). Thus, while raising the question of the resistance of workers as a barrier to managerial control of production, for obvious reasons Filtzer has little direct evidence to support his interpretation of the Soviet labour process, and tells us little about how production actually is organised or how workers actually are motivated to work.

Direct evidence of the social organisation of production within the Soviet enterprise has only become available very recently. Sergei Belanovskii and his associates conducted a series of fascinating interviews through the 1980s.[15] David Mandel has also published a selection of his extremely interesting interviews, mostly with worker activists.[16] However, valuable as they are, these collections comprise discrete interviews with usually atypical and somewhat marginal individuals (e.g. workers with higher education, politically active workers), giving us an insight into the social organisation of production, but only a partial picture.

The first Western sociologist to study the Soviet labour process from within was Michael Burawoy, building on his earlier experience of work in industrial enterprises in Hungary, the US and Zambia.[17] His first study, jointly with Kathryn Hendley, focused on management reorganisation in a Moscow enterprise, but in his second study, in collaboration with Pavel Krotov, he worked on the shop-floor in a furniture factory for several months.[18]

It is not surprising that with such scanty information there has been a strong tendency within the Sovietological literature to over-generalisation. We began our own research with a thorough reading of the existing Western literature, from which we emerged with the idea that our task was to identify the characteristics of the typical Soviet enterprise, against which to measure the changes taking place under the impact of the introduction of market relations. We soon discovered that it is very difficult to generalise about the Soviet enterprise, since every enterprise has a life and a personality of its own.

The problem of generalisation, or of identifying the significant determinants of variation, is not a lack of information, but the fact that there are so many important variables, and because the scope of informal relations is so great that personality can play a decisive role in defining the characteristics of a particular shop or enterprise. At this stage of the research we have therefore been trying to resist the temptation to generalise prematurely, and to keep our analysis rooted in the enterprises in which we have conducted our research, to provide a firm basis on which to generalise at a later stage of the research, building on the mass of materials we now have at our disposal, and seeing the patterns which emerge through a longer process of change. For the same reasons we have resisted the temptation to develop the comparative dimension of the research, for fear of dissolving the distinctive features of the Soviet enterprise by focusing on superficial similarities with enterprises in the capitalist world.[19]

WHY DO RUSSIAN WORKERS WORK?

The question that provided a central theme of the first stage of our research into shop-floor relations was: how, under Soviet conditions, are workers induced to work at all? This question arose for Peter Fairbrother and myself on the basis of our reading of the Western sovietological literature and our superficial knowledge of the conditions under which Soviet workers were compelled to work. But it also arose for our Russian collaborators, for most of whom the world of the shop-floor was almost as much of a closed book as it was for us. Although the majority of our collaborators came from working class families, and most had worked in factories as students, or for longer periods before going to university, most of them had acquired the Russian intelligentsia's disdain for the world of work and workers, thinking even of their own experience through the stereotypes of the intelligentsia.

According to the Western literature on the Soviet enterprise management would appear to have few levers of control over the workers. Although the KGB kept a close watch on the activity of workers and any public expression of dissent could be ruthlessly suppressed, management had few negative sanctions to wield against individual workers in conditions of acute labour shortage, where workers could simply leave to find a job elsewhere, so that it was often impossible to sack workers even for persistent drunkenness and absenteeism and workers had to be guaranteed a regular income more or less regardless of performance.

Even where disciplinary sanctions were available, in conditions of acute supply shortages, inadequate raw materials and frequent breakdowns and interruptions in production, the shop management depended not on the passive compliance but on the positive commitment of workers. However the formal payment system provided few positive incentives since it provided little connection between effort and reward in circumstances in which the worker's ability to meet the norms on which his or her pay depended was determined not by her own efforts so much as by external circumstances. Moreover, while the pay of shop chiefs and engineering-technical staff (ITR) depended on the shop and the plant meeting its monthly plan, the pay of workers depended only on their meeting their individual norms, which were not necessarily consistent with the overall plan, particularly if the shop in question was, as was often the case, understaffed.

The paradox is further reinforced when we note that not only did managers have few sanctions and limited incentives to induce the workers to work, they also appear to have enjoyed very little authority in the eyes of the workers. Although managers and ITR in general enjoyed better working conditions and more privileges than manual workers, until recently their pay was lower than that of skilled workers. There is a wide range of evidence to indicate that Soviet workers have a very sharp consciousness of their class position, based on the rhetoric of seventy years of 'socialism' which has defined manual labour alone as productive, and this evidence is confirmed by our own experience as workers regularly declaimed against the parasites in their offices, in the administration building, or on the fifth floor.

Nevertheless, although management lacked authority in the eyes of the workers, and appeared to have few positive or negative levers of influence over the workers, Soviet workers were not only induced to work, in often appalling conditions, but showed high levels of positive commitment to overcome technical and supply difficulties, frequently working double shifts and weekends without additional pay, in order to meet the plan month in and month out. Our initial idea that such commitment was driven by the fear of repressive sanctions was not confirmed by our interviews and observation.

For all of us involved in the research our interviews and meetings with shop-floor workers and line managers in the first stage of our research soon brought home to us the inadequacy of the stereotypes of the Russian intelligentsia and the inappropriateness of the Western model of the Soviet enterprise. Our collaborators were surprised at the articulateness and self-consciousness of the workers with whom they talked, and at the complexity, diversity and sophistication of the social relations and understandings on the shop-floor. Each of our collaborators soon acquired a close attachment and loyalty to his or her enterprise. We were all also surprised at the extent to which every shop and every enterprise has a character of its own, defined by its own history, the characteristics of the labour force, and the style and personality of its management, so that there is no such thing as the 'typical' Soviet enterprise. Nevertheless we soon came to identify three fundamental respects in which we felt that the orthodox Western model on the basis of which we had initially approached our research was inadequate.

First, the Western model has tended to be based on a view of the labour force as an homogeneous mass. It has long been known that conditions in enterprises of the military-industrial complex have been very different from those in light industry and services, with better working conditions, higher levels of pay and stronger discipline in the former branch. It has also been well known that within enterprises there has been a distinction between the core *aktiv* or *kadrovi* workers, who have participated in production conferences, socialist competition and Party and trade union activities, and the remainder of the labour force. However the basis and significance of these distinctions has never been systematically explored, either theoretically or empirically. We therefore started with the hypothesis that the internal stratification of the labour force played an important role in the management and regulation of production. This internal stratification is extremely complex, but we can indicate three key features.

First, within the ranks of manual workers there is a clear distinction between basic production workers, who contribute directly to making the product, and auxiliary workers, whether they be cleaners, store-keepers and loaders or highly skilled fitters, setters and toolmakers. Similarly, within the ranks of the basic production workers those who are closest to the finished product tend to enjoy higher status than those involved in the preparatory phases of production.

Second, within the ranks of the labour force there is a clear status hierarchy based on age and experience, with older and more highly skilled workers enjoying higher prestige and more privileges than younger or less skilled workers. The privileged position of such older and more experienced workers is also connected with their participation in networks of informal personal relationships with workers and managers in other shops and plants, right up to the level of General Director, built up over the years.

Third, the status hierarchy has a strong moral dimension based on the individual's personal qualities, often referred to as his or her 'cultural level', expressed negatively in drunkenness, lack of diligence at work, and the inappropriate use of bad language, and positively in activism and positive commitment both at work and in the social and political sphere. Such committed workers were prime candidates for promotion to managerial positions, because they enjoyed the respect of their fellow workers, but were not always willing to take the loss of pay and burden of responsibility that such promotion implied. The Party and trade union similarly sought to recruit such active and committed workers to their ranks, but this moral dimension of the status hierarchy was not necessarily coincident with Party member-ship – such active workers were not always willing to submit to Party discipline, while the Party was torn between its desire to recruit loyal and subservient cadres and its desire to preserve its authority by establishing a coincidence between the formal and the informal hierarchies.

Within the internal stratification of the labour force the more prestigious jobs were reserved for the more highly motivated workers, while those who did not show any commitment to their work tended to be restricted to unskilled auxiliary and routine administrative work. Similarly, the more privileged enterprises were able to select the best workers, while light industry and services had to make do with whomever they could find. Our initial hypothesis was that the threat of promotion and demotion within the hierarchy would provide a lever of managerial control.[20] However it soon became clear that there was relatively little mobility between these categories, with a fairly sharp cultural demarcation between the different strata.[21] Line managers relied on more subtle informal levers of day-to-day control, including such things as the allocation of more or less profitable work, discretionary payment of bonuses and the bestowal and withholding of a range of favours and benefits, the latter often in association with the trade union. However these more subtle mechanisms of managerial power are not sufficient to explain the positive motivation of Soviet workers. To explain this we have to refer to the ideological and cultural significance of labour in the Soviet system.

The second weakness of the Western model in our experience has been its relative neglect of the importance of the particular Soviet ideology of labour, which is connected with the strong moral dimension to the stratification of the labour force already noted. The ideology of labour is linked to the complex relationship between moral and material motivations of Soviet workers. Soviet survey data indicates that the primary motivation of less skilled workers is monetary, while more highly skilled workers derive more satisfaction from job content and job control than from their financial rewards. However, while such results would endorse the observations about the stratification of the labour force above, survey data is never a good indication of motivation, both because Soviet surveys have been strongly ideologically charged in their formulation and interpretation, and because of the gulf between what people say and what they do. The usual explanation for differences in motivation is to refer to the educational and 'cultural' level of individual workers, which is obviously correlated closely with skill level. However in our opinion the question of motivation cannot be addressed in such individualistic ways, but has to be related to the Soviet ideology of labour.

The Soviet ideology of labour is as much a moral as an economic ideology. The physical act of the collective engagement with nature is seen not simply as a means to produce goods to meet human needs, but more fundamentally as the means to achieve human dignity and self-realisation, so that the act of production has value in itself, regardless of the material rewards that might flow from it, and in extremis even regardless of the usefulness of its results. This ideology could not be more foreign to Western intellectuals, for whom the priority of mental over manual labour goes without saying, and for whom the measure of the value of labour is the monetary reward received by the labourer. However in Russia this ideology is not simply an abstract philosophy expressed in the rhetoric of the regime, but has been internalised by Soviet workers as the result of seventy years of systematic propaganda, despite the workers' scepticism and even contempt for the regime and its rituals, because this propaganda superimposed Soviet collectivism onto traditional craft and peasant conceptions of labour and of the interaction with nature, so that it is deeply embedded not only in workers' consciousness, but also in the everyday life and hierarchical structures of the enterprise. Thus, far from being atomised, individualised and alienated from their work, as some Western commentators suggest, the primary work group tends to show a high degree of solidarity and positive commitment to work. This orientation also defines a distinctive attitude to management on the part of workers.

The third major weakness of the Western conception of the Soviet enterprise was that it tended to be based on an implicit assumption that the plan played the same role as profit in defining a clear opposition of interest between workers and management. Although, as noted above, there is a lot of evidence that workers have a very clear consciousness of their class identity as productive labourers, and have a marked lack of confidence in management in general, at the same time there is equally much evidence to indicate that workers have a high level of confidence in their own managers, the degree of confidence being greater the closer they are to the manager in question. In our own experience workers frequently express their scornful contempt for all managers and specialists, only to make exceptions of their own managers.

This apparent paradox can be explained by the fact that, while workers see themselves as victims of an exploitative and irrational system, there are no clearly identifiable agents of this exploitation. The manager at each level has a dual role. On the one hand, the manager is an agent of the system in transmitting the demands sent down from above. But on the other hand the manager represents the interests of his or her subordinates, both in negotiating with higher authorities in order to minimise those demands and in providing the subordinates with the means to realise them.

At the level of the enterprise as a whole the General Director is the representative of the authority of the Ministry in ensuring that the labour collective of the enterprise realises the plan. However the primary function of the General Director from the point of view of the labour collective is to negotiate a realisable plan and subsequent plan revisions, to secure the necessary financial resources, equipment and raw materials to realise that plan, and to secure or divert the means to build up the social and welfare infrastructure of the enterprise. The primary function of the General Director is therefore to deal with the external relations of the enterprise to ensure that it has the resources it needs to enable the labour collective to realise its productive tasks. A 'good' General Director is not necessarily one who secures soft plan targets, but one who can provide the labour collective with the means to achieve those targets by showing strength in the face of other enterprises and central and local authorities. Within the enterprise the 'good' Director is the Director who is 'firm but fair', a Director who knows the technical production processes inside out, preferably having worked his (or exceptionally her) way up from the shop-floor, who regularly visits the shops and passes the time of day with workers and line managers, and who is accessible to those who have complaints and grievances.

The same kind of relationship is reproduced at the level of the shop, section and primary work group. The shop chief is responsible for ensuring the realisation of the shop plan, but his (or rarely her) primary function is to ensure that the supplies needed are forthcoming, that parts and semi-finished products are delivered from other shops, that equipment is delivered, installed and maintained, while filling in reams of forms and compiling endless reports. Thus the main focus of the work of the shop chief is not to manage the social relations of the shop in order to drive the workers to ever greater efforts, but to provide the workers with the means to do their job. A 'good' shop chief is not one who allows slack discipline, but one who enables workers to make or overfulfil their norms by providing them with the means to do the job. A 'good' shop in this sense is then able to attract more highly motivated and disciplined workers and enter a virtuous circle of harmony and prosperity. A 'bad' shop, on the other hand, is one with a weak shop chief who is unable to secure the necessary resources or maintain discipline within the shop, so that the better workers look for work elsewhere, and in the worst case the shop becomes a resting ground for 'drunkards, absentees and derelicts'.

A similar relationship obtains between the foreman and the primary work group. The foreman is usually responsible for the allocation of tasks to the workers under his or her command on a daily, weekly or monthly basis, but during the working day the foreman's primary tasks are to seek out raw materials, parts and supplies, to arrange the maintenance and repair of defective equipment, to monitor the technical coherence of production, to fill in more forms, and perhaps to assist less experienced workers. The foreman generally has very little authority over the workers under his or her command, depending for such authority on his or her proven skill at the job and ability to organise the production process.[22]

The result of this structure of control is that while conflict is ubiquitous, there are no clearly defined lines of vertical conflict within the enterprise and no clearly identifiable 'frontier of control'. The pace and intensity of work is determined by the plan, which is dictated to the enterprise and the shop from above, but within the limits of the plan the manager at each level represents the interests of his or her work group in securing necessary resources. The shortage of resources generates conflict at every level, as Ministries compete in Moscow, enterprises compete within the Ministry, shops within the enterprise, and sections, brigades and individual workers within the shops. The inter-dependence of production processes equally generates conflicts between groups which depend on one another – between customer and supplier enterprises as much as between production and auxiliary workers, or between shops or brigades which represent successive stages in the technological chain.

The outcome of this structure as far as shop-floor workers is concerned is that the source of their exploitation and oppression lies in the system as a whole, but within the system their managers tend to play the role of their representatives in securing the best conditions under which they can carry out their productive tasks. The concept of the 'labour collective' plays an important ideological role in defining the productive solidarity of the Soviet enterprise or shop as a unit of collective production. However production in conditions of scarcity means that the 'collectivism' of the labour collective is marked by a diffuse pattern of cross-cutting lines of solidarity and conflict, in which unambiguously solidary work relations are rarely found beyond the level of the primary work group, and in which competitive or conflictual relations tend to prevail once one moves beyond the level of the shop.

This ambiguous coexistence of solidarity and conflict defines the framework within which managers at every level have to use the formal and informal levers of influence at their disposal to induce the workers to work. It equally defines the framework within which conflict is articulated and diffused as workers maintain an ambiguous relationship of accommodation and resistance to the system. Although conflict is endemic to the system, the intricately cross-cutting lines of solidarity and conflict on the whole prevent such conflict from coalescing into significant collective mobilisations of the workers, since the tendency in the event of a conflict arising at one level of the system is to look to its resolution at the next highest level.[23] For example, workers aggrieved at their foreman will normally appeal to the section or shop chief, who will resolve the matter one way or another.

Within our own collective work we have tried to conceptualise this complex relation between accommodation and resistance, between solidarity and conflict, between the enterprise as a unit of collective production and the enterprise as the basic unit of a system of exploitation and oppression, in relation to the concept of paternalism. The idea of paternalism has been, and continues to be, the object of fierce debate within our group, and the term is perhaps inappropriate because its interpretation depends so much on one's understanding of fatherhood. Nevertheless we continue to use the term, sometimes qualified as 'authoritarian paternalism', because the exercise of power within the enterprise is closely associated with the rhetoric and symbolism of patriarchal authority.

FORMAL AND INFORMAL RELATIONS IN THE SOVIET SYSTEM OF PRODUCTION

The papers in this volume address the problem of formal and informal relations from a number of different perspectives.

The first two papers have both been written by Sergei Alasheev on the basis of his research in two large engineering factories in Samara, a city on the Volga dominated by the military-industrial complex.

In the first paper Sergei focuses on the role of informal relations in production, which he explains in terms of the inadequacy of the formal regulations to the requirements of production and of the producers. Sergei begins by describing the operation of informal relations in various spheres of production activity, and then classifies such relations in terms of the various deficiencies of the formal relations in response to which they arise. He goes on to identify three distinct types of informal relations: individual violations of established norms; informal relations which are embedded in systems of dependence and play a central role as levers of managerial control; and informal relations which have become institutionalised as norms of behaviour. He concludes his paper by examining the changes in the role of informal relations which are emerging as a result of the transition to a market economy. These changes involve a weakening of informal relations at the expense of formal regulation in some spheres, but also the emergence of new informal relations in other spheres of activity. However the most fundamental changes involve the replacement of ideological by monetary levers of management influence.

In his second paper Sergei addresses the question of the Soviet ideology of labour, his central thesis being the provocative claim that the specificity of Soviet production was defined by the fact that Soviet workers love to work. Work plays a central role in the lives of Russian workers in part because of the impoverished domestic and social conditions in which they live, in part as a legacy of the craft ideology which developed in the 1930s as workers had to make do and mend to achieve the targets set for them, and in part as a result of their internalisation of the Soviet ideology of labour. This orientation to work is expressed in and reproduced through the specifically 'non-technological' character of Soviet production, which stands in the starkest contrast to the rigidly technologistic conception that dominates the official ideology. Every technological process bears the mark of the worker who undertakes it, who has to use his or her skill to compensate for the inadequacies of equipment, parts and raw materials.

The result of such violations of formal technological discipline is not the high levels of waste or poor quality of production through which Don Filtzer believes Soviet workers express their resistance to the system, but the systematically non-standard character of production which makes it impossible to control the quality of the product. The outcome is not a uniformly low quality product, but a wide range of unpredictable variation, something which clearly creates acute problems in a plant such as that studied by Sergei, which produces precision bearings. Sergei concludes by raising the question of whether this ideology of labour is specific to the type of enterprise and categories of labour that he has studied, noting that such an ideology is much more deeply rooted in the older generation and in core production workers than among young people and among auxiliary workers. This ideology can therefore be expected to be eroded by the transition to the market economy. Sergei is now exploring this erosion by looking specifically at the impact of production for the Western market on the regulation of quality.

The third paper, by Petr Bizyukov, explores the complex relation between accommodation and resistance within the framework of the concept of paternalism. Petr's own research has been based primarily on coal mines in the Kuzbass in Western Siberia. He develops the concept of paternalism in close association with an examination of the role of coercion in the management of the Soviet enterprise, arguing that paternalism and coercion are two sides of the same coin of authoritarian management methods, with paternalistic elements growing from the 1960s following the relative decline in the use of coercive instruments of control, and being transferred from the state to the enterprise with the collapse of the administrative-command system. Petr concludes that the transition from paternalistic to market-oriented methods of management will be a slow, painful and conflict-ridden process.

Petr's arguments have been the object of considerable debate within our research groups. While the general framework of analysis is recognised as being fruitful, there is a widespread feeling that Petr's analysis of paternalism is too narrow in identifying the strength of paternalism with the material well-being of the enterprise and the prosperity of its workers, and characterising all other cases as instances of 'weak' or 'decaying' paternalism.

A more general view is expressed in the next paper, originally written by the Samara group in response to the first version of Petr's own paper. The core of this view is the argument that paternalism cannot be identified as a particular managerial strategy, which managers may chose to adopt or not, but has to be understood in terms of a particular form of social relation of authority and dependence which is deeply embedded in the structure of the enterprise and its forms of management and in the beliefs and expectations of its workers, which has deep cultural and historical roots, and which is reinforced by the state and the wider society. The Samara group argues in addition that paternalistic social relations have an asymmetrical structure, in the sense that there is no necessary concordance between the actions of management and the perceptions and responses of the managed, so that the structure of patriarchal relations is the negotiated outcome of the interaction of these two inconsistent aspects.

The implication of this latter approach is that the strength of paternalism is not necessarily associated with the provision of high levels of material well-being. Thus an impoverished enterprise may pay low wages, be unable to provide its workers with more than a bare minimum of benefits, and find itself laying off workers on a large scale without this necessarily undermining its paternalistic structure and ideology. The management can retain its paternalistic credentials if it is seen to be doing its best to protect the workers, for example by diverting all its funds to paying wages, by reducing lay-offs to the minimum, by offering short-time working or pay reductions as an alternative to lay-offs, by continuing to provide at least symbolic benefits to pensioners, and so on.

This approach also implies that Petr's identification of the strength of paternalism with the relative absence of conflict is questionable. Paternalism does not exclude conflict, but defines particular structural, cultural and ideological forms within which conflict is expressed and through which it develops. Thus it is quite possible for a strongly paternalistic enterprise also to be marked by high levels of conflict, while a weakly paternalistic enterprise may have low levels of conflict. Thus our general view is that Petr's paper provides not a final statement, but an important reference point for the further discussion of the character of Soviet paternalism.

The fifth paper, by Lena Lapshova and Irina Tartakovskaya, addresses the question of the position of women in Soviet production, based initially on research in a large Samara heavy engineering enterprise in which a bare majority of workers are women. Statistical evidence has long made clear the extent of horizontal and vertical discrimination against women, their inequality of wages and opportunities, their domination of the most monotonous work and of work in dangerous and unhealthy conditions, in violation of their proclaimed equality and of extensive protective legislation. However to the best of our knowledge this paper provides the first systematic exploration of the specific characteristics of female labour in an industrial enterprise.

Lena and Irina's paper provides a penetrating insight into the disadvantages suffered by women workers, showing the extent to which their subordination is embedded in the informal relations of the shop. However a major topic of debate within our research group has been the explanation of these disadvantages. At first most of our collaborators, male and female alike, were unwilling to accept that gender was a significant independent variable in defining the conditions of particular categories of work, a position which could be maintained because of the very high degree of gender segregation and the very sharp gender stereotyping of particular occupations. This means that it is certainly possible in principle to explain a large part of the disadvantage suffered by women in terms of features other than gender, although including the supposed psychological and physiological specificities of women. Thus women workers can be defined as being less ambitious than men, less work-oriented as a result of their domestic responsibilities, better able to tolerate monotonous work and work requiring high levels of patience and concentration, with lower levels of technical training, with more interrupted career histories, with higher levels of absenteeism and lateness as a result of domestic responsibilities. Women's domination of work in harmful conditions can be explained by their desire to augment low wages by earning the bonuses that such work attracts, their absence from better paid work a reflection of their lack of ambition and willingness to assume greater responsibilities.

Such arguments are still very familiar in the West, despite the impact of feminism, and so it should not be surprising to find them so strongly embedded in the deeply patriarchal Russian culture. In the West it has been possible to advance beyond such superficial explanations, to show that the supposed psychological, cultural and physical specificities that explain the subordinate position of women at work are merely complementary expressions of the subordination of women in society as a whole, but this has been not simply an intellectual exercise, but more fundamentally a reflection of the fact that women have increasingly resisted their subordination and sought to break through the supposedly insuperable barriers that confront them. In Russia women by no means passively accept their subordination, but their resistance and self-assertion continues largely to be confined within the limits of the role assigned to them, so that women are still almost as inclined as are men to accept the stereotypes with which they are branded.

Most of our collaborators still insist that age, education and skill are as important factors of social differentiation of the labour force as is gender, but they have come to recognise the importance of gender as an independent factor, and increasingly so as they have made gender an explicit object of their research. However to pose the problem is only to win half the battle.

The specific character of gender relations in Russia cannot be understood simply by chronicling the extent and patterns of inequality and disability suffered by women, and measuring their position against some universal scale. The historical development of gender relations in Russia in the course of industrialisation has been quite different from that in the Western industrial countries, so that the relations between men and women, the conceptions of gender identity and the forms of self-identification are different in quite fundamental ways. In particular, in the sphere of gender relations Russia did not experience the revolution associated in the West with the destruction of old structures by the rise of capitalism, but rather saw the transformation and reconstitution of 'traditional' gender relations under the control of the Soviet state, in which Soviet woman was ultimately the servant not of Soviet man but of the Soviet state. This raises fundamental issues of the relationship between gender relations and state power, and of the future development of gender relations with the collapse, and perhaps transformation, of the state.

Despite three years of radical and dramatic change, with the collapse of the administrative command system, the liberalisation of prices and mass privatisation, changes within the enterprise have been far less dramatic. The sixth paper in this collection, by Pasha Romanov, explores what should be the most fundamental area of change in the internal relations of the Soviet enterprise in the transition to the market economy, change in the role of middle management. Pasha's paper is based on his research in another giant engineering enterprise in Samara. He explores the traditional role of the middle manager in the Soviet enterprise, before looking at the subtle changes in the status of middle managers which are emerging as a result of the policy of senior management, on the one hand, and the growing insecurity of the workers in the face of unemployment, on the other.

Middle managers have traditionally been caught between the workers under their command and the senior management to whom they are responsible for delivering the plan. As the impact of reform opens up tensions within the enterprise between senior management, increasingly constrained to reduce costs, and the workforce, anxious to preserve living standards and jobs, middle managers find their loyalties divided. The danger for senior management is that in the event of open conflict the middle managers will align themselves with the workers under their control in resisting fundamental restructuring of the enterprise that will be detrimental to the workers. Pasha argues that senior management has tried to counter this threat by deliberately raising the pay and status of shop chiefs, while section heads and foremen have seen their authority and security increase as workers face the growing risk of lay-offs, short-time working and unemployment. On the basis of comparative research Pasha argues that this is a general tendency, although it is at present only at an early stage in its development.

This is a contentious issue, because there is some evidence from our studies that in the event of open conflict between senior management and the workforce middle management tends to align itself with the latter. Such conflict is usually linked to conflicts within the management team, particularly between the formerly dominant engineering specialists and the newly emerging financial, economic and marketing specialists, each of whom looks for support to the workers. It is in this context that middle management provides the link between the 'productivist' faction, which retains the traditional values of production for production's sake, and the mass of the workers, in resisting the more radical changes proposed by the more market-oriented faction of management.

In the seventh paper in the collection Marina Kiblitskaya focuses her attention on one small episode in the life of an engineering plant in Moscow to bring out the continuing importance of informal relations in the Russian enterprise. Marina considers a range of explanations for the dramatic failure of the plant to meet the plan in one month in 1993. First she explores a range of objective explanations, including supply and technical difficulties, which at first sight provide an adequate explanation for the breakdown. However she notes that such difficulties are normal for Soviet production, and affect the plant every month. She then argues that a more fundamental explanation for the failure to meet the plan was the collapse of the informal bargains that had enabled the plant to keep going in the face of objective constraints in the past. The failure to meet the plan then precipitated a conflict within the management team, between those who sought radical change in the systems of production planning and management and those who held to the traditional remedy of finding scapegoats and allocating individual blame, a conflict in which the latter emerged victorious.

In the last paper Valya Vedeneeva examines the example of a reform in one central aspect of the formal structure of enterprise management, the payment system. Her research is based in a small engineering enterprise which was one of the pioneers of privatisation under a radical management. The traditional Soviet payment systems have always established only a weak relationship between effort and reward. Although piece-rate payments have predominated, there has never been a close relationship between the established norm and the effort required of the worker, while output has depended far more on conditions of supply and equipment maintenance than the worker's own efforts. The result has been that the formal payment system has provided the framework within which informal systems have developed in which line managers use their power to allocate work, supplies and equipment and to misrecord work done in such a way as to give them discretionary control of the earnings of the workers.

In this case the management sought to introduce a new formal payment system which would overcome the limitations of the traditional system by moving to the payment of time wages, supplemented by formal bonus systems. However the result of this reform was disastrous. On the one hand, the workers were aggrieved because they experienced the new system as a loss of control and its results as a violation of their sense of justice. On the other hand, line managers had lost the informal levers of influence through which had been able to control the workers' individual and collective effort. The reform failed because it followed the traditional Soviet course of seeking a reform of the formal system of payment, without paying any regard to the informal systems of regulation through which production is really managed.

Each of the papers in this collection focuses on one aspect of the life of one post-Soviet enterprise. However the fact that each has been produced within the framework of a collaborative research project means that the whole is more than the sum of the parts. Each researcher has drawn comparative data from other enterprises that we have studied within the project and the analysis of each paper has been discussed collectively in the framework of the various other themes and issues that we have been exploring together. Taken as a whole the papers provide some insight into the complexity of the internal life of the Soviet and post-Soviet enterprise that derives from the pervasive role of informal social norms and relationships in regulating its activity.

Of course informal relations play an equally important role in Western enterprises. However in our view the fundamental difference is that in the Soviet enterprise the formal system was far more rigid, far more remote from everyday reality, and far more impervious to change than is the formal system of a Western enterprise, both because of the centralisation of the Soviet system and because of the enormous gulf between the ideology, which was perforce embedded in the formal system, and reality. Whereas in the Western enterprise the formal system can be gradually adjusted to bring it more closely into line with the informal system, the gulf between the two in the Soviet enterprise means that the two systems often have very little relation to one another.

The informal system itself is not homogeneous. On the one hand, as Sergei Alasheev argues, parts of the informal system are institutionalised and norm governed, with clear expectations on the part of workers and managers of what is the norm, both in a factual and a moral sense, backed by a strong sense of social justice. On the other hand, there is enormous scope for the exercise of individual discretion and the exploitation of personal relationships. This means that individual style and personality can play a determining role in the character of the social relations of a work group, a shop, or an enterprise as a whole. It is this feature that gives each enterprise and each shop a personality of its own, a personality that is identifiable almost as soon as one enters the plant or building. This human colouring of an inhuman system is what makes the experience of researching the (post) Soviet enterprise so satisfying, but at the same time it presents enormous problems for the sociologist seeking to generalise from this experience. For this reason, at this stage we prefer to present the reader with fragments which raise as many questions as they answer, and open up new avenues for research, rather than to try to pull them all together to draw premature conclusions.

CONTINUITY AND CHANGE IN THE RUSSIAN INDUSTRIAL ENTERPRISE

The industrial enterprise was the bedrock of Soviet society, but it was never an unchanging institution. Despite the high degree of continuity as the enterprise has secured its own reproduction, the industrial enterprise has adapted to and conditioned changes in the wider society from the utopian modernism of the Revolution, through the repressive coercion of the Stalinist period, to the repressive paternalism of the period of Khrushchev's reform and Brezhnevian stagnation, and the chaos of perestroika. The papers in this volume show us that exactly the same is true of the current period of development in Russian society, the so-called transition to a market economy, as the enterprise and those who depend on it struggle to find a place in the new world, but in struggling make their mark on the new world that is emerging.

The Soviet enterprise was undoubtedly an authoritarian institution which squandered human and material resources. Yet those who lived and worked within the enterprise nevertheless constructed their own world which expressed their own aspirations and their own values. The values of democracy, of solidarity, of egalitarianism, of justice, of the dignity of productive labour may have been empty rhetoric for the regime, but they were filled with human substance and a powerful oppositional content by those who lived within the system. This oppositional content was not expressed in political form, but it nevertheless pervaded the informal relationships within which people negotiated their subordination and that defined the fabric of their daily lives. These values were certainly distorted and deformed by the compromises and divisions through which subordination was reproduced, but they nevertheless provided many people with a reference point that gave some meaning to their lives.

'Market Bolshevism' is undoubtedly changing the industrial enterprise, as have the previous techniques by which Bolshevik power has sought to sustain itself. The papers in this volume show clearly that the pressures of the market economy are reinforcing the most negative features of the soviet enterprise, as job insecurity sets managerial authoritarianism on more secure foundations, fostering divisions within the labour force, eroding traditional values and diverting resources from investment and the provision for social need into speculation and crime. But at the same time it is not so easy for managers to establish control over a workplace which has never been within their domain, which is why the more entrepreneurial among them look to commerce and finance, speculation, theft and fraud to make their millions. Moreover the market economy is equally generating a response as it threatens the very survival of the enterprise and all those who depend on it, not only for employment and a wage, not only for housing and for health, welfare and social services, but also for the very definition of their social identity, for their dignity and self esteem as useful members of society. Just as the Russian enterprise adapts to the market economy, so will the market economy have to adapt to the Russian enterprise.

The transformation of the industrial enterprise will be as gradual a process in Russia as it has been in the capitalist world, and will not be determined by the schemes of politicians and consultants but by the outcome of the conflicts to which it gives rise, conflicts which take place within and around the formal and informal relations through which people live their lives. The theme of conflict and change is the focus of the second volume of papers from our project, which is currently in preparation.

NOTES

1   Most of the Soviet and Western literature on management focuses on this formal system. See, for example, A. Freris, *The Soviet Industrial Enterprise*, Croom Helm, London, 1984; W.J. Conyngham, *The Modernization of Soviet Industrial Management*, Cambridge University Press, Cambridge, 1982.

2   A search of articles in Sociofile, dating back to 1974, which includes coverage of the major soviet sociological publications, produced only two references to informal or unofficial relations. V.G. Vasil'ev, 'The Socialist Industrial Enterprise: Its Structure and Functions (Sotsialisticheskoe promyshlennoe predpriiatie: ego struktura i funktsii)', *Sotsiologicheskie issledovaniya*, 1974, 1, 1, July–Sept, pp. 41–50, contrasts the relation between 'official' and 'unofficial' structures in the work group, which under capitalism are supposedly opposed to one another, while under socialism they are generally in harmony (although Vasil'ev notes that they may also make up for deficiencies in the administrative apparatus even under socialism). Vasil'ev's recommendation that the proper study of such unofficial structures could help to strengthen the workgroup and the enterprise as a whole does not seem to have been taken up. The only other reference to such structures appears two years later, in R.K. Simonian's article 'Social Management of the Production Collective of a Shop (K voprosu o sotsialnom upravlenii proizvodstvennym kollektivom tsekha)', *Sotsiologicheskie issledovaniya*, 1976, 3, 2, Apr–June, pp. 93–97, which noted the need for shop management to use the informal structure of the shop to increase the efficiency of production.

3   The classic work of this generation was A.G. Zdravomyslov, V.P. Rozhin and V.A. Yadov, *Man and His Work (Chelovek i ego rabota)*, Moscow, 1967 (English version published by International Arts and Sciences Press, White Plains, New York, 1970). See also the collections edited by Murray Yanowitch, *Soviet Work Attitudes*, M.E. Sharpe, White Plains, New York and Martin Robertson, Oxford, 1979 and *Work in the Soviet Union: Attitudes and Issues*, M.E. Sharpe, Armonk, New York, 1985. The most interesting work is that of V.B. Ol'shanskii, who used methods of participant observation, working in a large factory for several months in the 1960s. V.B. Ol'shanskii, 'Personality and Social Values (Lichnost' i sotsial'nye tsennosti)', in *Sociology in the USSR (Sotsiologiya v SSSR)*, Moscow, 1966, Volume One. See also I.A. Ryazhskikh, 'The experience of using methods of participant observation in the research of the life of an industrial collective (Opyt ispol'zovaniya vklyuchennogo

nablyudeniya dlya izucheniya zhizni proizvodstvennogo kollektiva)', *Sotsiologicheskie issledovaniya*, 3, 1985.

4   The principal exception to this was the Novosibirsk school of industrial sociologists.

5   The most interesting research during the mid-1980s was that on the brigade system of organisation of labour and the newly emerging systems of 'self-management' and 'industrial democracy'. However this research still used the traditional methods of tendentious generalisation weakly supported by indices, typologies and correlations derived from simple questionnaire data.

6   R.V. Ryvkina, S. Yu. Pavlenko, L. Ya. Kosals, et al., *The Social-managerial Mechanism of Development of Production. Methodology, Methods and Results of Research (Sotsial'no-upravlencheskii mekhanizm razvitiya proizvodstva. Metodologiya, metodika i rezul'taty issledovanii)*, 467pp., Novosibirsk, 1989, contains a lot of valuable material, focusing on the socio-economic analysis of managerial interaction in agriculture and the agro-industrial complex and based on a large amount of solid research carried out at the local level, from ordinary workers up to senior managers, between 1982 and 1987. S.Yu. Pavlenko, 'Informal Management Interaction (Neformal'nye upravlencheskie vzaimodeistvie)' in T.I. Zaslavskaya and R.V. Ryvkina (eds): *Economic Sociology and Perestroika (Ekonomicheskaya sotsiologiya i perestroika)*, Progress, Moscow, 1989, pp. 190–202, is an interesting article which touches on informal relations, including those at the level of middle management, on the basis of a survey of managers. Yu. S. Gurov, N. F. Vodolazskaya and L. Ya. Tyangov, *The Labour Collective: A Sociological Investigation (Trudovoi kollektiv: sotsiologicheskoe issledovanie)*, Cheboksari, 1991, reports the results of a sociological survey of two enterprises in Cheboksary in 1989, using a range of research methods.

    N.V. Chernina, *Labour Behaviour in New Ownership Conditions (Trudovoe povedenie v novyx usloviyax khozyaistvovaniya)*, 205pp., Novosibirsk, 1992, is based on sociological research carried out by the author between 1982 and 1990, focusing on new types of behaviour characteristic of different categories of workers in leasehold enterprises. L.S. Perepelkin, 'Russian Workers in Contemporary Industrial Production (Russkie rabochie v sovremennye promyshlennye proizvodstva)', *EKO*, 3, 1993, pp. 119–132, is an interesting article defining the distinctive characteristics of the Russian worker, based primarily on an 'expert survey' and questionnaire data, which is relevant to Sergei Alasheev's second article below. Ya.M. Roshchina, 'The Private Sector: Entrepreneurs on the Problems of Ownership (Chastnyi sektor: predprinimateli o problemakh khozyaistvovaniya', *EKO*, 1, 1994, pp. 94–107 is an interesting article based on a survey of heads of non-state enterprises.

    V. M. Vologozhin, 'The Dawn of Soviet Shares (Utro sovetskix aktsii)', *EKO*, 1, 1989 and A.V. Vasil'ev, 'Perspectives for the Development of Shareholder Relations (Perspektivy aktsionernyx otnoshenii)' *Sotsiologicheskie issledovaniya*, 5, 1990, pp. 16–21, provide very interesting material on three pioneering leasehold enterprises. There is also a number of useful articles concerned with the miners' strikes, e.g. L.L. Mal'tseva and O.N. Pulyaeva, 'What Led to the Strike? (Chto privelo k zabastovke)', *Sotsiologicheskie issledovaniya, 6*, 1990, pp. 38–42; G.V. Kubas', 'The Kuzbass Workers' Committees' , *Sotsiologicheskie issledovaniya, 6,* 1990, pp. 49–53 and V.V. Yakunichkin, 'Contradictions in the Strike Movement in Western Donbass in the Spring of 1991 (Protivorechiya zabastovochnogo dvizheniya v Zapadnom Donbase (vesna 1991g.)', *Sotsiologicheskie issledovaniya* 12, 1991, pp. 87–9.

7   J. Berliner, *Factory and Manager in the USSR*, Harvard University Press, Cambridge, Mass., 1957. David Granick: *Management of the Industrial Firm in the USSR*,
    Columbia UP, 1954, and *The Red Executive*, Macmillan, London, 1960.

8   V. Andrle, *Managerial Power in the Soviet Union*, Saxon House, Lexington, 1976; A.C. Gorlin, 'The Power of Soviet Industrial Ministries', *Soviet Studies*, 37, 3, 1985,

pp. 353–70; S. J. Linz, 'Managerial Autonomy in Soviet Firms', *Soviet Interview Project Working Paper* No. 18, April 1986; S.J. Linz, 'The 'Treadmill' of Soviet Economic Reforms: Management's Perspective', *Soviet Interview Project Working Paper* No. 39, August 1986; Paul R. Gregory, *Restructuring the Soviet Economic Bureaucracy*, Cambridge University Press, Cambridge, 1990; Paul R. Gregory, Productivity, slack and time theft in the Soviet economy', in James R. Millar (ed.) *Politics, Work and Daily Life in the USSR*, Cambridge University Press, Cambridge, 1987.

Ed A. Hewitt, *Reforming the Soviet Economy*, Brookings Institution, Washington D.C. 1988, Chapters Three and Four, contrasts the 'formal' and the 'de facto' systems, but as usual has nothing to say about this contrast within the enterprise.

9   A more sophisticated analysis of the planning system as it actually operated has been developed by a group of Russian economists (including P. Aven, S. Belanovskii, V. Konstantinov, S. Kordonsky, V. Naishul', S. Pavlenko and V. Shironin), based on their own experience within the system and interview materials. They characterise the 'planning system' as the 'economy of getting approvals' ('ekonomika soglasovanii') or the 'administrative market'.

10   Granick, 1954, pp. 66, 81. Granick stressed the similarities between Western and Soviet enterprises in managerial structure and functions, although he noted that in Soviet enterprises the foreman enjoys the kind of power which in the US had already been transferred to higher management. 'The significant area of difference between the production work of managements in the Soviet Union and in the United States lies in the basis upon which decisions are made and in the relations of management to the workers of the plant and to other non-managerial organisations' (ibid. p. 34). In *The Red Executive* Granick reaffirmed the stability of the enterprise as the core institution of Soviet society, noted that Soviet enterprises had proportionately fewer managers, a much higher degree of decentralisation, and far more auxiliary and manual workers than US plants. While he noted the similar patterns of informal worker control of output and work schedules in Soviet and US factories, he also noted that different constraints on management, Soviet managers having to meet the plan with little regard for costs in a relatively stable environment. Granick also noted the relative decline in the power of the Soviet foreman, so that 'power over personnel has evaporated from within the foreman's fist' with the result that 'the foreman has achieved success only as he has taken up a position independent of both management and of the workers he supervises. ... In short the foreman must try to be the shop-floor mediator between management and the workers' (p. 279).

11   A number of texts discuss various aspects of the life of Soviet workers, relying primarily on Soviet published sources, though they barely touch on work itself. The most useful are Arcadius Kahan and Blair A. Rouble, eds, *Industrial Labor in the USSR*, Pergamon Press, Oxford, 1979 and Walter Connor, *The Accidental Proletariat*, Princeton University Press, Princeton, 1991.

12   The classic such work is John Scott, *Behind the Urals*, Indiana University Press, Bloomington, 1989, originally published in 1942. Michael Gelb's edition of Zara Witkin's memoirs, *An American Engineer in Stalin's Russia*, University of California Press, Berkeley, 1991, contains an extensive bibliography of such memoirs.

13   Mary McAuley: *Labour Disputes in Soviet Russia 1957-1965*, Clarendon, Oxford, 1969.

14   Don Filtzer, *Soviet Workers and Stalinist Industrialisation*, Pluto, London, 1986; *Soviet Workers and Destalinisation*, Cambridge University Press, Cambridge, 1992; *Soviet Workers and Perestroika*, Cambridge University Press, Cambridge, 1994. For the latter book Filtzer was able to supplement the published sources with some interview material of his own and David Mandel's for his discussion of the labour process (a selection of Mandel's very interesting interviews has been as *Rabotyagi: Perestroika and After Viewed from Below*, Monthly Review Press, New York, 1993),

which includes some material on informal bargaining, although his main concern in this chapter is to document the levels of waste and indiscipline, and the extent of output restriction and job control, as an indicator of the power of workers in the Soviet system, rather than to describe how production is possible at all in Soviet conditions. There is something of a tension running through Filtzer's analysis between the supposedly considerable power of workers in opposition to management, on the one hand, and what he claims is the extreme individualisation and atomisation of Soviet workers on the other. Our view would be that Soviet workers exercise a considerable degree of control, but within strict limits, that may vary considerably from one workplace to another, which the worker has little power to challenge (see Simon Clarke, Review of Filtzer, *Soviet Workers and De-Stalinisation*, *Sociology*, 27, 4, 1993, pp. 717–9; Simon Clarke, Peter Fairbrother, Michael Burawoy and Pavel Krotov, *What About the Workers*, Verso, London, 1992, Chapter One).

15 These interviews were eventually published as S.A. Belanovskii, *Industrial Interviews (Proizvodstvennye intervyu)*, Four Volumes, Moscow, 1991–3.

16 David Mandel, op. cit.

17 The richest material on the labour process in Soviet-type enterprises comes from Hungary. In addition to Michael Burawoy's work with János Lukács (Michael Burawoy and János Lukács, *The Radiant Past: Ideology and Reality in Hungary's Road to Capitalism*, Chicago UP, Chicago, 1992) and Haraszti's account of working in a Hungarian factor (Miklos Haraszti: *A Worker in a Workers' State*, Penguin, London, 1977), there is the pioneering work of Lajos Héthy and Csaba Makó, originally dating from the late 1960s (Lajos Héthy and Csaba Makó, *Patterns of Workers' Behaviour and the Business Enterprise*, Budapest, 1989).

18 Michael Burawoy and Kathryn Hendley, 'Between Perestroika and Privatisation: Divided Strategies and Political Crisis in a Soviet Enterprise', *Soviet Studies*, 44, 3, 1992, pp. 371–402. Michael Burawoy and Pavel Krotov, 'The Soviet Transition from Socialism to Capitalim: Workers' Control and Economic Bargaining in the Wood Industry', *American Sociological Review*, 57, 1992, pp. 16–38, and in S. Clarke et al. *What About the Workers*, pp. 56–90. A Russian version has been published as 'Sovetskii variant perekhoda k kapitalizmu ...', *Rubezh*, 4, 1992, Syktyvkar, pp. 107–138. There has been a very limited amount of other 'case study' research conducted by Western researchers in Russia, but this rarely amounts to more than questionnaire surveys of senior managers or reports of brief site visits. Wendy Carlin, John van Reenen and Toby Wolfe, Enterprise Restructuring in the Transition: an Analytical Survey of the Case Study Evidence from Central and Eastern Europe, *EBRD Working Paper*, 14, July 1994, is a brave attempt to draw conclusions from some of the available case study material.

In our own work we have benefited immeasurably from discussions with Michael Burawoy, Don Filtzer and David Mandel. Peter Fairbrother and I would also like to express our gratitude to the many Sovietologists who have provided encouragement and support to interlopers into their field, and particularly to Ron Amann, Judy Shapiro and Alastair McAuley.

19 The most productive foci for comparison seem to us to be, first, the persistence of craft traditions and shop-floor control in the development of factory production in the capitalist world and, second, the reproduction of paternalist and patriarchal structures within industrial enterprises, particularly, but not exclusively, in East Asia. The importance of informal relations in Western enterprises has been much under-researched, although it has been brought out in several classic studies of piece-rate bargaining and work organisation (especially those of Donald Roy and Melville Dalton), and above all in recent studies of gender relations at work (especially that of Cynthia Cockburn).

20 Clarke et al., *What About the Workers*, pp. 20–22.

21 Mobility seems primarily to involve younger workers, who wait their turn for recruitment to the more prestigious jobs, and older workers, who are transferred to light work when they can no longer keep up with the pace of core production work.

22 The foreman until recently usually earned less than the workers under his or her command. Most Russian enterprises now work according to the brigade system, in which the brigadier has taken over some of the functions of the foreman, particularly in the allocation of labour and organisation of the production process.

23 This analysis is confirmed by the pattern of Russian strikes, which still tend to have a spontaneous character, without any organisation or any coherent set of demands (Simon Clarke, Peter Fairbrother and Vadim Borisov, *The Workers' Movement in Russia*, Edward Elgar, 1995).

2. Informal Relations in the Soviet System of Production

Sergei Alasheev

The starting point for this article was provided by a question posed by Simon Clarke. In a letter to one of the research groups he wrote that it was difficult to understand how production workers were able to work in Russia. Our workers receive little pay and work in difficult conditions. The official trade unions are not interested in defending their interests, but are merely additional levers by which the administration exerts pressure on the workers, and all this in conditions of political instability and economic crisis.

In the present article I cannot answer this question completely, but I will try to explain to some extent how it is possible to manage the production activity of workers in industrial enterprises, and how informal relations play their part in the organisation of production.

The source for my reflections was interviews, group meetings and observation carried out by a group of Samara sociologists in two large industrial enterprises in Samara, interviews with workers and observation in other Samara factories, and also personal impressions. The interviews quoted in this article were conducted by myself, Irina Tartakovskaya, Lena Lapshova, Pavel Romanov, Vadim Borisov, Simon Clarke and Don Filtzer.

INTRODUCTORY REMARKS

Our research aimed to get a view of the problems of production from within. Perhaps we managed to see production problems from within, but we still saw them with our own eyes; this is our opinion. We spent a year and a half in the enterprise but all the same we could not penetrate the understanding and mood of the people working in the factory themselves. Indeed, we saw the problems of production from the point of view of the workers and managers of the enterprise, but this is our vision (conditioned by our cultural values, theoretical knowledge, our understanding of the situation in the country, in the city, in general our level of understanding people). Although we did not have any fixed theoretical position, nevertheless we clashed with paradoxical, impossible opinions, with the illogicality and inconsistency of people's actions, even the language of the respondents we sometimes translated into our own language, considering it to be 'common'.

It seems to me that we could only understand those moments which corresponded with our own experience, only those which we had experienced ourselves (or something similar). Thus it is quite possible that a person with a richer or broader experience elsewhere could discover more and penetrate more deeply. To a considerable extent, in studying the factory, we were trying to understand ourselves.

Undoubtedly, the true understanding of the problems of production is to be found among the workers of the factory itself. And in order to reach this understanding, it is not enough to spend every day in their work place – it is necessary to work in their work place, and it is necessary not only to work, but even to live their lives. We did not do this. So all our investigations not only cannot make claims to truth, but can only claim to be one of many possible understandings, explanations of life in a Russian enterprise.

INFORMAL RELATIONS IN PRODUCTION

Besides the formal relations laid down in job descriptions, instructions, orders and rules there are informal relations. These are the real relations, appearing in the unwritten rules of people's relationships in production. These rules, traditional norms of behaviour, play the role of regulators of the productive life of the enterprise; they are just as inalienable a part of the life of the factory as the formal norms. The failure to fulfil this or that demand can be attributed equally to formal and informal relations.

The system of formal norms is incomplete, it does not take into account the diversity of real life situations, of the entire richness and changeability of human life. Informal relations compensate for this shortcoming.

In this article we are particularly interested in informal relations, but this is not in any way to underestimate the role of formal relations in the process of production.

Instead of giving a more precise definition of informal relations, we will cite several situations that we were able to observe during the course of our case study. These examples are fairly typical and allow us to define those spheres in which one can identify informal relations. Several of them are quite interesting.

So under what conditions can one speak of informal relations in production?

PRODUCTION ACTIVITY

We managed to uncover informal agreements arising from a wide range of causes in the process of production itself: at the stage of distribution of work, its carrying out, methods of providing incentives for quality and the fulfilment of the plan.

Here is the reply of a shop chief to a question in May 1993 about how the section foremen distributed the better paying work:

— How does the foreman distribute the work? [referring to the better paid, more profitable work, S.A.]
— In general, he obviously tries to put the more highly skilled people onto this work, those he considers that he needs to hold on to. And of course he gives them this work. This is a serious question. This question is related to justice. And they receive very different amounts, it is clear that if they are working on improvement work they receive only basic pay, but on this work they receive basic, and a bonus, and even more depending on how much work they do. And, of course, he gives preference to those people on whom he can rely in every respect, in the sense of quality, and everything, everything.

The distribution of work, handing out production tasks in the section to each worker, is the responsibility of the foreman. But the workers can distribute the work amongst themselves and without reference to their immediate manager, the foreman. The foreman in his turn shuts his eyes to the existence of such practices. A forty five year old worker of one of the large enterprises of the military-industrial complex spoke in May 1993 about the system of distribution of profitable work:

— We still had such an agreement amongst ourselves. We are six fitters. One part pays very well – that is how it is normed; another pays badly. And we agreed amongst ourselves like this: A, you take the good part, and next time B will take it.
— Understood.
— The thing is that we regulated it among ourselves. We did it. But this again is a situation in which all the fitters have a single grade, the same level of qualification. If someone is weak, then, of course...
— And what in that case?
— Well, we would give them the good parts, but not as often.

So the workers themselves distribute profitable work on the basis of informal agreements, arising from their own perceptions of justice, so that everybody receives approximately the same amount.

There are absolutely no regulations concerning the distribution of work: the distribution of profitable and unprofitable work is not provided for in any of the rules, which are replaced by informal agreements between workers and the foreman who distributes the work. And this becomes one more of the levers of pressure on the workers.

The following extract from an interview describes how the foreman distributes work. It is interesting that the foreman himself has apparently not really reflected on the distribution of work as an agreement reached between the workers and himself.

— All in all, what are your relations with the workers like? Do they like you or not? How are they?
— Well, let us say that when I had only just arrived in the shop, my relations with the workers were difficult.
— Please can you give us an example?
— I had two brigades. In one brigade was a person who was a jack of all trades, but, as they say, he drank a little. And in the other brigade were strong young people who did not drink, but had little experience. And there was an argument between them because I gave profitable work to one brigade and unprofitable work to the other.
— And had you really done that?
— No. At least I tried to give work equally, but if I felt that not everyone could do this work, or the work had to be done quickly, then, of course, I gave it to those who could do it the best. If this is very complicated work, then it is also very well paying, we call it 'kalym' [literally bride price]. For example forging rollers – it is a very capricious part, very expensive work, it has to be forged with interleaved filaments; if I forge it wrong it will go through every stage, but by the end of the operation cracks will have appeared.

— Well, for the workers it is kalym, but what is the advantage to you?
— None.
— So you just give the kalym to whomever you feel like? And you get nothing out of it?
— Nothing. Absolutely nothing.
— I think that the brigade which gets the profitable work must be grateful to you in some way?
— No. It is not that. Absolutely not that. Only gratitude means better relations with me, and a willingness to carry out my requests quickly, in good time. That is all.
— For example?
— An example. In the work process in another shop a part was smashed. It had to be made urgently. I come to my workers and I tell them to put their work aside — they are forging some other part, they had it in the furnace – and they urgently did what I asked them to do. Naturally it was not for me, but for production, but nevertheless it was my request. Moreover the workers lose pay through this, or have to stay after work for it. All this is only possible because they have a good attitude to me. (July 1993)

The foremen complained that formally they had no financial resources to provide incentives to the workers to carry out the work set for them. There is a Foreman's Fund, but it is an insignificant sum. However they have plenty of informal methods of controlling the fulfilment of tasks. We had an interesting conversation in May 1993 with a worker in one of the factories about one of them.

— And does the foreman have any additional levers, monetary, with which he can influence workers?
— No. No, unless he creates some kind of fund of his own unofficially.
— How does he do that? Is it the foremen who create the unofficial fund themselves?
— It is the foremen who do it.
— But what is in the unofficial fund? Is it money, alcohol or what?
— No. One could say that it is money, because it is accounting for work done. Let us suppose that the technologist introduces some kind of additional operations in the technical process at the request of the foreman, which the workers do not in fact carry out. But it is paid for, it is in the price schedule. The workers do not receive it. They used to do this, they did this earlier, not now. Now he goes cap in hand to the shop chief, the shop chief then gives orders to the chief of BTZ (Department of Labour and Wages), and he searches for some resources.

In many enterprises that we know about there is an unwritten rule: do not overfulfil the plan by too much, so that they do not cut the wage rates. The practice of annually slashing the pay norms gave rise to a corresponding reaction: the concealment of a percentage of the month's production, and the redistribution of orders from month to month so that in the accounts the fulfilment of work for each month appears as around 100 per cent of the plan.

This is a pretty widespread practice in workplaces which pay on piece-rates. In this situation non-fulfilment is a violation of the formal accounting norms. We know of cases in which workers have hidden orders for a month which they considered to be sufficient, but in fact part of the order was hidden for the following month. Let us suppose that this month I have worked well, but next month I intend to take time off, then I will conceal not the whole order, but an amount which enables me to receive my normal pay, and part of the order I will keep for the following month, so that next month I will not receive any less, because I intend not to come to work for a few days. All this goes on without the approval of the foreman, although he certainly knows about it.

Observation of this informal rule is not only welcome to the workers, but is also to the benefit of the foreman. A significant over-fulfilment of the plan means that he will be faced with an increase in the work norms, and this in turn can lead to a non-fulfilment of the plan in some months, and consequently the non-payment of his bonus. Moreover he may have to force the workers to work more intensively. So the foreman also supports the secret agreement not to fulfil the plan by more than 103 per cent, for example, which would become disadvantageous. Here is what a foreman from one of the factories said about this in June 1993:

— Can a chap produce more parts than are laid down by the norm?
— Yes. But the plan defines how much should be made in a normal hour. OK. We cannot overfulfil it by much because, well, here we have to think about the norm-setter. He will think that the norms are too low. If there is a substantial overfulfilment they will chop the time allowed for this part, they will reduce it. Well, correspondingly, say, there are a lot of these parts, then it will be unlikely that we could fulfil the plan with these fabricated norms.
— So you keep an eye on it so as to hit it exactly, so that it will be more or less 100 per cent
— That's exactly it. We keep an eye on the plan so that it will be fulfilled by 101–102 per cent
— And if you feel that it is going to be more?
— Well, I simply do not push it.

— And, as they say, put it on the side somewhere?
— Yes, to the following month.

The shop chief is equally involved in the redistribution of accounting for tasks. Thus, in another factory a shop chief told us in October 1992: 'so as to make sure that everything is paid for we register this month the balls which were not handed over last month'.

The shop management, which has a wide range of means available, has other methods of combating the reduction of work norms, avoiding the consequential effect on pay. The same shop chief continued:

> Earlier, five or six years ago, each year they set a target for the reduction in labour intensity. Let us say it was two per cent. Whether you like it or not, you have to reduce it. So, for example, they tell the factory to review the norms and to reduce labour intensity by two per cent. And so everybody was ready for this in advance, because they all knew that at the end of the year (in December) they would be ordered to reduce the labour intensity. If it was done according to the rules then, for example, if we installed new equipment we had to review all the norms, but we did not do this because we knew that at the end of the year they would order us to review all the norms in any case, so we just endorsed the proposed norms (and did this for all of them, whether they were right or wrong) – one could even say that this review only took place on paper. How? For example, because our balls are made with various degrees of precision, we announce, for example, that we can make the balls with a high degree of precision, but they should increase our pay correspondingly. And they slash the rate for the 20th degree of precision, knowing that the following year we will make balls of the 10th degree of precision, much higher. In this case we played around with the final stages of processing.

DISCIPLINE

Informal relations in the immediate process of production are strongly connected with interactions concerned with discipline.

Violations of production discipline were always one of the most severe problems of Soviet enterprises. In the enterprises we have been studying this continues to be one of the most difficult problems faced by the administration.

In the area of attendance at work, the life of the worker is strictly regulated in large industrial enterprises. The time of arrival and departure from work is noted. The procedure for receiving permission to be absent from the workplace is pretty bureaucratic. For example, to get permission for absence from work – so-called administrative leave – it is necessary, in the first place, to do this in advance, then to discuss it with the brigadier, then to fill in a special form (or a written statement) which has to be signed by the foreman and shop chief and then given to the timekeeper. These people, as a rule, are scattered about, will be busy, will not always be in their offices, so that one has to wait and explain the reasons for one's intended absence to each of them. All this takes a lot of time, working time, since it has to be done during working hours. There are established norms for absence from work, three days for a wedding, three days for a funeral. But all these days are not paid. If the worker has worked overtime (and that is taken into account), then he can use it (sometimes within a definite period – a month for example) and take time off for the time worked earlier.

However permission for administrative leave can be organised by somebody else in place of the worker, most often the foreman, although this is not part of his duties. Administrative vacations are often authorised retrospectively (interview with a foreman, June 1993). We know of cases in which the foreman arranges time off and puts a drunken worker in the passage, so that he will not lose pay, so that the shop chief will not punish him and so as not to impair the performance of the section.

In some cases it is impossible for the worker to plan his absence from work for a day, and this is understood by his fellow workers, although formally it is considered a violation of discipline. A foreman described the situation in July 1993:

> A situation that arises very frequently is one in which a worker comes up to me and asks to leave – it is very urgent. I give permission. But he is still concerned that I might let him off today, but because nothing is written down, tomorrow I might say that I had not given him permission to leave and I might report to the chief that he went earlier than the proper time.

Lateness for work is also a disciplinary offence. But such offences are rare. In some of the enterprises in which we have done research workers arrive as much as one and a half hours before the start of the shift.

Absenteeism is a pretty widespread phenomenon, in most cases as a result of drunkenness. This subject can be illustrated by a conversation about absenteeism with one of the foremen in June 1993:

> — Do people sometimes ask you to cover for them afterwards, i.e. to register them as having been here?

— They do. But they do not ask themselves, the foreman does it for them. You see it is practically impossible to keep quiet about every absentee, the foremen themselves look after it, the administration. They decide whether they want to or not.

— The foremen or the administration? Do you mean that you can fail to report this matter, so as not to exaggerate it, to resolve it at your own level, to deal with it as an administrative vacation?

— Yes, the foreman can.

— And what would happen if a worker turned up in the section drunk?

— If he was very drunk, then he would be sent to sit somewhere until the end of the shift to sober up. In general we try not to make a fuss about it, because if we punish somebody for being drunk, if we dealt with him very strictly, then that person would be sacked within a month, let's say.

— Have you faced such a situation? Have you had to sack someone who is a regular drinker?

— Well our people are not regular drinkers. It is simply that there are occasions on which people have a few drinks. Or it happens when he has a bit of money, has his pay packet, simply when he is in that kind of mood.

Well, there was a case not long ago when we had a lad who was absent for three days. Well, we looked into the situation. He was committing an offence and he had not been given leave. You see he had been upset. As a result he began to drink and, possibly, he would have gone on drinking if we hadn't gone to his home and told him to get back to work!

— Was this someone from your brigade?

— No the foreman went ... Well he [the absentee S.A.] is a responsible lad. He works well. As a worker, as a specialist he is not bad; that is to say he works, if he works, normally, well.

Recently punishments for disciplinary violations have become much more rigorous. This is related to the reduction in the number of workers in the enterprises, and serves as a reason for dismissal. Thus in one of the factories lateness leads to the loss of all bonuses and an application to the administration for dismissal. In the enterprises in which we have been researching all the interviewers have noted the improvement in production discipline. Cases of drunkenness have fallen on account of the sacking of the completely hopeless alcoholics, and the rest only drink rarely. Absenteeism and lateness has been reduced because the workers are afraid to lose work, leading to a process of self-discipline.

The reaction of workers to punishment for disciplinary violations is calm, they accept it as appropriate, and there are no conflicts arising from it. Workers found guilty of misdemeanours (lateness, absenteeism, drunkenness) 'do not stand on their rights', but accept their guilt and are sorry (shift foreman in mechanic's department, January 1993).

RECRUITMENT AND PROMOTION

Relationships with friends and personal contacts were extremely important for getting a job, not because it was difficult to find a job (there were always a lot of vacancies, especially for workers with a trade, and they could choose from among a number of places to work), but because it was important to make your own choice. In fact the person was choosing his whole future, because work is a large part of life, it will be the social environment of the person for many years.

The shop chiefs are practically independent in the selection of the people they recruit to work, the Personnel Department of the factory only does the formal preparation of the documents. Recruitment and sacking are carried out through the shop chief (his stamp is required on the documents), and he knows almost all his workers. By contrast to the Personnel Department, the shop chiefs relate informally to recruitment.

One shop chief told us in October 1992 that he hardly ever recruits people to his shop off the street, usually someone brings a newcomer along (that is someone already working in the factory). Or here is an extract from an interview with the head of a Personnel Department in April 1993:

— What is the mechanism of recruitment and selection of personnel?
— The subdivisions give us a statement of their labour force requirements. We report to the Labour Recruitment Bureau, we used to put out advertisements as well. People come to us, and we direct them to the subdivisions. We still do what we did before, which is to recruit 'from below', when the worker comes to someone he knows in the shop, and he is taken on there.

Although we have not observed any kind of fully developed recruitment policy, nevertheless the shop chief has an interest in recruiting qualified people, who are willing to work and are not too active politically. There is evidence of cases in which the shop chief has got rid of one of these dissatisfied 'trouble-makers'. But here we want to turn our attention to the method of placing people in work and forming the collective. The process was described by a shop chief in October 1992:

— Do you have any troublemakers like B. in your shop?
— Yes, there are, every family has its freaks. We 'sold' one to the neighbouring shop, then he gave them a hard time, just as he had given us a hard time earlier.
— And how did you 'sell' this tearaway?

— Well, like this ... He had to be put on light work, but I said to him that I could not do it, because all the work in this shop is heavy, but he knew all the laws better than any lawyer. We signed lots of bits of paper for him, all according to the law, a whole list, together with the lawyer. As a result he signed a document for us stating that he had turned down all the work offered to him, and we sent him to the Personnel Department where they found him work as a foreman in shop 1, where he sat quietly for the first two or three months, but then he began 'to wind up his machine' again.

— But what was it he wanted?

— Well, he would never ever agree with anything: I gave him an instruction, and he would consider that it is improper and demand that I change my orders, but our lawyer is terrified of these trouble-makers. But I also do not have the patience of Job, so I refused to change my orders and proposed that he take his complaints to the Director of the factory. But he left me alone all the same. But still the deputy Director of the factory signed some kind of paper cancelling the order.

— But have you got any of this kind of person left here now?

— Well, who made trouble for us? There were some in the third section. The collective was undisciplined, the senior foreman could not cope with them, and I moved this foreman (found him other work in the shop), because people had got out of his control. A manager without his own ideas is not a manager. A manager cannot manage if he supports every point of view (and the collective has forty people), there will never be a general opinion, he will just dash from one side to the other. He agreed with me and this subdivision was reorganised because there was already complete anarchy there, and so I amalgamated two departments. I explain something to him here in the planning meeting, and there he explains the opposite, he misleads people, well that is what happened. It is not the people who are to blame, it is all the fault of the manager. This relates to both production questions and opinions. It is true that they were discontented, they spoke up a bit, some of them left. But basically now it is normal. There aren't really any people who try to stir things up without any reason. There is one here, a new one turned up for me, although she is ill at the moment, but I met with her this week.

Although the shop chief has quite a lot of discretion in the organisation of the collective of his shop, at the stage of recruitment he often relies on those already working in the factory. This patronage in recruitment provides some protection for those who are brought into the shop by the patron, who can show the newcomer some of the weak points in the organisation of production, and provide knowledge of the norms of behaviour and interaction in the factory, shop and section. Strictly speaking it is difficult to call this influence patronage. In fact the jobs available in such a case are neither prestigious nor profitable, although there is some possibility of the new recruit choosing the most desirable job out of those available, depending on his criteria of desirability. Patronage in the majority of cases takes the form of friendly advice on the side. There may be a lot of such advice, but most often you do not have to listen to those who recruit the best, but to those who are closest to you.

From time to time a positive or negative attitude to the patron affects the protégé. But in any case the newcomer acquires an informal status, for example 'the foreman's man', or 'the Chief Engineer's man', but most frequently is defined by the surname of the protector. Fairly quickly the new recruit receives his own name, not related to the name of the patron, and already his name may appear in the role of patron. The hierarchy of informal status does not always coincide with the hierarchy of formal responsibilities, that is to say a person in this or that formal post may be related in various ways to higher levels of the hierarchy of posts and can have a higher or lower status of his own. A good example of this is the fact that in one shop the chief may not have any respect among the workers, but in another he may have an unquestioned authority, at the same time as a manager of a higher level – the Director of Production – enjoys no respect.

The worker who introduces a new recruit to the factory, as·it were takes on various obligations towards management on behalf of the person he has brought; the status of the patron in such a case serves as a guarantee. The worker helps his protégé to find a place in the structure of production, both formal and informal. In his turn the protégé is considered to be indebted to his patron in various senses. He can show his gratitude to his patron by giving him presents, bringing him some drink or helping him in some other way. However this does not always go far. None the less this obligation to somebody who helps you find a job exists, even if is it only psychological. This is demonstrated, in our opinion, by the fact that in interviews, when people talk about their labour biography they often talk about their gratitude to those people who 'brought them into the factory', helped them to acquire a trade.

We have spoken a lot about patronage, although it was quite possible to get a job on one's own initiative, without any connections through friends, family or anybody else. But in this case it would be necessary to be very strong-willed, confident in one's own ability, in order to get to grips with the specific features of the relationships in production, to make a name for oneself without depending on any patronage. This is a fairly attractive way to do it.

Apart from finding a job independently and finding one through a patron there are other ways of getting a job. In the majority of cases your future workplace was predetermined by where you received your education. The system of allocation of jobs after finishing Institute, technical or professional-technical school left practically no room for independent choice. However in the new work place the new arrival finds a mentor: sometimes this is established formally and the mentor is nominated by the management, sometimes it is the immediate superior, but in some cases these functions are performed by one of the workers. In these cases the mentor fulfils all the functions of patron about which we have already spoken.

Here is a story of the violation of the existing system of allocation of jobs after finishing education, where the husband of the person who has come to work is in the role of patron. The story was told by a foreman in July 1993:

— How did you come to be in this factory?'
— After Institute I was sent to a factory in Penza. I went there, but they did not give me anywhere to live. But my husband already worked in this factory [in Samara S.A.]. I went to this factory, sent a letter to the Ministry of Agriculture, went there, made an application and so I came to be in this factory. In accordance with a letter from the Ministry of Agriculture. They simply transferred me to the other Ministry, administratively.

I came to the factory, found out what kind of specialists they needed, at that time the Chief Metallurgist's Department (OGM) needed technologists, they gave me this letter, I took it to the Ministry and got from them an assignment here.
— What did your husband work as then?
— At that time he worked as a senior foreman.

I should have gone into the OGM, but then my child was ill, and I looked after him for two months, but when I came back my job had gone. I should have been a metal technologist in the instrumental shop. And they sent me there ...
— When you came to work here did it make any difference that your husband was working in this factory?
— Yes, I think so. Although he had not worked here long, only three years, but, as they say, he had established a good reputation.
— Where? With whom?
— At work. With his shop chief. With his immediate superiors.
— But you went to work in another shop ...
— The factory is not large. When I arrived, everyone knew about me already, even though I did not want them to know about me.
— I would like to know how all these informal aspects affect the recruitment of people to work?
— Very much. Above all, now people only ever get the good jobs through acquaintances.

Now, as a result of the reduction in recruitment and difficulty of finding work the significance of informal relations (relatives, friends, personal contact) to get work has considerably increased. Even for relatively low-skilled work one can only get a job 'through an acquaintance', 'through *blat*'. You would have 'to be a Solomon' for the management to take you without a recommendation.

Patronage is no less important for promotion. The widespread existence of promotion through patronage is illustrated by a passage from an interview with an inspector of the Personnel Department in May 1993. One should take into account the fact that the interview was concerned with the question of the position of women in production and, in our opinion, the situation is somewhat exaggerated since the respondent was very excited and somewhat indignant:

— Do women have any prospects of promotion?
— What promotion! Women have families, children. If they are sick of working in one place, or have worked for many years in harmful conditions, then the woman can transfer to another shop (that is not a promotion but a transfer).

There are female foremen. But you have to have a special kind of personality, strong-willed. It is difficult to work with men – they use foul language and so on.
— How are people promoted? Is there any chance of promotion for female ITR?
— There is a limit for women – engineer, very rarely senior engineer. Women are hardly ever promoted.

Promotion is determined by the 'hairy hand', connections. If there is not some powerful person behind one's back, in order to be promoted here you have to have the character to become stronger. And some people work here and then leave, or stay the whole time in one post. They usually promote men from the production sphere (from the shops) into leadership positions.

In our department they promoted G. [a woman who was head of the ITR group in personnel management] to the vacant post of deputy head of personnel management, but she refused the job. They put in a man who had never worked in personnel but was somebody's protégé.

The question of promotion of men was not asked, this judgement only concerns women, but women make up half of the workforce in the factory.

I know of one case in which a protégé turned to her patron (her head of department) to resolve a conflict with her immediate superior, who did not give her a gift agreed for all the workers.

Patronage has a pretty widespread influence not only on production activity, but also in other spheres of people's life. In popular consciousness there are even terms to designate these kinds of family, friendship and personal relationships, patronage without reference to the specific source of support – this is called the 'hairy hand' or the 'shaggy hand', or the 'long hand' or simply the 'hand', which refers to the idea that a person has a 'hand' which supports him, promotes him and so on. It is not acceptable to refer to the source of this support, especially as this is often hidden.

Strictly informal relations are made concrete in the informal status of the worker, which is, as it were, the 'output' of the informal relations.

Informal status in the process of production changes in the course of work, depending on the behaviour of the individual, on his fulfilment of formal and informal instructions. The most important role in the future development of a person's status is played by the quality of the person's work, his capacity to work and the quality of tasks carried out. His communicative qualities are also important.

For the most part status includes precisely these characteristics. We can hear them when we ask about this or that person: Who is that? Then, for instance, criteria related to a person's capacity to work serve as status characteristics: 'a good worker', 'always helps', 'with him you can not skive', 'he closes his eyes to this or that breach of discipline', 'constantly lectures people', 'an arse licker'. That is, when we ask in the enterprise about a person the reply describes features of his informal status. Most often these refer to:

- work qualities, which evaluate him as a worker – 'all-round expert', 'inexperienced'.
- attitude to work, labour discipline – 'skiver', 'drinker' ('good worker, but drinks', here 'good' is a work quality, but 'drinks' is about the attitude to work, disciplinary qualities).
- moral-ethical qualities: helps others, justice, 'self-seeking', trouble-maker.
- relations to management, i.e. characteristics in the system of superior-subordinate, or place in the formal hierarchy – 'defends workers', 'ingratiates himself to management'.
- extra-labour characteristics – 'trade union organiser', 'cheerful lad', 'sociable', and so on.

Speaking here about informal status we are referring to the statuses of the workers in the factory. But apart from these there are undoubtedly informal statuses attached to posts, such as the status of foreman as a post, which define what the foreman can demand of the worker and what he cannot, which matters he must refer to the shop chief, and which he need not, and so on. The statuses of the posts, obviously, have their hierarchy so that, for example, for the worker it is much more important to have a good relationship with the storeman who issues special clothes or tools than with the technologist who works out the norms for the issue of special clothes and tools. Here we are referring to the informal statuses of workers in the factory as a whole, as much as about personal informal statuses and relationships.

SPHERE OF DISTRIBUTION

The enterprises in which we have been researching have a developed social sphere (*sotskultbyt*). Both enterprises have dozens of kindergartens, a polyclinic, sanatoria, holiday camps and so on. The enterprise often buys goods for its workers with its own resources. For these same purposes the funds of the trade union are often used. Apart from this in conditions of inflation and the crisis of non-payment barter deals are widespread. As a result the enterprise has a large number of goods to be distributed (since there are not enough for everyone) and sold to the workers of the enterprise.

There are formal procedures for the distribution of all these goods among the employees of the factory. The number of these goods and the frequency of their supply depends on the workers' labour contribution, length of service in the enterprise, the number of children the worker has, the age of the worker, participation in the war and so on. At the level of the shop the distribution of these goods frequently depends on the joint decision of line managers and President of the trade union committee (interview with President of shop trade union committee, November 1992).

However in real life access to these goods often depends on personal relations, acquaintance with those people who carry out the distribution. Sometimes the distribution of social goods is carried out with the aim of getting some benefit, receiving a bribe or a reciprocal good turn. Such abuses violate the principles of social justice, and even if they are not criminal offences they are socially disapproved of. Traditionally the trade unions play a major role in the distribution of social goods. This is how the leader of the independent trade union Solidarity, who was previously the President of the shop committee of the official trade union in one of the enterprises, evaluated the distributional activity of the official trade unions in September 1992:

> You know that the basic function of the trade union was distribution. And they always stole everything, that is to say they shared everything for their own benefit, people sat there for decades, and by the way, nothing has really changed. I also had to carry out distribution, and it was very difficult not to compromise myself in front of the workers because distribution is connected with theft.

And this is what he had to say about the principles of distribution through trade union channels:

> — Have there been any attempts on the part of the administration or the official trade unions to cut people who join your trade union off from receiving the goods and services that are distributed?
> — There have. But this is not done openly, but is more like a gradual strangulation, because they remember that I know the law. If they did this officially, for example through a declaration or an order to cut us off, I would be very pleased because I could take it to court. For example, literally yesterday they handed out cigarettes. They gave the shop the agreed quantity. But they gave four packs to members of the official union and only two packs to us. This may be trifling, but it is strangulation. They cannot express their favouritism on a global scale. It's difficult, you hammer everything out, but at any moment they can say that there are no more *putyovki* [passes to rest homes and tourist bases], well I cannot get hold of their documents to find out whether or not they have really run out.

Abuses and violations in the sphere of distribution are considered to be the norm and are clearly viewed negatively by those among whom the benefits are to be distributed. This is precisely because those responsible for distribution try to underline their justice and lack of bias, even if they have not admitted to any violations. The administration and trade union committee try to overcome the dissatisfaction of the workers by publishing details in the factory newspaper of how many of which goods have been distributed to each shop.

Violations in the sphere of distribution are carefully concealed, camouflaged by the observation of all the formalities. It is very difficult to find out about it. Nevertheless sometimes such violations are publicised. Thus one of our respondents unearthed violations by the administration in favour of their own people in the distribution of imported fur coats, automobiles and the construction of garages.

In one case in 1992 the administration of the enterprise transferred four flats in a building under construction to the account of the city administration, for which the enterprise received a large credit. In the same year another enterprise transferred the right to buy automobiles on privileged terms to one of their suppliers, which in return fulfilled an order to supply industrial raw materials.

In general the system of mutual favours between enterprises which depend on one another is a necessary condition for the functioning of the enterprise. For example, one of the Samara enterprises sold its scarce products to a Novokuibyshev enterprise which produced alcohol, which in its turn sent alcohol to an enterprise in Kazakhstan which needed alcohol for the production of cotton. The enterprise in Kazakhstan in its turn supplied raw materials for our enterprise in Samara (interview with chief accountant, April 1992). This is one of the simplest examples of the chains of mutual collaboration.

Among all the examples in which informal relations are connected with distribution, we are particularly interested in those cases in which informal relations in the sphere of distribution are used for the purposes of production. For example, a shop chief told us in October 1992 of a case in which he wanted to hold onto a high-skilled worker who wanted to move to another shop, so he got the administration of the enterprise to give the worker the right to buy a motorcycle.

In those cases in which it is formally forbidden to raise the pay of essential workers informal methods of taking account of their labour contribution and non-monetary incentives are used, for example, moving up the queue for flats to transfer to another shop, or being put at the head of the queue to receive an automobile as the incentive to transfer to another subdivision.

In general the shop with the best production record has the biggest rights to receive privileges in the distribution of goods and services between the shops, but the importance of the position of the shop in the technological chain and the professional composition of the shop also play a part. All these factors play an implicit role in the negotiations with management and contribute to the decision-making about the distribution of various privileges to the shops.

The argument of the President of a shop trade union committee in October 1992 about the desire of workers to leave the official trade union is interesting in the context of informal relations:

> When they say that they want to leave the union I dissuade them; 'wait until spring, nobody knows what is going to happen in the future'. Nobody in our

shop has left the trade union so far. But this, for example, is what Nikolai Kukushkin says: 'What has the trade union given me?' He wants to leave it. But you know we, the trade union, once sent him to work at Kirkombinat and for that he got an apartment. And we could just as well have sent somebody else.

Through distribution in the first place they look after people with twenty years or more of service. Over the past two or three years they have supplied practically every worker in this category with a Malyutka washing-machine which is produced in our factory. Of course the market price is twice as high as that at which it is supplied. I myself usually do not take any of the things which are distributed. You can come to my house and have a look.

The sphere of distribution in enterprises at the present time has been significantly reduced, it has practically disappeared, so the informal relations around distribution have also been reduced.

So. Here we have described cases of informal agreements – the most frequent and easiest to observe. Informal relations are, of course, much more widespread than this. The areas in which informal relations appear can be categorised theoretically so as to group together the cases which we know about.

THE FUNCTIONAL FOUNDATIONS OF INFORMAL RELATIONS

In some cases the sphere of informal relations is subject to strict regulation by formal norms, for example, legal means of taking time off. Here literally every one of your actions has to be recorded, regardless of the fact that the shop chief might be stupid, that the worker might not want to explain why he has to take time off, and regardless of the fact that when those on time wages take time off they lose pay, even if they carry out the work by the appointed time, i.e. they are paid not for their work but for the time spent at work.

In other cases, for example in the distribution of work, there are virtually no regulations governing the activity: there are no rules providing for the allocation of tasks, they are all farmed out by the foreman, depending on his moral and ethical qualities. But the workers' interests are still not taken into account.

Informal relations compensate for the deficiencies of the formal rules governing production relationships. In some cases informal means of resolving problems are possible despite the existence of regulations. It seems to us that the emergence of informal relations does not depend on whether formal regulation is weak or strong, but arise where this regulation is unsuccessful, because it does not take into account the interests of all the people involved in these inter-relationships.

The examination of a number of examples of informal relations will show that they can arise on various foundations.

I. *In some cases they arise as a result of the inadequacy of the formal norms to the demands of production because the formal norms have been established without taking any account of the quality of the equipment.*

Thus, in one of the factories in which we carried out our case studies the operation of many of the machines does not correspond to the operating standards laid down: the foundations of several of the machines are not sufficiently massive and independent so that the machines interfere with the reliable operation of other equipment, as a result of which they have to be re-adjusted twice as frequently. In this particular case this was not a reason for the emergence of informal relations because the adjusters do not know about the norms for adjustment, but consider that their job is to keep the machines working, not being concerned about the frequency or the amount of time required for adjustment. The technologists cannot (and do not want to) rebuild the foundations and so they try to represent this situation as the result of the inadequate quality of the adjustment or slipshod operation.

Work with old equipment (which has sometimes been written off) gives rise to top-up pay (*pripiski*) both on the side of the workers, to persuade them to work, and on the side of the foreman. In the following extract from an interview with a foreman in July 1993 it emerges clearly that the reason is precisely the condition of the equipment, and not the quality of the workers' work, or the norms according to which they are paid.

— For example, take these cutters, who are my lowest qualified workers: the equipment on which they work has already been written off. I have got three perforating machines left, of which only one works. People want to work, but they can not do so because of the inadequacy of the equipment. So I have got two cutters (for this particular kind of work – one of them can not manage it), they are constantly swearing at one another about who will work on this machine, because they both want to work. It could come to blows, although it hasn't got that far yet.
— But why should it come to blows?

— Well, the workers are on piece-rates: they are paid according to how much they produce. If he works on an automatic machine he can earn good money. If he works with a saw on its own, he earns half as much. Either he has to top his pay up, or ...

— How can a worker top up his pay himself?

— The workers try to work on the large rings first of all. A large ring pays 35 roubles and it takes 20 minutes to cut, so he can cut some more faces – several cuts have already been added. I might glance at it in passing, and he writes down three or four more cuts. So, let us say he now has 100 roubles, even more because we now have a coefficient which increases it, so he has made good money. That is how he can top up his pay.

— That is very interesting. Do you have any control over this process of topping up?

— I do.

— But you do not always notice it?

— Yes, and sometimes I even try not to notice it.

— And does this happen with all the workers, or only selected ones?

— With absolutely all of them. I cannot work if I have two cutters in my section constantly swearing at each other.

Work on worn-out equipment is pretty widespread. This is precisely the reason why workers who are able to produce high quality parts on low quality equipment are so highly valued in production, as much on account of their technological nouse, being able to sort out the machines, to fine-tune their adjustment, as on account of the idiosyncrasies of their operation (hitting the machine a couple of times with a sledgehammer in the right place). Such workers benefit from privileges in distribution out of respect for them, and sometimes can use their position to get all sorts of indulgences – they can always say to the chief: let's see you try to work with this machine! This argument worked because it was vital for the chief that the plan should be fulfilled, especially in the past, as a result of which this is not his problem, but a matter for the worker. As far as the foremen are concerned, they tried to find out why the equipment worked like this, but such an understanding often depends on experience rather than on the technological knowledge of the foreman.

II. *In other cases formal demands do not take any account of the conditions of operation of the enterprise.*

Earlier these were the conditions of a planned economy. Then the managers could only secure the fulfilment of the plan targets in time by using informal methods of stimulating the workers (so-called 'spiritual grease'), fines (they allocated less profitable work as a sanction), encouraging them with the use of time-honoured punishments.

The use of strong methods of management also required such methods of encouragement. The production managers did not have the financial resources to stimulate the workers to the regular fulfilment of the plan, and so they had to use incentives not anticipated in the instructions. And here, to ensure the fulfilment of targets in time, the shop chief (through the foreman or in person) uses the so-called 'spiritual grease', that is to say he pours out a certain amount of alcohol which is drunk after work or on the job. The term 'grease' itself leads to the well known saying 'if you do not grease, you will not eat'.

Now the situation is one of unstable demand and falling production. And here managers are already using informal methods: the allocation of more profitable work while sending those for whom there is no work at all on compulsory leave.

III. *In still other situations the formal demands, which emphasise egalitarianism for ideological reasons, do not take into account the real differences in effort, in the labour contribution of the workers.*

'Of course, not everything is perfect in the distribution of pay. Sometimes it does not correspond to the expenditure of labour', was the opinion of the President of a shop trade union committee.

If a person has worked at the factory for twenty or twenty-five years, then formally he has particular privileges as a result of his long service in the allocation of flats and automobiles, the distribution of goods and so on. The President of the shop trade union committee quoted above spoke about this in an interview. But the formal demands do not take into account a whole range of factors, for example that even though a worker may have worked for a long time he may be very mediocre, that the worker might just be a trouble-maker and to work with him might be a constant hassle, and so on. All these factors have to be taken into account. As the trade union President, who is responsible for distribution, put it: 'You have to know about each person's family situation, what are their domestic concerns, how much they earn, how they get to work (the kind of transport), what they live on, you have to know everything.' When we characterised the informal status of a worker, in our opinion it also included and accurately expressed these various aspects of the real life of the worker.

IV.   *In other situations informal relations arose on the basis of the impossibility of the workers being able to carry out all the formal demands.*

This is what a foreman in one of the shops had to say about this in June 1993:

— Do workers in your workplace often violate the instructions?'
— It happens, of course.
— In what area as a rule?
— Well, we have got poor quality technology. That means that a technical process is specified for us in writing, but there is some kind of deficiency. Let us say that a part must be heated up to a particular temperature, but the workers can see from their own experience that if they follow all the instructions it will not turn out like that. They do it in their own way.
— Does it take longer?
— No, it is nothing to do with that. He produces a part, to make it, to make it appropriate. But if he works according to the instructions, an appropriate part will not be produced.
— How often does this happen?
— Very often.
— And is it possible to resolve these problems with the technologists?
— We try not to emphasise it, because in the end we are not expected to maintain the technological processes, we are expected to turn out the products, without interruptions. If the inadequacy of the technology does not stop production, then we work there and then with the technologist: we say to him, we ask him why, how.

A foreman in another factory spoke in July 1993 as follows about violations of the technological specifications:

— It is the same with the free forgings. These are parts which do not really need to be forged, which have to be forged with a manipulator, which were not forged in the past. This blank weighs eighty to ninety kilos, so it cannot be forged by hand. Of course I bear the responsibility, I am in a straightjacket, I pray to all the gods that everything will turn out. Because the equipment is very old, and sometimes the hammer strikes two blows instead of one, this hot blank could fly out and kill someone.
— If you are not required to forge these blanks, why do you do it?
— Because everything is connected with everything else. If it is carted off to another factory this takes a long time and is very expensive. And I know that if I approach a worker and tell him to make a good forging of up to 80 kilos he will forge it for me, but this is only a highly skilled worker. If I knew that they could not do this I obviously would not approach them.
— But why do you have to do work that you are not required to do?

—Money. I depend completely, my pay, my bonus depends on the output of the shop, I am tied to the shop. If I were tied to my own section – then I would get a 40 per cent bonus tied to the output of the shop.

— Why do you constantly violate the norms: on your equipment you can make things within a certain range, but you often go beyond these limits, what forces you to do this?

— The requirements of production, because either there is not the equipment or it is very old. I just ruin the hammer, the equipment. I simply know what I can make and what I cannot.

V. *Now and then the reason for the emergence of informal relations is the elementary carelessness of a worker. This carelessness takes both disciplinary and technological forms.*

The case of defective products can serve as an example of the violation of technological discipline. If a worker allowed faults or defects in the process of production of parts, the foreman would give that worker a 'bruise', which means a 20 per cent, 50 per cent or even 100 per cent loss of bonus. Such a 'bruise' is applied for violations of those processes, for the culture of production (not tidying up the workplace after work), turning up for work drunk. However the people who allowed the violations may have been 'approached' by the foreman, so that when it comes to the moment of working out their pay the 'bruise' is not imposed. When we asked why he acts like this he put forward two arguments in explanation – pity and the fact that the 23rd February holiday was beginning. It is very likely that this is an excuse, but the important point for us is that the worker is not always punished for violations, even if he is found out.

The woman foreman of another factory said to us in July 1993 that if the chief wants to 'put a spoke in the wheel' or to try to remove her ostensibly for some offence (she is sometimes late for work, when she takes the children to school and fetches them), then she can always reply to him that he violates production discipline much more frequently and seriously than she. And she knows this about him, but for the time being everyone closes their eyes to it. For example, he uses the factory's resources for his own purposes (his car spent a whole week being repaired in the factory, some parts for it were made out of turn at the factory's expense, and so on). She also gave us another kind of example: she herself repairs her car during working time or goes out to do her own things when she needs to – well she is also a chief – she is able to! But always, at any opportune moment, he taunts her with the fact that she is often five or ten minutes late coming back from lunch, although he knows very well that she has two small chil-

dren whom she has to fetch from school and for whom she has to prepare lunch every day.

> — But doesn't anybody report on what he is up to?
> — But why? I would do it if he began to blow anything up against me, but
> everybody has all kinds of little shortcomings, so that is why nobody is going to
> report him.

There are two points of view about informal relationships, just as
there are two global reasons for the existence of informal relations: 1)
formal relations do not take account of the whole richness of human
life; 2) people have to breach formal norms in the conditions of
Russian reality. We propose that the reader resolves this dilemma for
herself: whether it is the people who are bad, or the formal relations
which are bad. In our view informal relations fulfil the role of corre-
lating the real lives of people with the conditions and demands of
production.

THREE TYPES OF INFORMAL RELATIONS

We think that there are three types, three large classes of informal relations in production. They are defined not so much by the character
of the action as by the way in which they are understood by the
worker and by the consequences they entail for him.

1)   Individual Violations

Practically every worker commits violations of some or other formal
production, technological or disciplinary requirements. Moreover this
can occur not only as a result of the carelessness of the worker, but
also as a result of the impossibility of meeting all the formal demands.

A person is late for work, exceeds the tolerances in working on the
machinery and so on. If the violation is not noticed, and he gets away
with it all, the worker feels no pangs of conscience. On the contrary,
he is even pleased that he has 'cheated' the factory. It is normal for a
person to be in something of a sweat with the factory. In this kind
of relationship formal norms are violated without any application of
formal sanctions, and although the worker knows that he has committed a violation, within himself he feels that it is permitted. Here we
find the philosophy that if one is not caught there is no crime.

In the examples examined above there are very few cases of informal relations of this type, and that is understandable because workers try to conceal them, but nevertheless such violations exist. Doubtless there are also unrevealed violations in the sphere of distribution. Here one should also include the frequent cases of theft from factories.

One of the factories acquired an imported packaging system for finished products. However the plastic cassettes were so suitable for seedlings that the cassettes and all the reserves for some incomprehensible reason vanished from the factory. The only way to resolve this problem completely was to arrange the production of cassettes for the stacking system in the factory itself. However it turned out that such packaging did not correspond to world standards, production was cut back, and the cassettes were replaced by wooden packaging.

One can judge how widespread is this phenomenon not only by the size of the figures which appear in the statistical accounts of the enterprise but also by the common joke of the workers: someone asks you at the end of the day, 'what did you make today?' – in reply you tell them or show them what you took away from work today.

Such violations not only occur in discipline and distribution. Here is an example of a violation of the technological process. We discovered in an interview with a worker in May 1993 that the workers can violate these processes without the knowledge of the foreman.

> If I have confidence in myself, if I know what I am doing, I by-pass the adjustment control for this operation, I fix it directly on the bench, and I only test it when I have finished. In that way I immediately cut out two transfers.

The violation of formal requirements may arise not only to the detriment of production, but also at the expense of the worker's own health in order to earn higher wages. In this way piece-workers in one of the factories themselves instituted a more intensive pace of work, going in on Saturday so as not to lose pay ('we were idlers here – now we make up on Saturday').

In this type of relationship the worker feels some anxiety in relation to those people who could reveal these violations, but he does not experience any similar feelings in relation to the enterprise.

2)   Informal Relations as a System of Dependence

If violations come to light, formal sanctions do not always follow. The foreman may not impose the corresponding sanction in relation to this or that offender, and sometimes leaves the violation unpunished, and in this situation the offender is considered to be obliged to the foreman. The one who has incurred the obligation has to repay the person who hides the offence in some way, and this is retribution due to a particular person, to the foreman personally. This person then has a right to demand of the offender in due course that he does something beyond the norms (not anticipated in the formal requirements). The worker has become dependent on the foreman, on his good mood and disposition. These may often be production demands, for example to make parts in a very short time because the customers are in a hurry. Nevertheless these demands arise as a personal request, and not as a production requirement (and correspondingly are not paid). Moreover the repayment for a violation often has a personal character, for example to make some kind of part for a private car, and so on.

This deal takes the form of a verbal agreement, sometimes immediately the violation is discovered. For example, the shop chief might meet a worker who is arriving late and say: 'So! You are late?!' The worker, hanging his head, is quiet, or begins to justify himself. The chief continues: 'Well, OK then, you can sharpen some cutters for me'. If the worker continues to justify himself or the chief is indignant with him there is no deal. But if the worker continues to keep quiet and goes off, then the deal is done. Now and then the chief's demands on the worker as compensation for the violation seem to be excessive and the worker asks for additional conditions, seeking some additional privileges for himself. He may say, for example, 'Yes, but my grinding wheels are old, where can I get some better ones' or 'the cutters are very hard'. To which the chief will reply 'I will give you some wheels!' or something like 'Fetch the cutters yourself – you aren't a child – I can not create them. You know very well ... what did you smell of the day before yesterday. I will cut out your overtime!'

One often hears of other cases in which the violation is simply covered up, and no conditions at all are set. The worker is simply considered to have incurred an obligation, an obligation to show his gratitude sometime in the future, to finish off his work. The retribution is separated from the violation. Such a situation establishes the violator in a position of dependence. If sometime in the future the worker-violator refuses to carry out the demands of the chief (i.e. does not recognise the system of relations that has developed), he will either become an outcast in the collective, or he will be faced with the formal procedure for his sacking or punishment.

The system of dependence is personified. If the foreman does not punish the worker for a technological violation, then the latter is personally obliged to the person who covered up this violation, not to foremen in general. The worker has no obligation to the shop chief who authorised him to take a day off when his relatives visited, but the worker is personally obliged to Ivan Ivanovich, who held this post and helped out. If another shop chief comes along this obligation to Ivan Ivanovich is not transferred to him. But this obligation to Ivan Ivanovich remains, even though he is now working in another shop. It is interesting that when a shop chief moves from one shop to another in the factory, other workers follow him to this shop because their whole system of informal relations is transferred with them (interview with a shop chief, October 1992).

The system of dependence does not require an immediate repayment. If the repayment followed, then the person would become independent. The person who holds the other in dependence is inclined to stretch out the informal retribution for as long as possible, in order to prolong the condition of dependence.

The foremen do not like to apply sanctions to violators. But knowledge of violations provides him with a definite power in the informal system of interdependence. For example, one foreman who was asked in an interview in June 1993 how he dealt with violations said: 'I always try to make a note of it. Even if I do not say anything, I will make it clear that I have noticed that he is drunk, and he should try not to do it again.' A worker in one of the factories said 'the chief is pleased when he sees us drunk', then he can force the workers to do some job or other. Because he has not applied any formal sanctions the chief establishes the dependence of these people on him and can demand that they carry out additional work (fetch something, send them somewhere and so on).

Dependence is not only established vertically between levels of the production hierarchy, but also in the opposite direction. The foreman in the factory is dependent on the worker, on the quality, quantity and speed with which he carries out his work. Thus in an interview in May 1993 a worker declared:

The foreman is more dependent on the worker than the worker is on the foreman. You see. He needs him to fulfil the plan. He has a particular set of things that he must get done. There are deadlines that he must meet and if he does not meet them he has to go to the workers and ask them to come in on Saturday ...

In the background is the fact that the workers can consciously extend the time they take to fulfil their tasks. The foreman in another factory complained to us that the managers ask the foreman about getting the products out, he is responsible to the management for this, but the worker finds a load of excuses, and what's more they never appeal to the worker, you see there are many of them but the foreman is on his own.

Such mutual relations exist not only from above to below (the subordinate depends on the chief), but also from below to above (the chief turns out to be in a position of dependence), and also horizontally at one level of the hierarchy.

The person who uses his influence to recruit someone to a job, introduces a newcomer to the shop, helps a protégé enter into the structure of relations in the factory, receives in exchange his share of dependence.

The system of mutual (or one-sided) dependence actively functions at one level of the production hierarchy (between workers, for example, or between shop chiefs) or at neighbouring levels (worker-foreman, foreman-senior foreman). However there are also multi-level relations of dependence, for example the Director of the factory may have 'his' fitter, 'his' chauffeur, and so on, and these relations may be maintained for quite a long time in a suspended form, but can be activated when they are needed.

The system of dependence is sufficiently strong that it can also be mobilised for activities unconnected with production. Activities beyond those normatively prescribed may be called for in the most varied spheres: production, in social activity (speaking at a meeting), lend money, go to fetch some beer, supply a 'bubble', render other services.

We have recorded a curious example of the operation of these systems of informal dependence. A shop chief had to make a fence around the grave of a relative, for which he received the appropriate permission from a manager. But when he sent his technologist to shop 3, which does this kind of work, the latter refused, ostensibly because of the absence of materials. Then the chief asked one of his fitter-adjusters to go to the third shop. When the fitter approached the chief of shop 3 with the order to make the fence, the latter said 'I guessed whom he would send!' and met the order. The point was that the fitter was a childhood friend of the chief of shop 3, and the latter 'simply could not refuse him'. It is true that conditions were laid down in response – three bottles of vodka, on top of which this work was accounted in the planned tasks and the workers who carried it out were paid accordingly (interview with a fitter, July 1993).

The system of relations of personal dependence may be created not only on the basis of violations (as retribution for them), but also on the basis of the conscientious fulfilment of formal demands, particularly in those situations in which it is not possible to provide incentives for it. For example a worker may be moved up the housing list for good work, even though this is a violation of the rules.

The relations between the foreman and workers in one of the factories is built on mutual concessions, according to a foreman in an interview in July 1993. Moreover, good deeds are not only recognised by similar good deeds in return, but also are done in the hope of establishing a reciprocal relationship. The foreman understands that good relations are not built out of nothing, but arise from a feeling of a good relation to oneself. The workers will not submit to the foreman, and the foreman will not hold onto workers, if he does not pay them. Thus we speak about a system of mutual dependence.

In such circumstances any activity beyond the norms is not perceived simply as normal, but as providing the possibility in the future of demanding compensation for a good deed (i.e. establishing somebody in a position of dependence). This is the psychology which has developed. In general, activity beyond the norms which cannot be explained from the point of view of relations of dependence is regarded as nonsense ('What are you doing? Do you need something?') or with great distrust ('Who sent you?'). It is thus no accident that the management of the factory regularly try to represent pay increases as personal good turns: 'I published an order to increase pay' (Director), 'I got an increase in pay' (shop chief), 'I demanded that the management increase our pay' (shift foreman) – all explaining one and the same fact to the workers.

We have often heard the way in which deals over production questions are fixed through consultations over the intercom between the Director and heads of shops and plants in one of the factories. When the Director urgently demands that a particular task be carried out, the chief of the relevant shop sometimes comes out with his own demand: I do not have any oil, or something else needed by the shop. And as a rule he gets the Director's approval or a promise to receive what he wants. In this case the repayment for dependence is made immediately, and the form of payment is stipulated. In other cases the repayment is postponed. It is simply that the Director remembers the fact that one particular shop produced a batch of parts ahead of schedule, and then when automobiles are being distributed the shop chief might remind the Director about the fact that he once made a batch of parts for him (as though it were his personal request). If the Director turns out to be forgetful then the next time there is a risk that his instruction will not be carried out on the basis of goodwill alone.

Thus the informal structure of the shop or factory is a branching system of the most diverse dependencies and interdependencies, built up on the basis of personal relationships. It would be incorrect to characterise these interrelationships as being of the 'you–me' 'I–you' type, with the idea that I will not do anything for anybody unless I get something from him in return. It is something quite different: I do something for somebody, but if he does not do something for me when I need it then I will be hurt and offended.

It is likely that informal relations with a person are reflected in the informal status of their post. Although they are not likely fully to define the status of the post, they certainly have an influence on it.

These personal relations permeate functional links and relationships in production. And often production is ensured only thanks to this system of informal relations. Relations between people who at first sight hardly know one another appear as personal, friendly, comradely.

We are inclined to consider that in the majority of cases informal relations function as a system of personal dependencies. Above all, the system of personal dependencies, most probably, is extended to the framework of private labour activity and embraces the widest range of events in people's lives.

3) Established Norms

Here we refer to those informal relations of whose existence the worker is not even aware. If a violation of the requirements of production is permitted, and this does not have any consequences, despite the fact that in principle everybody knows about it, then it becomes an informal norm.

For example, one is supposed to be at work at eight o'clock, but generally people would only be coming through the entrance at that time. And people do not even think of this as a disciplinary violation, although they should already be at their workplaces at eight o'clock. Periodically (once every few years) the managers of one of our factories would remember this, and would conduct a campaign to register the time at which workers arrive at and leave their workplaces, control over which fell to the shop and department chiefs, with the application of fines. At these times the workers would try to arrive at the entrance ten or fifteen minutes before work began. However everything quickly reverted to the normal course. In another institution there is a norm of lateness: thus, one can be thirty minutes late, but to be an hour late is considered improper.

In several enterprises there is an informal tradition of marking workers' birthdays at work, sometimes with the consumption of alcoholic drinks – informal norms touch on many aspects of the life of workers in the enterprise.

An interesting judgement on the permissible differences in pay between a skilled and an inexperienced worker was expressed in an interview with a foreman in July 1993: 'There may be a difference in pay of between one and one and a half thousand in favour of the more experienced worker. And if the less experienced worker signs for extra work without crossing this limit then I shut my eyes to this.'

Informal norms relate not only to violations of formal instructions, but also to the conscientious fulfilment of production tasks. Thus it is considered normal that if a person has worked for a long time and considers himself to be a specialist, then he should understand the equipment on which he works, so as to perfect it and, in particular, to become a rationaliser.

The participation of workers in various political actions remains normal: the organisation of an election campaign, leaving work for a demonstration or meeting, participation in voluntary civilian detachments to maintain public order.

The violation of traditional norms of interaction leads to a negative reaction, and may put someone in the position of an outcast in the collective.

An example is the way in which the behaviour of the Director of one of the factories, which did not conform to the traditional style of informal relations, was perceived. (He spoke his mind at a meeting of the labour collective, but he did not pass the time of day with people in the factory.) His disdain for the traditional norms reduced his authority and his popularity with the workers. A shop trade union President expressed his indignation in November 1992:

The words of the Director must be weighty, not like mine. But how can one say something, and then not do it? He promised every worker imported underwear, but what came of this – it was terrible! There was one bra for every six workers and one pair of pants for every five. The workers were coming into the factory when they met the Director. So why did he not even greet any of them?

Normative representations concerning the level of pay are particularly interesting. The shop trade union President (a man who has worked his whole life in the factory) continued:

> I know that some people have low pay and some people have high pay, but there should not be such differences. Of course they have graduated from the Institute, they have studied for many years, and they used to earn less than a loader, I do not agree with this. But if he is highly qualified, a machine operator receives too little. It seems to me that in terms of pay they should be somewhere closer together. Well there will be a little difference. Of course, those who have only recently arrived and begun to work on the machines should earn less, but there should not be such differences.

We have heard an enormous number of opinions about what should be the pay of this or that category of worker because this is a very acute problem today. However none of these judgements is based on any economic evaluation, but provide interesting material about the criteria according to which pay is considered fair and just in the understanding of workers.

In general normative propositions about the level of pay are based on an understanding of justice. There is a deeply rooted idea of equality in popular consciousness: not the American idea of equality of opportunity, but the Soviet idea of equality of outcome. Evaluations are accompanied by an almost unconscious philosophy: if things are bad for me, then they must be bad for others; if they are good for me, then they must be good for others too, it is just that they conceal it! If workers in one and the same job working in different enterprises or different organisations earn different pay, the explanation 'because they work in another enterprise' will certainly not satisfy the person who is paid less, he is not going to be satisfied with the argument that he had an equal opportunity when he started his career: he will compare his situation with that of the worker in the enterprise which is paying more now. He demands equal pay, without looking at the different economic positions of the enterprises, or the level of development of production, or a thousand other reasons which distinguish one enterprise from another. If his neighbour earns less, then this says something about his inability to organise himself, arouses contempt, or at least pity. But at the same time there is an idea of a minimum subsistence level, an income lower than which provokes a uniformly negative reaction.

The types of informal relations that we have identified differ in the consequences for the workers of the action in question, depending on how it is perceived by the workers, not on the properties of the action itself. One and the same action (for example lateness for work) may be linked to the first, second or third type depending on its consequences. For example, if the lateness of a worker (which is a violation of formal norms) is ignored and has no effect on work, then we identify it with the first type. If the lateness is punished, but the formal mechanism of punishment is not invoked, and the person who was late becomes to some extent dependent on the person who did not invoke the sanctions, then we consider it a case of the second type of informal relations. If the worker does not even know that lateness for work is a violation of the formal norms, so that lateness has itself become an informal norm, then we consider this a case of the third type of informal relations.

Pavel Romanov considers that informal relations operate in the reproduction of every aspect of the working life of the enterprise. That they, being an inalienable part of production, themselves reproduce the process of production equally with the formal norms.

In our opinion this view is absolutely true, but only in relation to the third group of informal relations. Indeed, established as stereotypes, the norms of mutual relationships between workers support the rhythm of work. Informal relations with the foreman or brigadier, having taken on the form of fixed stereotypes, also serve to reproduce the process of production. This group of relationships plays a conservative, stabilising role in the process of production. They preserve the production process unchanged.

The second group of informal relations, in our view, only reproduces the basis of the status relations of the producers (workers and managers). The functioning of the system of dependence secures the high status of the foreman or shop chief and, correspondingly, enhances their ability to manage the workers. It provides a reserve with which to manipulate people, for the strengthening or weakening of the formal demands.

The system of dependence is a basis for the restructuring of production, for the possibility of its change. The established system of dependence may contradict the formal requirements of production. And it may be destroyed by the system, formal and informal, at a higher level (when the post of foreman was abolished in one shop). At the same time the system of dependence modifies the traditional norms of inter-relations in production.

The first group of informal relations is close to the third, but the workers are more conscious of it. This group not only does not reproduce production relations, but is in direct violation of them. In this sense it forcibly destroys the production process. But a new tradition can be created even with a single case.

So informal relations are simultaneously a conservative force, factors for change and destructive of managerial power in the sphere of production.

The conflict and interaction of formal and informal relations is not the only source of development and change in relations to production, but also within the informal relations there are fairly contradictory, fairly destructive and stabilising moments, which indicate not only the impossibility of their withering away, but also the impossibility of their independent development, independent functioning.

ON CHANGES IN INFORMAL RELATIONS

In describing informal relations in various spheres of activity of the enterprise we have touched on those changes which have come about in recent years. Here we would like to say something about the most significant changes in the area of informal relations.

I. *The most obvious tendency is the weakening of the traditional sphere of informal relations. Informal relations have most recently given way to formal relations*

This has been affected by the fall in the volume of production and the reduction in the number of workers. The administration does not want to support a large number of people at work and tries to get rid of the surplus labour. Thus if it is possible to apply formal sanctions to violators, they use them so that they do not have to pay the workers who have been sacked the redundancy payments which are due to those who have been made redundant as a result of cuts in staff. As production falls, so does the need to reproduce informal relations, or to reproduce them to the same extent.

However the process of reduction of the number of workers is not necessarily related to a decline in the sphere of informal relations. Thus, when the plant is working at low capacity, the closer the worker is to the foreman the more chance he has to get work. Or, for example, in one of the factories the voluntary redundancy of the fitter-adjusters meant that the workers had to repair their machines themselves, and the foremen had to try to find ways of influencing and stimulating them. In the area of recruitment to work informal relations (personal connections, patronage) continue to play an extremely important role (interview with a foreman, June 1993).

Although the traditional sphere of informal relations is narrowing, nevertheless informal relations are not disappearing, they are beginning to emerge in new areas of activity of the enterprise. It would be more accurate to say that the sphere of informal relations is changing (informal relations are spreading).

One can see a new sphere of application of informal relations with the beginning of the process of privatisation. Already at the first stage of privatisation of the enterprise one can cite examples which indicate that informal relations will have an important future in this sphere. Thus, in one of the factories in which we have been researching, a situation arose in which the administration drew up the list of representatives on the shareholders' council of the enterprise and proposed them to meetings of worker-shareholders of the factory. At one of the meetings that we attended the participants in the meeting did not adopt the administration's list, but the list proposed by the meeting clearly did not suit the administration. According to all the evidence the resolution of this problem was only possible through some exceptional, informal means (they will probably activate existing interdependencies, personal relations, and so on). Moreover the process of privatisation itself is inadequately formalised, even at the level of the legislation.

II. *The development of informal relations leads to their formalisation. In their operation informal interrelations are perceived by workers as duties, as norms of behaviour, they get used to them and it is possible that the informal norm will be reproduced in specific instructions as a duty, as a formal demand.*

Our hypothesis is that the three types of informal interrelations which we have defined amount to three stages in the process of development of informal relations. Beginning with individual cases, they then take the form of informal interactions (dependencies), and finally become norms of behaviour. The gradual establishment of informal norms may be fixed in documents, i.e. included in the formal framework.

Informal means of recruitment of workers and promotion through connections with relatives are reflected in such completely official factory documents as the 'Regulations concerning labour dynasties', according several privileges to these groups of workers (labour dynasties).

We found such a situation in one of the factories in which we conducted our case study. We spoke to people in the Personnel Department about the list of people designated as reserves for promotion – normally the reserve for the post of Director is the second most important person in the factory, the Chief Engineer, but in our enterprise it turned out that it was the Deputy Director for Production who came from a factory dynasty, which was probably what defined his status, although a former Director had also held the post of Deputy for Production. What is important here is that the formal norm – the reserve for promotion – took account of the personal characteristics of the person, and was not related to his post. The form itself – reserve for promotion – is expected to take all these features into account.

Having begun this article by posing the question how do workers work in Russian enterprises, we have inevitably touched on the question what is work for Russian workers. Furthermore, speaking about the changes in informal relations in production which have been going on in the most recent period, we have to note that attitudes to work in general have changed. The internal disposition of the worker, in our view, is now changing.

III. *What was work for Soviet people in the past? What was it? A habit. A means of self-realisation. A way of providing the means of subsistence. A meeting place, a circle of friends and acquaintances.*

Maybe it was all these things at once. But now we sense that to this has been added a feeling of fear – fear of losing all this, fear of losing one's job.

IV. *In the last several years the role of ideological levers in the management of workers has significantly decreased. The ideological support for managerial influence, backed in the past above all by the Party line, has significantly weakened.*

The shop chief in one of the factories told us in October 1992 that now nobody is responsible: earlier they could call on the Party Committee to tear someone off a strip, and this had an effect on people. The Chief Engineer of another factory complained about the absence of the Party Committee as an additional lever of power.

The disappearance from the enterprise of such ideological structures as the Party and Komsomol organisation removed the ideological content of labour, although appeals to the value of labour as such and the factory as one's 'native' enterprise persist.

Now the receipt of work, wages, payments and so on, is not reinforced by the influence of the Party Committee, the consequence for the production life of the shop is that the informal relations which exist in this sphere have lost their ideological support and become important for their own sake. They have become stronger. The point is that earlier one could take a complaint to the Party Committee (whether about wages, the distribution of work, about a negligent worker or a tyrannical boss), but now there is nobody to complain to. Both the foreman and the shop chief – God and Tsar, have seen an increase in their importance and authority.

There is an interesting example of the part played by the ideological component in informal relations. The President of the shop committee of the trade union told us with some pride about his ability to represent the domestic problems of workers as problems at a factory level, or affecting the position of the factory, branch, state and so on. As President of the shop committee he went to the Director of the factory to try to resolve the domestic problems of the workers. He had thought out his speech very carefully, and used examples such as the following: 'A worker from our factory comes to work and every day sees himself on the Board of Honour, but he cannot invite guests home because he lives in a hostel'.

V. *Money enters into informal relations and has begun to play a noticeable role.*

Here is a fairly extensive excerpt from an interview with a worker in one of the factories, reflecting on the changing motivation of labour in May 1993, against the background of conflict between older and younger workers. This conflict is primarily at a moral level, but it often comes to the surface over questions of money and payment.

— What are the biggest changes around you in the section. Can you give us an idea of what has happened over the past year or two, or maybe three?'
— About what in particular?
— Well, in general, do you think: yes things have changed here, or that everything remains as it was before.
— Now I think that things have changed for the worse. Earlier it was ...
— In the general atmosphere?

— Yes, that's exactly it, the general atmosphere. Let me tell you about these two lads who, as a matter of fact, came to us like this: our section is mechanical milling-machine operators, fitters – it was one shop. But these two lads worked (well, at that time there were not two, four or five people worked there) in another shop, they also had a separate section. But they were real grabbers, born grabbers. So when they were combined with our section the young lads who worked with us tried to keep up with them, they became grabbers. Now, I tell you, if you want some help – no way! Help – money!

— Was this within the brigade? Give them a bottle and then ...

— No, not within the brigade, but between us it has become like that now. Not everyone, I say, not everyone. People who have worked a long time have not changed, but the young lads basically look after themselves.

— Is this at the everyday level? Does one worker say to another: I will do this for you, and you give me half a litre or something?

— Yes, yes, yes. I will help you – but you must do something for me in return? That is all there is to it.

— Was there a lot of cohesion in the past?

— Yes, extremely strong cohesion. I tell you I just do not recognise these young people, I simply do not understand them you know. Some of them are just here to earn money, it is all me–me. Already they do not think about other people.

— But it could hardly just be these two who corrupted them. Probably it happened to all of them. Probably the atmosphere got worse.

— No. It only began with those two. But those lads began to grab for themselves. Everybody saw that they were grabbing for themselves.

— Did this lead to any kind of condemnation?

— At the beginning it did. But then these two 'big specialists' got the management under their thumb – you know it got to the stage where the lads even set conditions to the shop chief: I will not make these parts for that money, you pay me double and I will make them for you.

— And how did the chief react to that?

— The chief has power. At first, of course, he began by threatening them, I will punish you! But then – time is short, time is short – the result of all this was that they got him under their thumb.

— Maybe this also happened in the past, but on a smaller scale? When workers said to the chief: OK, you give us something and we will make the plan?

— No, it was not like that before. Relationships then were completely different. Absolutely different. There were absolutely no negotiations, none at all.

Here we will identify some general features of the restructuring of relations between managers and workers in production. Some workers are **already** prepared for the kinds of interrelations that one can call capitalist: they are ready to work **for money**. Monetary incentives have become extremely significant for them, and they try to use them. The management of the shop itself is still attracted to strong management methods, and does not use monetary incentives in production (it is true that in the majority of the cases they do not have any such incentives at their disposal). As a result there is a dual selection, a selection of those workers who hold on to the traditional norms of interaction, which are built on the customary methods of management, based firstly on influence and orders, secondly on the charity of a good chief and thirdly on the ideological conception of collectivism.

The considerable significance of money in the productive life of workers is indicated by the fact that the theme of money and pay comes up all the time in workers' conversations. Almost everybody we interviewed complained about the low level of their pay.

The low level of pay was the cause of every strike that we know about, with the primary demand being for more pay. Money – that is the hobby-horse, the main argument, of the new independent trade unions for the recruitment of new members, although it is true that this runs alongside the defence of the interests of workers. Workers are attracted to the new trade unions because they assign much more money than do the official trade unions to visiting the sick, to relatives' funerals and so on.

It is difficult to illustrate this influence with material from interviews, but our feeling is that the mentality of the workers itself is changing. Now money is seen as the purpose of work. In the past the idea of work was **to work**, including the importance of such factors as good relations in the collective, the acquisition of the skills of a trade or profession, high pay – but pay primarily as an index of your needs. But now the idea of work is **to earn**, that is to get a lot of money. The value of work is changing. In the past workers were proud of their professionalism, that they had mastered their machine, that you could not work it without them, that they had worked in the factory for their entire life and they were valued for their work. Differences in pay were not very large. Now money is important for its own sake and differences in pay can be fantastic.

Nevertheless personal relationships continue to be very important. But if in the past it was important to have acquaintances, connections with Komsomol, Party or trade union bureaucrats (the biggest distributors), these organisations have either vanished or their distributive functions have been curtailed, but connections with the management of the factory, with the shop chief or the foreman, within the production structures, remain important. At present consumption goods, which are distributed in the enterprise through trade union channels, cost more and more in the shops (which in the past had only a small mark-up on goods, so they were cheap) and there is not such a shortage of goods. The significance of the trade union as a channel of distribution has fallen sharply. Now it is not so important to be close to a bureaucrat: if you have money, you can buy goods!

It is also noteworthy that for money people are even ready to do work which is not a normal part of their trade.

3. On a Particular Kind of Love and the Specificity of Soviet Production

Sergei Alasheev

One can often hear or read in the mass media that (former) Soviet people, including workers, do not know how to work, that the quality of production is low and does not in any way correspond to western standards, being at a lower level.

Scientific works (those of Don Filtzer, for example) also claim that Russian production is a process of reproduction of waste and of low quality products.

In my opinion this is not quite correct. In this article I want to put forward my view of production in enterprises. In the course of carrying out our case studies on the restructuring of industrial relations in Russian enterprises I began to think about the untechnological character of Russian production, about the absence of any well-defined technological regulation of the production process. Here I will try to provide some foundation for this point of view.

The article is based not only on interview materials but also on observation of work in shops and the activities of managers. The basic source of this article is provided by research materials from only one enterprise in Samara. This is a large ball-bearing factory. Although I will support my arguments with observations from other enterprises, nonetheless it was precisely immersion in the atmosphere of factory life in the course of the research that led me to the hypothesis proposed here.

First it is necessary to examine the aspects of the production process which affect the quality of the product and technological discipline. In my opinion the most important factors are: attitudes to work, the condition of equipment, the quality of raw materials and the technology of production in the strict sense.

ATTITUDES TO WORK

After spending eighteen months in one factory, including many meetings with workers and managers the following picture has emerged.

Soviet (and now Russian) workers do know how to work! Yes indeed! They really know and love their job, their work.

Work is one of the most important values in people's lives (on a level with their family), according to opinion polls. According to my observations people quite often value their work above their family life. Workers get more satisfaction from carrying out their work responsibilities, and sometimes much more, than from the time they spend with their families. This basically concerns male workers.

This is all the more the case because the living conditions of the majority of workers leave something to be desired. (Quite often they live in communal flats or in rooms in hostels, but even if they live in their own flats this is not much good because the majority of workers are elderly people and the best ones have been passed on to their grown up children.) Five thousand of the twenty thousand people working in the factory are in the queue to receive housing.

The housing problem has an important influence on the activity of workers, and the distribution of housing is one of the levers by which the administration and the trade union committee puts pressure on employees. Thus in one of the sections of the factory all the workers joined an alternative trade union, but the foreman, who was a supporter of the workers, did not join this trade union in March 1993. The behaviour of the foreman is explained by his unwillingness to leave the old trade union because he did not want to lose the chance of receiving housing. In this way he formally displayed his loyalty to the management of the factory ('he has worked for four years for an apartment and now he is waiting for them to give him an apartment, so he does not want to do anything rash').

Even those whose housing conditions could be considered satisfactory are not usually dying to get home at the end of the working day. This is because of the low level of comfort and poor conditions for rest in our apartments, and also the lack of development of leisure facilities in the city ('after work there is nowhere to go').

Yura is a metalworker whom I know very well. He has worked at the factory for 36 years. He has two years to go to retirement, and he continues to work in the factory, despite the attempts of the administration to cut the number of workers without a formal process of redundancy. Despite a significant fall in pay (in comparison to the growth of prices), Yura does not under any circumstances intend to leave his job, explaining his decision by the fact that, firstly, he is used to it and, secondly, he is convinced that the administration is holding down pay because it is trying to cut the numbers, but that later production will return to normal and then, as a high-grade specialist who knows the equipment inside out, he will earn normal pay.

So Yura lives in a little room of twelve square metres in a communal flat for seven families. He lives alone, he is not married. Now and then he stays behind at work for an hour or two to finish repairing a machine (so that 'it doesn't hang on my heart'). He has a permanent and long-lasting relationship with a woman, but it is not too burdensome for him. His basic activity in his free time consists in helping his common-law wife, who has a separate one-room apartment where she lives with her sick mother. He busies himself fitting out her apartment, using materials taken from the factory and tools made in the factory. He considers that there is no point in ennobling his apartment. The rest of the time he spends looking out of the window, in conversations and quarrels with his neighbours, and in drinking together with his relatives and colleagues (now and then with people he has met on the street – one cannot drink alone).

He goes to work with great pleasure. There he has many friends and acquaintances, and there are many things to talk about. At work he feels himself to be a professional, not that he is irreplaceable, but that he is needed. He speaks with great enthusiasm about some unusual breakdown, which he comes across all the more rarely because the majority of them are already well-known to him.

Confirmation of this loving attitude to work is provided by the fact that in one of the shops in which the case study was carried out, the workers come to the shop one and a half hours before the beginning of the shift, and spend the time chatting together about a wide variety of things.

The workers find a 'safety-valve' in work, because they live in such conditions that work, if you like, is the single socially approved possibility of self-realisation.

One can provide examples of people gladly giving up their free time for their work, the family life of people sometimes counts for less than the environment of their work life. A small episode from the biography of the shop chief of one of the subdivisions of our factory seems to me to be very revealing, as does the commentary on it by the author of the official history of the factory.

> She lived not far from the shop, on Vodnikov Street, and the whistle of the Andion machines as they worked grinding grooves carried to the window of her room. This meant that at night, if the machine stopped for any reason, Savel'eva would immediately be woken up by the sudden silence and, hurriedly dressing, would run to the shop, find the reason for the fault ... this was not during the war years, but the middle of the 1960s. If one can put it like this: you do not lose your feeling of personal responsibility for everything for a single minute, whether or not it is your job, this is the most conscious discipline. It is the lack of such discipline that we are all starting to mention in our complaints about the difficulties of present-day production activity. And it is by no means only the particular behaviour of the specific shop chief P.V. Savel'eva that we have in mind, this quality was typical and normal for practically all her colleagues (E.E. Astakhov, *Zhizn' prozhit'* (*A Life to Live*): A Documentary-Artistic Narrative, Two volumes, Samara, 1991, Vol. 1, p. 23).

As a result of such a responsible attitude to work, people can develop unique, phenomenal professional capacities. Here is a quotation from an article in the factory newspaper which struck me:

> A complex multi-axis automatic machine was stopped for repair. When it was stripped down it appeared that it needed a replacement shaft, the pinions were worn out, and the ball bearings had also served their time. In another shop this would have required the machine to stand idle for repair because the repair base would only get down to making parts when they had received the drawings.
>
> But here they instructed the brigade of fitters headed by V. Barinov. The machine was repaired not only quickly, but also to a high standard.
>
> Barinov, a universal turner, can make any part without a drawing, using a sample. Take him a spindle and he will make one similar in every detail.
>
> Only a person with considerable production experience could do this. And the turner Barinov has plenty of experience and practical knowledge. He has worked at the factory for fifteen years, and has repaired equipment for the whole of this time.
>
> V. Barinov has another noteworthy quality: in addition to doing his turning well, he knows grinding inside out and on these operations he over-fulfils the norms for the shift by two to two and half times. (Astakhov, Vol. 1, p. 223)

It was our impression that clever individualistic people who carry out not only their own narrow tasks, but who are also universal, with a wide range of skills, are respected in the factory (particularly among the veterans).

Clear evidence of the committed attitude to work is provided by the movement of worker-rationalisers. Now, as in the past, one can find many worker-rationalisers. The technologists of one shop spoke of the large number of rationalisation proposals put forward by workers, affecting both the technological potential and the efficiency of the equipment.

Here is an example from the official history of the factory, which recounts the story of the rationalisation proposal of a fitter, the fitter of grinding machines G.I. Kon'shina according to the description of another fitter in the same shop, K.I. Ivleva.

> I cannot omit to describe one invention on which we worked together. In the ball-making shop there was a big breakdown as a result of 'burns' during the grinding of balls. These burns happen because the balls come into contact with one another when they move at high speed between the cast-iron disks through concentric grooves. In this shop, in order to avoid this, they began to use wooden and aluminium balls as 'padding' for the manufacture of large balls. This reduced the breakdowns slightly, but did not completely eliminate them, and as a result productivity fell – because half the capacity was made up of 'buffer' balls. We tried out many ways of resolving this problem and, finally, a successful idea came into Kon'shina's head – to replace the concentric rings on the disks by multiple spirals. In them the balls move at increasing speed, and as a result of this they cannot come into contact with one another. The results of practical experiments had the hoped-for result; the way to grind without 'burns' had been found. (Astakhov, Vol. 1, pp. 186–7)

Or here is a quotation from the newspaper:

> The growing requirements of the Soviet engineering industry demand an increase in the output of ball-bearings from massive rivetless separators...
>
> On the initiative of the shop mechanic P.M. Isakov they decided to create their own design of extruding machine with a motive power of one ton and to build it directly in the shop. The task was carried out by the forces of the collective of the mechanical service of the shop, since the design of the machine had been worked out directly by P.M. Isakov. The new machine has undoubted advantages over existing production models. It is simple to adjust and repair, and provides increased speeds of extrusion – ten metres a minute, while the usual machines are only rated at six metres a minute ... Now the mechanic Isakov is working on the creation of a new design of high capacity machine, intended to extrude windows in massive separators. (Astakhov, Vol. 1, p. 224)

Workers' rationalisation proposals were encouraged by moral stimuli: the handing out of certificates, the display of photographs on the Board of Honour, the award of the title 'best rationaliser in the factory', and so on, and also small monetary bonuses. It is significant that despite the insignificant material stimuli, large numbers of rationalising proposals and inventions were put forward.

In an interview in August 1993 I asked a fitter (former deputy chief of the shop with responsibility for technical matters), why so many people are involved in rationalisation and invention:

—Why do you have to do this?
—You see this reflex is still working. I still burn with it. I still cannot exist without it. I walk around and I look and I want everything around here to work as well as possible. Even though I do not have to do this ...

So, on the one hand, the love of workers for their work is an inescapable feature, and on the other it is an energetic love and not a contemplative admiration. Thus workers love their work, dedicate themselves to it completely, although in discussion they often curse it. To put it figuratively, it is the worker's 'difficult love', not simply sex or fleeting passion.

Of course, in the factory there are many different kinds of people, with the most varied attitudes to their duties: there are also idlers, and dimwits and careerists and so on, and so on, nevertheless the dominant quality of the majority of workers, it seems to me, is precisely this love, their commitment to their work. Even in those situations in which the real behaviour of workers is at variance with the proposition that they love their work, this attitude persists as a value of ideal behaviour; even in those situations love of one's work is considered necessary, normal and proper. 'Love' is expressed as a cultural norm, called forth by objective causes.

Those workers with whom we have met in the factory are not only good specialists: maybe they are not always high grade specialists, but specialists with specific training. They can do their work in any conditions, getting satisfaction from this. As one of the old hands at the factory said accurately of the *kadrovi* workers: 'these lads are made of a special stuff. They are one-offs ...' They can do their work in the kind of conditions in which nobody works in the West, and even in impossible conditions. We need to document this.

A few years ago one of the shops being researched produced almost 10 million rings of 250 different types each month. Every day they got through about 130 tons of metal. Around one thousand people work here. The measured level of noise and the fumes exceed the permissible level by two or three times. The uneven floor levels between the

buildings makes it impossible to introduce mechanisation and auto-
mation. Shavings are removed on handcarts and electric trolleys. In
summer it is extremely hot because the ventilation does not work
properly. Twice a month the cooling system has to be cleaned of
emulsion, soda. Because of the cramped conditions it is not possible
to provide the workers with a place to get ready for their shift. In
some operations the workers have to move around ten to twelve tons
from one place to another!

That description comes from the appeal of the shop collective to
the administration of the factory and deputies of the city Soviet in
September 1990, but it coincides with our first impressions on visiting
the shop.

In the shop there is a constant noise. But this is not the noise of rain
or of surf, this is the noise of the ripping up of metal, the sound of
blows, blending into a continuous monotonous howl. One can talk, for
example, in the 'smoking room' – this is two or three benches placed
around a bucket full of cigarette ends in the corridor between departments, through which the electric trolleys pass.

In the work places themselves, in the sections, it is impossible to
talk, one has to shout, and then you may attract the attention of the
workers, who are accustomed to the cascade of surrounding noise,
provided that they are less than twenty feet away. Then you can shout
into one another's ear and can understand the words.

The workers in the shop have worked out a special way of speaking
– in a very low tone, but with a kind of rich, powerful sound. This
ability to suppress unnecessary sounds is a great help to the trade union activist working in the shop, when it is necessary to stop
unnecessary discussion, attract attention, or at a meeting in the general
din to say a necessary word.

People with such 'specific training' are becoming fewer and fewer
in the factory. This is what the director of one of the workshops in the
factory had to say about this in an interview published in the factory
newspaper in April 1993:

> It is no secret that it takes years to train specialists for our production. Compli-
> cated kinds of press-mould dies for the separators, moulds for consumption
> goods – all these are made on universal equipment, finished and polished by
> hand.
>
> It needs diabolical patience and the highest qualification to do it. The average
> age of our workers – of the basic specialists – is already more than 50. The ear-
> lier famous dynasties of Denisov, Archakov and others have died out and new

ones have not emerged ... Thus we lay special stress on the introduction of new equipment, on which people with lower levels of qualification can carry out their work.

In the framework of this article there is no intention to examine the distinctive orientations of men and women to their work. Nevertheless we can make some comments on this question on the basis of our observations.

There is no difficulty in finding extracts from interviews in which foremen and shop chiefs provide examples to illustrate their view that women are worse workers than men, with various explanations for this: either their limited physical abilities, or because they are sick more often and take time off work as a result of the sickness of their children, or are more frequently absent from work as a result of domestic problems.

However it seems to me that the statements of managers (most often men) do not always provide an objective evaluation.

My impression in the factory is that work is as important in women's lives as it is in the lives of men. The fact that women traditionally carry the larger share of caring for the home, family and children is another matter.

Nevertheless, work also plays an enormously important role in the life of women. I know from many conversations with women that many of them were only able to create a family thanks to their work: the social circle of working women sometimes does not extend beyond employees of the factory and neighbours (often in factory hostels). Moreover the free time of workers is also organised around the factory, so that she is likely to meet her future husband at a social event in the evening, on shop excursions, or through contact during working hours. This is another aspect of the specifically Soviet organisation of the social sphere through the mediation of the enterprise: the workplace, as it were, defined the whole complex of people's vital needs, and was people's exclusive life-support system. For women this specifically Soviet system was particularly significant because state social subsidies (payment for maternity leave, payment for time off to look after children, family allowances, provision of schools, and so on) are provided through the enterprise. Thus work in the life of women (just as much as for men) is not simply work, it is not simply the possibility of earning money, but also the state's social guarantees, a circle of friends, a generality of interests, a source of information, political news, gossip and so on.

There is more than this. It amazes me how much patience and concentration is required of the women who carry out the visual inspection of the quality of production in one of the shops in the factory, where defects are identified by the brightness of the finished products. After watching them work for ten minutes I was dazzled by the dozens of absolutely identical shining balls. The female inspectors do this for the whole of the working day. Men as a rule do not do this job. In another shop in the factory women machine operators work on machines which are not even semi-automated, but are entirely manually operated with a very monotonous working rhythm, 'which men cannot stand'. Several machine operators work a double shift, that is to say they work on this equipment for sixteen hours at a stretch.

Above we quoted an episode from the labour biography of a woman shop chief, who abandoned any domestic activities and rushed to the factory if any kind of fault arose.

Thus, despite the fact that working women have much more to do at home, with the family and the children, and, naturally, they 'cannot be at home with the family and at work at the same time', nevertheless the feeling of a love of their work exists among the women working in the factory.

Of course, if one judges the woman's love of her work by such criteria as a knowledge of the equipment, the skill of understanding its finer points, and so on, it is weaker than the man's love of his work. However if one judges it by the patient and painstaking way in which they carry out their work, their willingness and ability to carry out manual labour, their discipline and reliability, the absence of drunkenness and absenteeism, then women's love of their work is markedly stronger. It seems to me that the conditions of Russian production and life do not allow women to have any less an interest in work than men. Other things testify to this loving, committed attitude of women to their work: they do not understand the finer points of the construction of the machines very well, but on the other hand they use them very carefully, keep them clean, keep them in order.

I am inclined to see the global explanation for these differences in the particular position of women in society, not in production. In Russia history has given women a secondary role in relation to questions which fall outside the family, including those related to work. And women's relations to work are to a considerable extent defined by men! They are subordinated to the established norms of this relationship, they copy and reproduce male stereotypes of working behaviour. And in those cases in which conditions allow them to devote themselves fully to their work (if a woman is on her own, or the children are grown up, and so on), then in such circumstances the woman reproduces the (male) stereotype of a loving relationship to work more clearly and more openly than men. Moreover they receive much less in return: they earn less, they steal less from the factory, it is enough for them to hold low positions, while being the real executors of the work, it is enough for one person to pay attention to them now and then, without receiving recognition from the whole collective. Judging by their heckling at meetings, women are the most categorical exponents of the norms of a conscientious attitude to work.

At the present time a conscientious attitude to work has a considerable influence on the threat of losing one's job, which is particularly real in our enterprise precisely for women, because they find it much more difficult to get another job.

EQUIPMENT

Turning to equipment the first thing to note is that it is very specific. Our factory, like many large industrial enterprises, has its own machine construction department. More than 35 per cent of the stock of machines was made in the factory itself. The factory has its own design department, whose job is to design new equipment.

> The designers of equipment receive orders from the shop listing the necessary technical-economic specifications for this or that piece of planned equipment, and if there is the slightest doubt they may go to the shop, department or section in which this equipment will be used and introduce the necessary corrections. Thus the technologist-machine builders know well both the production and labour capacity of the production shop, and the materials which are going to be used on the given equipment. The designers of the machine building workshop work in close contact with mechanics and workers in the shop, and they adjust and finish off the equipment in the shop (interview with chief engineer in the factory newspaper, May 1993).

For this reason, one can say without any exaggeration that the equipment is produced at the workplace, almost for each specific worker. The machines acquired thus have their own (factory and shop) finishing touches and adaptations.

We can cite this interesting description by the chief engineer of a shop of the process of adaptation of equipment bought by the factory for the specific conditions of the shop in an interview in August 1993.

We do it like this. We bought the machines, we made a proposal, we say [to the designer of the machine building shop S.A.], lad, have a look here, give us the working drawings of this machine. We have our own drawings for the production of new parts. We get these drawings, through the Chief Engineer, through someone or other, and we ask for it to be made. We have a machine-building shop, we give this set of drawings to them, and they prepare the machine for us according to our drawings. Naturally we introduce our own corrections, of course, not without the authorisation of the Chief Technologist's department, but they again pay heed to us, they come to us and ask us what and how to improve it. We have just modernised a filing machine, but not completely, we intend to make a new group of machines, so we met with the head of the design bureau's mechanics' department – well, the specialists met – and they said, here, when you correct the drawings, pay attention to this and that, correct something here, and so on. They wrote down our remarks. Then they make drawings, they consult us without fail. I have a look to see if everything is as we said, or if something comes into my head while I am working I can say: add something else. When I tested the rollers, I found that something had been removed, I say correct this bit, they rectify it, and I am then absolutely confident that we will receive the machine that we need. Thus everybody is satisfied: the repair workers, the setters, that it will be efficient and convenient to work on, and elegant

The machines on which Russian workers work are fairly old. In one of the shops the shop chief considers that the machines, which have been working for twenty years (and were obsolete after ten), are completely serviceable, that is to say that they produce to the necessary quality. And there are some machines which have been working since the time of the Swedish concession (1924). And they work well. Some of them only work on a wing and a prayer, but they work (interview with shop chief, October 1992).

Here is an example of how old equipment is used in production told to us by shop engineers in August 1993:

There are some other SH-90 filing machines with exactly the same defect. They were made somewhere in the year dot, one could say that we had basically written them off and thrown them out. But now we find that we have got to make some small balls, millimetres, [this is an order for an American company – S.A.] and there is nothing to machine them. We returned to these old ones. They were pretty well smashed up ...! Well, we did it, patched it up. And on this basis I am now making drawings, according to the type which we have on other models, which I am putting into this design. I am now restoring this equipment, I have made a single modernisation, it is not what I had planned to do, but the first step.

The equipment works thanks to the fact that the worker knows it inside out. It is HIS (or HER) machine, it is almost her child. *Kadrovi* workers know how often and where it has to be lubricated, what exactly it is necessary to adjust and when, where and how it should be hit (with a sledgehammer) to eliminate a defect. The setters in the shops work on the readjustment for new types of parts, which will not happen more than once a month, and may not happen for several years, the day-to-day setting up is done by the operators themselves. We often hear talk of this or that machine having its own character, arrogance, that each one needs an individual approach.

Thus, in order to become familiar with the work a certain amount of time is necessary. So in the ball-making shop newly arrived workers are paid average pay for a full year, they are not expected to be able to make the norm (plan) without defects. After a year they begin to wonder what to do with him, will he be able to work, or to earn real wages – and then he leaves (interview with shop chief, October 1992).

The process of mastering the equipment, working conditions and relationships arising in the labour process takes three to five years, although sometimes a year is enough. To be accepted into the collective takes even longer. But then one is an important specialist who knows: 1) exactly how much to tighten every nut on his machine; 2) how much wadding must be put in his ear to muffle the sound of the machine, while at the same time being able to hear the shouts of his comrades; 3) just what to say to the storewoman so that she will give him the protective mittens he needs and not be offended; 4) how it is necessary to behave with the chief and foreman so as to make sure that they do not hassle him and do not give him a bollocking if he has a hangover.

The Director's idea of rotating workers' jobs, which he picked up on a visit to Japan, seems to us to be cut off from Russian reality. Workers have been immersed in this world of the shop, section, work place for many years, making it their second home. And then do it all over again? In another work place, on new equipment?

The mastering of the equipment, the finer points of the technology, this whole system of relationships allows the worker to have some time in reserve to make parts. Having mastered the finer points of the machine, the workers become practically indispensable, almost appendages of the machine.

We came across an interesting situation in one shop in February 1993. As a result of the reduction in the volume of production the situation in the shop and in the factory was one in which the administration was laying off pensioners 'of their own free will', and some of the workers were sent on compulsory vacation. Nevertheless in the third department to everyone's surprise a pensioner, who had worked in this shop before, was taken on. We asked the senior foreman why this had come about. It turned out that the pensioner had been specifically invited into the shop. He had restored two machines which were very old and had already been written off. On these machines he began to make parts which were now exactly what were needed. Now he works and makes the plan on this equipment. Nobody is going to take his work away from him because he rebuilt these machines himself and he services them himself and he practically never makes any faulty products. Since now, in the difficult economic conditions faced by the enterprise, it is impossible to buy new equipment, and they have to fulfil new, non-traditional orders, this was the optimal resolution of the problem for the shop.

The other feature of the equipment is that it is very 'Soviet'. Foreign equipment is finished off and adjusted to suit local conditions. Thus foreign machines which come into the factory are initially looted, and then parts are made in the factory by the local skilled craftsmen. As a result the new parts do not quite fit, and they have to remake the original parts too, and it turns out to be a completely different machine.

As an example one can describe the arrival of a new machine in the shop. For about a month it stood on the site while they studied the documentation, looked for a place for it, and prepared a foundation. During this time the machine was partially dismantled (looted): workers (and anyone else you like) unscrewed several lamps, removed instruments, the repair kit, other parts, control buttons, various nuts were all removed bit by bit to work places or home. Even the boards from the packaging went off somewhere – for example to a dacha, where they can come in useful. When the machine was installed, it had to be finished off, completed with inadequate parts. As a result it already did not operate at the rate at which it should have done.

Here is a quotation from an article by a senior mechanic in the factory newspaper in June 1993, describing the work of machine and tool production in one of the large subdivisions of the factory. Here it is important for us to underline that the 'restoration' of American machines ends up changing the mechanical parts of the machine and completely replacing the electrical parts. In our view, after such a major reconstruction the machines can only conditionally be called American.

> The major repair of home-produced and imported equipment, which the factory is not in a position to buy today, is going on constantly. Over the past five years the American Bryants for ball-bearing rings have been restored. In the various subdivisions there are 120 units. This includes five machines which have been written off from the main factory. They replaced the electrical parts with controllers, and the mechanical parts were reconstructed. At the same time in 1992 the restoration of 10 Japanese Komiyami machines for making balls was completed. At the present time we have started to repair model 1261 Kiev lathes. In the next two years we plan to repair 50 of them.

We mentioned earlier the rationaliser's proposal to change the form of the loading window on the grinding disks. To carry out this proposal it was necessary to cut out of the cast iron disks an opening of a different shape, which entailed changing the speed of rotation.

Here is a description of the way in which a fitter in the shop finishes off the equipment in the course of its use, which shows that this is a constructive activity.

> I come back to the filing machine. We have six rollers supporting an elevator ring. I looked it over and it was in a disgraceful state – the elevator did not work, I made a sketch, showing the general view, but without measurements. I took it to the mechanics' department – lads will you make me a neat drawing of this picture? They drew it. We made an order, we made it, and now it has been introduced on every machine. It can happen here that I, a fitter, can give a job to the designer, I come and say lads, just draw! And we will introduce it. Here the thoughts of the designer arrive too late for the workers. (Interview with senior shop technologists, August 1993)

The technical rationaliser's mentality of the workers does not always appear in the form of rationalisation proposals. Sometimes the realisation of their finishing touches has a personal character: the skilled craftsman does not formulate his refinement as a rationalisation proposal, but realises it independently. Moreover, they keep quiet about some of the refinements, because they lead to loss of production, but are advantageous to the worker, for example because they make it possible to save time (at the expense of quality), or because they reduce the amount of work (at the expense of the economy of raw materials).

RAW MATERIALS

The quality of the raw materials has a significant influence on the quality of the finished product. Metal arriving at the factory often does not correspond to the requirements of the production process. As a result the factory has a whole preparation workshop, which is responsible for monitoring the quality and preparing the incoming raw materials. Depending on the condition of the metal received and on which shop the metal is going to, preparation may include the following operations: repeated annealing, straightening, roughening, drawing out. There is also a smithy in the factory, where small quantities of metal can be smelted if necessary.

> If there is no metal of the necessary diameter – if they have not received any – what can you do? It needs to be drawn out from one dimension to another, and after drawing it out we anneal it ...
>
> You ask how we manage to make high quality balls out of low quality metal. That is another matter. In various ways ...We make the diameter of the balls let us say 0.5 millimetres larger so as to remove the defects in the metal. As a result an excessive amount of metal is used, increasing the time needed for machining. The consumer does not suffer from the fact that we have made balls out of defective metal. Only we suffer. But the final result is that it corresponds to the demands of GOST (All-Union State Standard). (Interview with shop dispatcher, November 1993)

The workers and technologists explained to us about another problem with the metal. The fact is that the metal that they receive is unevenly tempered along the length of the rods out of which the blanks are stamped; the quality of the parts turned out depends on whether they are produced from one end of the rod, from the middle, or from the other end. It is practically impossible to eliminate this defect: the rod would have to be tempered again, this is uneven along the length of the rod depending on the amount of tempering of one end or the other, but then there is a big risk of overtempering the whole rod. Thus they have to set the machine to some average level of tempering so as to achieve a high quality result in the middle part of the rod, then the finished parts made from the ends have to be rejected.

Auxiliary materials which arrive are also sometimes not those necessary for production.

In one of the sections a problem arose related to oil and paste. The precise kinds needed for production were not available, as a result of which there were a lot of rejects. They got MD-12 oil from Novokuibyshevsk, which is very thin, so the brigadier improved it himself by adding stearin and nasadka – a type of glue. As a result they suffered from harmful fumes.

A particularly acute problem of quality of raw materials has arisen recently in connection with the breakdown of the economic links between the countries of the former Soviet Union, and correspondingly with the re-orientation of the enterprise to new raw materials markets. In our factory, in place of Ukrainian metal as the main material, they began to use metal from the Urals. The quality of the new metal was equally low, but it also had different dimensions. As a result, despite the efforts of the preparation workshop, the operating conditions for the work of the equipment which had been perfected over the years had to be changed. The shop (machines and workers) was used to working with one metal, then they had to change the operating conditions of the equipment and their skills to work with the new metal.

TECHNOLOGY

Some of the shortcomings in the quality of raw materials are revealed by checks when they arrive, but some of them are not identified at that point. Every technological inadequacy of the equipment and shortcoming in the quality of the raw materials comes to light immediately in the workplace. The machine operator is faced with unexpected defects and has to decide either to remove them (1), or to ignore them (2), or not to carry out the task as a result of the failure of the raw material or the machine to conform to the norm (3). Let us say that the worker has to choose between the second and third variants. If he chooses the third variant, not to make the part, and refers the matter to his manager in accordance with his duty to conform to the necessary procurement requirements, he wastes time and loses work, and it is quite possible that after reviewing the question the chief will demand that he carry out the work with the material that he has all the same (because there is no other, and it is not possible to remove the defect). Moreover the chief himself often knows about the low quality materials. If the worker stands on his principles, the chief will give the work to somebody else; if not, the time spent sorting it out will have been lost, which will affect his pay if he is on piece-rates.

If defects uncovered during working time are ignored, the worker loses nothing, although it is probable that these defects will have an effect on the quality of production which will show up in those parameters which are monitored. Then the defects may be exposed by the output control and as a result the part will be rejected and the workers' pay will be reduced. You can try to prove that the failure was not your fault, but as a result of all this the part has to be completed again by the worker, if the defects can be rectified.

Thus workers most often try to neutralise defects which arise in their work on their own initiative by some means, not risking the second approach, and not turning to their immediate superiors. It would be more likely that they would turn for advice to a more experienced worker (or instructor). The neutralisation of defects may be done with the aim of eliminating them completely, or of eliminating them partially, just enough to pass the output control. In this way workers correct the production technology of the parts depending on this or that inadequacy of the raw materials, equipment or components. The workers work out their own methods of removing this or that defect. Very often the foreman, senior foreman or setters told us that workers themselves know what to do and how to do it. Some of the tricks of the trade are secrets of the workers' craft.

The technology of producing one and the same part used by different workers in our factory is different. Machine operators carry out the functions of the setter. And every time the worker arrives at work for his shift he readjusts his machine.

In an interview a section foreman told us in May 1993:

> Every worker tunes up his machine for himself. One may set the cutting knife not in the extreme position, but a little nearer (a few millimetres), and regulate the dimensions of the cutting of the rod with the support. His replacement will arrive, set the knife in the extreme position, and his balls come out too 'hollow', then he readjusts the machine again by controlling the support.

Thus every worker adjusts the equipment in his own manner, and makes the products in his own particular way, so that the technology of production of the parts is very individual.

This technology is so individual that the foreman who took me around the shop did not know how each individual worker did it. As a result the quality of production is very varied, and not necessarily bad.

Here is the story of the creation of very high precision bearings in our factory. In the shop a series of category N bearings are produced, which conform to the highest category of precision laid down by GOST, according to which the whole engineering industry works. Earlier in the production of bearings pattern diaphragms were used, set to the necessary precision for the parts produced to the level of category N. However sometimes this processing, quite by chance, produces parts of an even higher category of precision, many times more precise than category N. When these are separated out they turn out to amount to between three and five per cent of the total number of bearings produced. This possibility of making bearings of a higher category of precision consequently leads to the production of new types of bearings of higher degrees of precision: categories P, V, S and higher (Astakhov, Vol. 2, pp. 49–50).

The development of the rationalisation movement among workers also facilitates the search for individual methods of work. When I mentioned the rationalisation proposals of workers earlier in this article, it was important to note that the very conditions of life of Soviet people (and ideological propaganda) forced workers to take a creative approach to their duties, which gave rise to a large number of rationalising proposals from workers. Here I would like to add that the material stimulus (often unconscious) to rationalising activity through the absence of fixed horizontal links between similar workshops strengthens the individuality of production in each workplace (and the untechnological character of production as a whole).

The technologists of the shop told us in April 1993 that they receive a large number of rationalisation proposals (even more in the past), and although two thirds of them are nonsense, nevertheless one third are intelligent suggestions and many of them can be used. The rationalisation movement develops the workers' inventiveness and encourages the development of methods of working in individual ways.

We can confirm the fact that fixed, stable links between those working on exactly the same equipment in the factory are absent by quoting the words of a former deputy chief of shop in August 1993.

Incidentally, we were on a business trip in Chimkent, and we met Dzhyudash-villi, who was the Moscow Technical Director, and I told him about the deficiencies. We work in completely the wrong way – every factory keeps itself to itself. This is completely wrong. Thus I travelled to a factory in the Far East for a top level meeting, and they did not use the XSh-36 filing machine which we use! Why not? Because they thought with their heads and devised a modernisation, produced them and now they are working. They still need to perfect them. But they work. I asked: why does not Vitebsk, the chief enterprise which provides all our machines, not give them to us? Why doesn't it give us such equipment? Our needs are simple, they are our own needs. They may not correspond to contemporary conditions abroad, but we do not have such highly qualified staff – we do not have the training. Thus I told them – this was my idea – I went to another factory – we put all the suggestions together and said the machine must be like this. This bit is no good, what do you suggest, this, this ... It will be an ideal machine, I guarantee. Then there a rough draft was drawn up so that almost all the leading specialists could meet in Vitebsk to talk about this issue. The proposal was very reliable, it was the best.

The non-technological character of the production process affects the system of training of workers in the specialisms required for their jobs. Young workers who have completed professional-technical school (attached to the factory!), and who have to work on this equipment, cannot work it immediately to its full capacity because they do not know the specificities of this concrete equipment.

Here is a fairly typical account of the quality of training of those arriving at the factory, told with a strong touch of nostalgia by the same former deputy chief of shop.

You explain to them, and they do it – they do not know what to do! Do you call this work? They just play at studying. Nobody teaches like they did before, apprentice, then first grade, second, third. But now they turn up. Someone arrives at the factory – I want to work as a fitter; we say – you haven't got a trade, we'll put you on the third grade; he says – it's not enough money, I do not agree. But I need people. So I think: maybe take him, something will turn up, it means putting him immediately on a higher grade. But he cries that he is a fitter – what, him a fitter?

For a new person to master a specific piece of equipment requires the development of skills, techniques, precise movements which take years to acquire. The craftsmanship of the worker and his individual methods of work is based on knowledge of the properties of production, the design of his own machine, the peculiarities of working with this or that raw material. Traditionally craftsmanship is the pride of the working person, and people share the secrets of this craftsmanship reluctantly: not because they do not feel sympathy or are afraid of losing something, it is simply that there is no powerful stimulus to transfer work experience other than personal sympathy.

Thus in reality the only way of obtaining a specialism and the transfer of experience is through apprenticeship. Then the transfer of the knowledge required for qualification is also very personal. The workers transfer their individual work skills and the secrets of their craftsmanship to their apprentices. Friendly relations between the teacher and apprentice pay a very important role in the process of training. During this time the apprentice who has a creative attitude to his work thus acquires his own tricks, distinguishing him from other workers.

However the system of training in the workplace has its own particular features. The training of the worker is very often a test of his nouse and quick-wittedness. If the pupil understands the first time, or picks up quickly, what to do in this or that situation, if he grasps it, the training is going well. If the young worker grasps how to work on this equipment, with these raw materials and this technology, then he can work, but if not he moves on to other work or leaves the factory.

Moreover, not only training, but also everyday working life is also a test of quick-wittedness. Here is a notable example reinforcing this thought.

When the foreman accompanied me to the section after an interview in May 1993, we passed a machine that was not working and I asked 'why is this machine not working?' The foreman went up to the machine with a resolute air. I noticed a little ball lying on the machine and asked again, 'why is there a little ball lying on the machine?' 'When a little ball is put there, it means that something is wrong', he replied. 'So what is wrong?' The foreman looked for a long time, rolled the ball in his hand, and then answered, 'I do not know. It is not obvious from outside. Maybe the ball is too 'hollow', or the wrong way round, or the metal is bad, or it is too large … But if you want I can go to the shop laboratory, measure it and find out the reason if necessary.' I declined his offer, and the foreman put the ball back: the workers on the second shift will investigate when they arrive.

The idea of the little ball lying on a machine that is not working is that workers on the first shift leave a defective ball for the workers of the second shift so that they will not start the machine straight away, but will inspect this ball, see what is wrong and eliminate the faults in the machine. The foreman could not immediately understand what was going on. For my sake he suggested going to the laboratory and taking measurements so as to find out what was wrong. The workers of the second shift obviously do not go to the laboratory, and determine the defect at a glance and work out how to remove it. Workers on the first shift equally certainly do not go to the laboratory, but detect the defect at a glance. Thus the workers on the one hand warn their colleagues, and on the other hand set up a check. Such tests of professionalism are not rare. It is their kind of game: to put their skill, their professional craftsmanship, to the test.

From the point of view of their attitudes to their work, such tests of professional ability are one more peculiarity of their love of their work. There is a sense in which this love of work demands a public display of heroism in the name of love.

The source of this phenomenon of tests of quick-wittedness, both in training and in work, it seems to me, can be seen in the history of the factory. We can make an historical excursion, drawn from an extract from the memories of a veteran of the factory which appeared in the book by E. Astakhov, published for the fiftieth anniversary of the factory. We would like to convey the atmosphere, the working spirit of the factory.

After the beginning of the Patriotic War a Moscow ball-bearing Factory was evacuated to Samara, which subsequently became the factory in which we carried out our research. However its history began earlier, with a concession enterprise in Moscow.

At the end of the 1920s, before the ball-bearing factory was first built, bearings were produced in small volume in Moscow. The bulk of foremen, highly qualified workers, machine setters and engineers were made up of foreigners, but secondary and auxiliary work was carried out by Muscovites.

And today in the factory there are still people who began as young people with the concessionaires. The situation in those days had its own peculiarities. There was absolutely no training, transferring production experience, tricks of the trade, and forms of speech. The foreign craftsmen stood aloof and revealed their professional secrets to nobody, even more so as they did not know Russian.

A similar style of relationship was also established from the beginning of the ball-bearing factory, where a large number of foreign specialists were employed. They knew their work well, carried it out intelligently, but they did not allow those interested to get close to it.

There was envy and annoyance, remembers one of the veterans ...

I remember in '33 a German worked at the factory, an extra-class fitter. At that time I worked a lathe, and the German did not hold much back from me. He obviously thought that as a turner I had no particular interest in his fitter's secrets. I wormed my way into his trust and bit by bit followed how he worked his magic in his enclosure, thoroughly investigated the secrets of his cunning. And just after that I immediately gave them to my friend, Yashe Feinstein was his name. Yashka worked as a fitter. He noted down everything and put it into practice. Thus we learned from the German with our four eyes.

This method of spying was, unfortunately, the basis of the mastery of the stock of complex machines which were fitted out for the Moscow GPZ by an Italian firm, which was participating in the planning of the factory, in installing the equipment and in its initial setting.

> then we young people often wanted to take our foreign instructors down a peg or two, their condescending attitude was very offensive to us, their confidence in their immense superiority over us. Usually we tried not to show this resentment. We hid it in the depths of our hearts. We tried to learn the tricks of their trade from the foreigners as quickly as possible, and most important to understand how their machines worked.
>
> It was a sin ... But the specialists dragged out the repair of machines or did not immediately investigate a fault thoroughly, we, who had already begun to get some experience of the method: lo and behold the more sharp-sighted make a good note, we successfully replaced these aces. We were frantic with our aspiration to know and to do. I do not want to compare or to reproach but the majority of today's young people do not have such an obsession. With sorrow and regret those of us of the older generation understand this obvious fact that to accuse only our young people is unjust and incorrect. (Astakhov, Vol. 1, pp. 18–22)

We find confirmation of the persistence of this peculiar tradition of spying in our interview with a former deputy chief of shop in August 1993:

> For example, I was in one of the enterprises linked to the factory: this was not any kind of industrial espionage – I am walking around, I take an interest; I looked at the repair group – some parts lying around there, but there is something unusual, I tried to find out what was going on. And I thought to myself, why can not we use these ideas in our production, so I come back here and made drawings.
> — Did you make these drawings yourselves?
> — Yes
> — And did they tell you what those parts were for?
> — I asked: for which machine? And the thing is – I know that we have identical machines, we have the same ones as them. Maybe they have hit on something, and I took it as the basis and added something of my own. As soon as I got back I began to use a variant on our existing machines. But with our measurements and settings.
> — Did you introduce that part?
> — Of course! They work now, and we sigh with relief, because earlier our machines did not work – the design of the machine was set up completely incorrectly, a blunder of the designers. This cutting machine was a calamity for us. Our whole factory was turned upside down, they held a meeting there, gave everyone orders to improve somehow, because without a cutter all production

was stopped. These were machines made in our factory. They were made on the basis of a machine which was invented, or manufactured, in the Kharkov factory. Being a mechanic I brought these four machines, we bought these machines. Our designers, mechanics, we copied, to put it crudely, we stripped one down, inspected it, drew it, and made them here in the factory with our own resources. Well! In Kharkov they are alongside the Tractor Factory, and so have copied a lot of the parts from there, in particular the conical drive, which was borrowed from the tractor factory. There the module was stronger, the technology of machining higher, maybe there they made tanks, shorter pinions, the stability of their use was higher. So that when we with our petty shortcomings made them in our factory they began to crack like nuts. We worried ourselves sick with this transmission. Until I went and took a look ... then it began to work. We do not have this problem. Now we have introduced a series of their novelties. We do not have this problem any more.

In this excerpt from the interview it is once more important for us to underline that 1) there are no set technological relations between enterprises which work with one and the same piece of equipment, there is no organised exchange of technological information and 2) our factory workers do not simply copy parts, but are sufficiently creative to go as far as the invention of others, and specifically: when this part is changed it becomes the basis for changes of other parts, and so for the construction of a new machine.

So, let us draw some conclusions from our review of the process of production in the enterprise. EQUIPMENT – 'Soviet', old and very SPECIFIC. RAW MATERIALS – bad and DIVERSE. TECHNOLOGY – INDIVIDUAL, which has its source: WORKERS – love their work because to work on SUCH equipment, with SUCH raw materials and for SUCH pay, and on top of that living in SUCH conditions is only possible if YOU LOVE YOUR WORK.

SPECIFICITY OF PRODUCTION

The review of the technology of production, the condition of equipment, the quality of raw materials, and attitudes to work – all of this comes down to saying that the quality of the finished product depends not on the firm (in the sense that it has some kind of specific technology, although that is possible) but on all sorts of production and non-production factors in the production process. Here a much more significant role begins to be played by such immediate nuances as the mood of the foreman, the sobriety of the workers, the feelings of the shop chief, their commitment to the particular concrete order. And this not only concerns the immediate process of production, but also the quality of raw materials, the quality of materials used, the quality of the sets of parts, all the same factors in the supplier and customer factories.

Returning to the beginning of the article, we want to say that it cannot be said that the quality of the products of Russian industry is low (because the equipment is old, the raw materials bad, and the workers drunk, and so on), just as it would be incorrect to say that it is higher than anywhere else (because workers love their work, understand their equipment, which was almost hand-picked for each worker, and so on). The point is that it is varied, amazingly varied (even in one and the same batch of goods). In fact it turns out that every successive part is made anew.

The quality of each part depends on thousands of factors, on the raw materials, the equipment, the attitude to work, the personal technology of the worker and so on. All these factors do not compensate one another, do not act to cancel each other out, and the products turn out to be varied. One can never predict the quality each successive time, because the raw materials might change, the equipment might be put out of action, or the machine might be swapped for its neighbour, as a result of which it is not known precisely which of the workers will make it and on which shift, even if it is the very same person, it is not known what his mood will be, or the mood of the setter, brigadier, foreman, immediate manager. The correlation of all these factors gives rise to production of the highest quality and at the same time of a very low quality.

Precisely as a result of these peculiarities of our industry the television that I bought broke down within two weeks of buying it, but my neighbour bought his television in 1962 and it still works (it has been repaired twice, the first time after seventeen years of use).

Thus, we say that production is non-technological, every part can be made, but they are always varied. The production of each part is a highly creative process, not giving itself up to technological regulation. We find a reminder of this kind of activity in Marx and Engels in *The German Ideology*, it is a true example of handicraft production. This activity is akin to artistic creativity. It is not the product of training and the close observance of instructions, but the result of one's own craftsmanship; the workers work everything out themselves and themselves improve their knowledge and develop their skills.

... every man who wished to become a master had to be proficient in the whole of his craft. Thus there is found with medieval craftsmen an interest in their special work and in proficiency in it, which was capable of rising to a narrow artistic sense. For this very reason, however, every medieval craftsman was completely absorbed in his work, to which he had a contented, slavish relationship, and to which he was subjected to a far greater extent than the modern worker, whose work is a matter of indifference to him. (K. Marx and F. Engels, *The German Ideology*, FLPH, Moscow, n.d., p. 67)

Thus we consider that this untechnological, unduplicable, unreproducible character of the production methods of each worker and the uniqueness of every part is the specific feature of Russian production.

Every factory service of technical control is called upon to smooth over this individual variation of the workers, but the controllers are also people, and they also have their individual differences, so this process is not always successful.

In one of the shops the quality control is fairly strict. In the shop there are around 100 controllers for 370 workers (203 production workers and 167 auxiliary workers). The large number of controllers, it is true, is not only related to the need for thorough examination of the products, but also for technical control – so-called visual control. A fragment of a report of a visit to a section gives an impression of the way in which the control works.

After each heat treatment the balls are tested by the Department of Technical Control (OTK). After stamping the balls are taken away by the OTK every hour. After the finishing process the OTK carries out a 100 per cent control of the balls and picks out rejects depending on the series, thus there are two methods of control – final (on the second floor) and operational.

In spite of this strict control there are many rejects. The first inspection lets through only 76 per cent of the balls. As a result of this the section regularly suffers a reduction of bonus. However this rejection is not final, many balls are then brought up to the required standard. 'Balls of a suitable standard' are sorted out in the foreman's office on special racks. This is basically connected with bad components: unsuitable paste and oil. But it may also be a fault of the setter.

Despite the strict technical control there are various ways in which workers can deceive the controllers. Situations in which the controllers are deceived with the open or tacit agreement of the foreman or shop chief are also common.

For the controllers and the workers the quality standard is set by the demands of the state standard (GOST). In the factory we were often told that GOST is the law! However in the course of the research it became clear that the requirements of the state standards can be changed, even by the enterprise itself. In conditions in which each separate shop in the factory is a monopolist in one or another kind of product the head of these shops (of course through the services of the factory) turned to Goskomstat with a proposal to change the standards. As a rule they were successful. They did this with the aim of increasing the required norms (in relation to the low quality of raw materials for example), or with the aim of reducing tolerance in those circumstances in which, first, there is a possibility of making a higher quality product and, second, if increasing the degree of precision of the work leads to an increase in the rate of pay for this kind of work (interview with shop chief, October 1992). Thus one can say that in fact the control of quality was according to the achieved (real, average) level of production.

We asked the controllers whether they could distinguish the products of different workers. Experienced controllers can identify the products of separate brigades, shifts, various batches of raw material and some even of separate workers. And the majority of controllers know in advance which production defects to expect from this or that group of workers. In fact, from the product they can tell out of which raw material, on which shift, by which brigade, on which machine and even precisely who made a perfectly round shining ball. Nevertheless the production managers struggle with this situation (or, as they sometimes say, cover themselves against it). For them this is a necessary reaction to the existing conditions.

The struggle with the untechnological character of production in their enterprise is the job of the OTK services. In the factory there is a weekly meeting to discuss quality at all levels of management. Any kind of centralisation within the framework of the enterprise (supply, repair, machine building, preparation of raw materials) also makes possible the universalisation of production.

The struggle with the untechnological character of production in supplier and associated enterprises can be carried on in two ways. The first is through the creation of their own finishing workshops. Thus in our factory there is a preparatory workshop, which prepares all the raw materials received for use in the factory's shops. More over, similar preparation is carried out at the shop level. One shop in which we carried out research employs one foreman and two workers, working on the quality control and finishing of metal for the shop in other shops in the factory. Another shop that we know also has a whole section for the preparation of metal.

The second possibility of struggle with the untechnological character of production in supplier enterprises is quality control immediately in the workplace. In another enterprise in which our group has been carrying out research representatives of the customers are to be found immediately in the shops and monitor the quality and evenness of supplies for their own enterprise. In our factory even separate shops keep 'pushers' in supplier factories for this or that purpose. 'In every metallurgical factory we need to keep a pusher, incurring large expenses for business trips' (Deputy General Director for Economics). This method has its own particular feature – personal contact with the executors, with the possibility of influencing them not by administrative means, but by informal methods and stimuli.

And there is one more method, which as it were supplements the first two, although it is not always possible to use it, and this is personal contacts. One can get high quality goods through *blat*, through acquaintances. This method is pretty reliable, but is most often used for a single delivery for a specific person, and not for the factory and other impersonal subjects.

NON-TECHNOLOGY AS A CONDITION OF EXISTENCE

Speaking of the non-technological character of production in this article I have looked at it almost as a general feature of the whole of Russian industry. The reader may raise the question. How is it possible to live in such general untechnological conditions? How is it possible to live when a person can have no confidence in the things he buys, which might be high quality or useless. Isn't it impossible to live with constant breakdowns? It is impossible to live normally without being able to have some confidence that the next thing that you take in your hands will not disintegrate. That going out into the street a balcony will not fall on your head. That the car in which you are sitting will not start to fall apart at the most inconvenient moment in the most inconvenient place. That sitting at home the chandelier will not shatter, the drains will not burst and so on.

Nevertheless it is possible to live like this.

It is possible not only to live but also to control this process.

Naturally the untechnological character of production is controlled in every workplace. That is to say, if the workers want to they can make very high quality parts (for themselves for example), using their own supply of high quality raw materials, and using the equipment in the appropriate way. All the different kinds of factors affecting the quality of production can be taken into account and made to correspond to the necessary requirements by the worker, provided that he is sufficiently motivated to get from the foreman (or through his own channels) a high quality set of parts and materials.

The manufacture of products of this or that quality can be controlled at the level of the labour process. That is to say a worker can approach other workers and ask them (or persuade them in some way) to make this part well, or even track them down.

Such regulation can also occur at the level of the foreman. The foreman in our factory has sufficient levers of pressure to make the worker work well. In such a case the foreman must, through the chief of shop or independently, obtain the necessary parts and raw materials (which is not always possible) and he must have the authority among the workers to get them to carry out this task to a high quality (particularly if the raw materials are not of the required quality).

At the level of the shop chief, he can also influence the worker to give him high quality raw materials, to organise the setters to adjust the equipment, and to follow the task through to completion. For this the chief must have sufficient influence in the shop and somehow provide an incentive to carry out the task to a high quality, now and then referring immediately to the workers.

The Director of the factory can also regulate the untechnological character of production. Part of his duties is to regulate this process throughout the whole factory; in some circumstances the Director can secure the production of a batch of high quality goods. And he can go personally to the workplace and by one means or another secure high quality work.

Thus there are various levels of regulation of the process of production in the workplace.

There are various ways of influencing the untechnological character of production to secure an improvement in the quality of the product. The worker can ask, pay for or demand reciprocal favours (bartering a favour or goods). The significance of material incentives in making it possible to influence workers has increased in recent times.

Thus it turns out that every individual person, with enough acquaintances, friends, relatives and personal contacts, either through having enough money or through having enough favours (or goods) to give in exchange, can get control over the process of production of this or that article, acting through the foreman, through the chief of shop, through others working in the factory, or personally.

Incidentally there is one other way of acquiring quality products – 'personal' production, which is pretty widespread. A machine operator can fix any kind of broken part on a lathe, or sharpen the cutters himself, or grease the machine himself, and so on, that is to say he can do other jobs than his own. One of the shop chiefs had personally repaired the roof of the building when it began to leak again immediately after it had been repaired. Indeed it is well-known that in our daily life it is sometimes better to make something oneself than to use industrial methods. This is particularly the case with services. Thus, it is much better to rebuild or repair your car yourself than to use a garage. The view that a man should be able to do the basic things in life himself is widespread in mass consciousness; for example, to change a broken light bulb, bang in a nail, hang a peg, repair electrical goods, repair a clock, make repairs around the home (in general to do a man's work in the home).

In this process – the process of regulating and influencing the non-technological character of production, making use of this untechnological character as a whole – any kind of informal relations are mobilised to a full degree, both outside and inside the workplace (including informal relations in the process of production, which is discussed in the previous chapter).

My reflections have been constructed primarily around materials from only one factory, in which we carried out a case study during 1992–3. Nevertheless our hypothesis is not contradicted by the materials with which we are familiar from other enterprises in Samara. The situation described seems to me to be typical of many factories, particularly in large enterprises in the military-industrial complex. In any case, this hypothesis can be tested with data from other enterprises.

The features of Soviet production noted by us can obviously be accounted for in many cases by the specific features of the enterprise in which the research was carried out. So we should indicate the specific features of this enterprise. It is a large enterprise of the military-industrial complex. Conversion has had a painful affect on its economic-technical position. It has a large social and welfare infrastructure. The administration maintains a paternalistic policy in the distribution of work, the supply of goods, the amount of pay and is maintaining its surplus labour force. The collective of the enterprise is fairly old (the average age of workers is 47). On the whole any kind of change has had little effect on the enterprise and its workers; it represents an example of the preservation of traditional kinds of interrelations and interaction in large industrial undertakings. With the fall in production and the difficult economic position pay in the shops has been falling and it is the experienced workers who remain, who already find it difficult to change their workplace. The collective is made up of older workers who grew up in the tradition of the battle for the plan.

Moreover the factory has a long tradition of heroic labour, as much after as during the war years, in the vanguard of Soviet engineering – the factory is one of the largest in its branch and was always in good repute. The traditions of self-sacrificing labour are transmitted through the existence of worker dynasties in the factory, and also through its own form of recruitment of labour, when the novice is brought (introduced to the management, invited to come) by somebody already working there.

Thus it is quite possible that the untechnological characteristics noted by us are related to this factory, in which old experienced workers and specialists dominate. And this is partly confirmed by the fact that young people, according to the old workers, do not understand the finer points of the equipment, do not have such a responsible attitude to work and to the fulfilment of their duties. And they understand their duties differently: the young person is inclined to do only his own work, but the veterans consider that their work embraces a much wider range of activities.

Taking these points into account, we have designated the specificities of production in the title of the article as SOVIET, since it is true that the specific features of Russian production will differ from those described (in the form of a higher degree of alienation of the workers from the process of production, if one follows Marx).

4. The Mechanism of Paternalistic Management of the Enterprise: the Limits of Paternalism

Petr Bizyukov

Observation of the activity of contemporary Russian enterprises leads us to note the increased role of non-productive functions over the last few years, connected with the attempts to maintain as high a level of earnings of the employees as possible, sustaining a manifestly unprofitable social sphere, supplying workers with scarce consumption goods at low prices ... In poor enterprises this is achieved only on a very small scale and at the expense of the development of the enterprise, but a prosperous enterprise can achieve something more significant, for example building cottages for all its workers. The burden of social problems only adds to the difficulties faced by management, who confront quite enough economic and production problems as it is. Nevertheless, hardly any enterprise managers refuse to involve themselves in this sphere, on the contrary they are turning from managers of enterprises into guardians of their workers, and the activity of the enterprise as a whole is oriented not just to production, but to supporting every aspect of life, to paternalism.

The evaluation of this development is not simple. Some people interpret this as an expression of the goodwill of the managers, but others see it as a means of manipulating people. In any case, Russian enterprises today are marked by a particular direction of activity connected with the subsistence of the members of the collective, going beyond the limits of purely productive activity. The most appropriate term by which to characterise this activity is 'paternalism', that is the guardianship of the collective on the part of management.

Paternalism is the sum total of managerial activity, the essence of which is contained in the realisation of guardianship on the part of the subject of management in relation to the object of management. Usually by guardianship we mean caring for incapable people, the young and the sick. But it can also exist in relation to ordinary people if it rests on something that gives one person superiority over others. The essence of guardianship over the collective consists in the fact that the manager-guardian defines the circle of needs of his employees which can be satisfied, and either satisfies them immediately, or assists in their satisfaction.

Paternalism was the most important feature of state management under socialism. From the very first years of its existence, and continuing through the whole history of socialist society, the state and its various organs tried to determine if not all, at least the majority of the important spheres of the citizens' lives. Having monopolised practically every sphere of activity, the state assumed all the functions of guardianship and decided exactly which needs would be satisfied and which not, to what extent they would be satisfied and, of course, defined the principles of distribution of goods between social groups.

In this article I will try to analyse this phenomenon as it appears in the activity of contemporary Russian enterprises. The basic material has been collected over several years, and primarily in the Kuzbass coal industry. But I have also used the results of research in other Kuzbass enterprises, in the chemical industry, light industry and various others. The question arises of whether the conclusions reached are typical only of Kuzbass? I think not. Having at my disposal the materials and results of the research of colleagues in other regions of Russia provides a basis for some confidence in this judgement. However in presenting my conclusions I have tried as far as possible to use the results of research in which I have participated personally, and use those examples which I have observed myself.

COERCION IN THE SOVIET ECONOMY

Guardianship and coercion are two phenomena which are in their essence closely related. In both cases there is a status inequality. The difference is only that in the case of guardianship the object really cannot manage without subordination to the subject and one or the other recognises the expediency of inequality (for example the guardianship of the old over the young), while in the case of coercion the subject imposes his inequality on the object and maintains it by force.

On the whole, then, one can consider guardianship as a mild form of coercion. However the boundaries between guardianship and coercion are not well defined, so guardianship can develop into coercion and vice versa.

How Coercion Took Root in the Soviet Economy

Coercion under socialism has a rich and tragic history. In the system of the GULAG, created in the middle of the 1920s and lasting to the middle of the 1960s the state operated by openly coercive methods. The idea of using forced labour was one of the favourite schemes of the Bolshevik theorists. Thus, if at the beginning forced labour was considered as a means of improving society – an educational measure used 'equally for parasitic elements and for backward elements of the peasantry and the working class', it fairly quickly extended to punitive labour for enemies and for those who 'do not want' to be re-educated. But this was not very significant, since it only affected a small part of the population. A new impulse for the widening of the sphere of forced labour came from Trotsky's idea of a 'labour army' expressed in his theses to the Central Committee of the Party:

> Those who have been freed from urgent tasks in the military sphere, right up to large military formations, must be used for labour, as one of the transitional forms in establishing a universal obligation to work and the widest application of the socialisation of labour.

And this is not all:

> Socialism requires the compulsory participation of all members of society in the production of material values ... In the immediate period those who must be involved in an obligation to work will be primarily those age groups which were less caught up in war mobilisation, along with, as far as possible, the drawing in of women.

Here he also lays down the methods by which this should be achieved:

> In the transitional stage of development of society, burdened with the legacy of such a hard past, the transition to systematically organised social labour is unthinkable without coercive measures ... The instrument of state coercion is its military power. Consequently, a degree of militarisation of labour ... is an unavoidable feature of the transitional economy founded on a universal obligation

to work. (L.D. Trotsky, 'How the revolution was armed. On the mobilisation of the industrial proletariat, the conscription of labour, militarisation of the economy, and the use of military units for economic needs. Theses of the Central Committee of the Russian Communist Party')

During the first years of Soviet power the universal obligation to work became a reality, expressed in the law on the obligation to work, which prescribed criminal penalties for the evasion of the obligation to labour and the labour book as the personal document which ensured that people belonged to the ranks of workers in state enterprises and organisations.

Forced Labour in the GULAG

Despite the fact that the obligation to work had already become universal in the middle of the 1920s, the process did not stop there. The need to observe elementary civil liberties prevented the use of a 'labour army' but at the same time the state, which was acquiring more and more totalitarian features, needed cheap labour power. Unable to transform its citizens into 'labour soldiers', the state decided to turn them into convicts. The GULAG was created for this purpose, established during the 1930s and beyond in places where there was no alternative but forced labour. The scale of the phenomenon of the GULAG is still not appreciated today. The available evidence allows us, particularly at the emotional level, to judge how large and terrible was the violence committed against people and to provide a very rough estimate of how many passed through the Stalinist camps and how many died there. Moreover the GULAG exerted an influence not only on those who were inside it, but also on 'free' people. It was precisely in this period that labour legislation acquired a truly draconian brutality. One only needs to cite a few facts characteristic of that epoch:

The working day in summer reached 16 hours! When the brigade did not meet the norms only the escort was changed, and the hard-workers stayed in the forest with searchlights until midnight, only coming back to the camp in the morning and eating supper along with their breakfast before going back into the forest.

There was nobody to tell of this: they all died. (A.I. Solzhenitsyn, *Gulag Archipeligo*, Vol. 2, Chap. 7)

Nobody knows to this day how many people passed through the GULAG. According to the official data of the KGB in 1953 there were not more than 2.5 million prisoners in the *USSR* *(Sotsiologicheskie Issledovaniya*, 6–7, 1991). But Solzhenitsyn quotes I. A. Kurganov's figures of deaths, according to which

> between 1917 and 1959, excluding war losses, only from terroristic extermination, repression, the increased death rate in the camps and including the losses due to the reduction in the birth rate – 66.7 million people. (without these losses – 55 million) (A.I. Solzhenitsyn, *Gulag Archipeligo*, Vol. 2, Chap. 1)

These are only the figures for deaths. The majority of those imprisoned survived. But here order is important. Even if we trust the figures from the KGB archives, the numbers passing through the Stalinist camps is measured in tens of millions of people – deaths and survivors!

Coercion after Stalin

After Stalin's death and the execution of Beria the GULAG system began to be cut back, although many elements of forced labour remained. The most savage forms of forced labour, such as strict regime prison camps, mass arrests of innocent people, required to populate the concentration camps with fresh labour power, began to disappear. However measures related to the coercion of people who remained at liberty were preserved unchanged. And this was the majority of the population, even if tens of millions of people passed through the camps. First, the legally enforced obligation to work. People who did not work were liable to criminal prosecution and could be convicted. Second, people were tied to their place of work, registration of their place of work appearing not only in their labour book, which had to be kept in the Personnel Department of the enterprise, but also in the passport of every citizen. Third, it was only in the middle of the 1960s that every citizen became entitled to a passport, until which time people living in the countryside in general did not have passports and without the agreement of the manager of the collective or state farm they could not get one (and consequently not only could they not move elsewhere, they could not even simply go on visits anywhere). It was not so hard for city dwellers, but they also had difficulty in moving from one place to another. It was necessary to work out a certain period before leaving – at different times it was from one week to two months.

Ideological Coercion

At the same time 'shock construction' became a popular method of attracting labour power, attracting people with the help of propaganda slogans to the idea of opening up new regions (opening up the virgin lands), building new industrial complexes (the Bratskaya hydro-electric power station), and so on. Being unable to command labour power by force, the state began to use ideological methods, whose object was above all young people, with their thirst for romance, with illusory representations of the conditions, instilled in schools and institutes. Once they faced the reality of 'shock construction' many began to protest, but here in place of the prison escort the mechanism of ideological pressure began to operate – 'you do not want to help your motherland', 'you are betraying your comrades', 'you do not understand the conditions faced by the country'... In place of crude coercion another mechanism began to work, but the aim remained the same: to force people to work in those conditions to which the state had assigned them.

For a long time the state could not manage without forcing people to work. All those 'shock constructions' which were begun by young romantics were completed by convicts and special military construction detachments – 'construction battalions'. But more and more often the state had to take a gentler role, rejecting the dictatorship of the proletariat to become the state of all the people. It became the usual practice, when providing the minimum level of welfare for its citizens, for the state to pass off any, even the most minimal increase in the volume of goods as a display of its care, even if this affected only a very small group of people.

THE ILLUSION OF CARE

A powerful ideological mechanism underpinned the image of the 'caring' state. This image was theoretically grounded. For example a whole complex of social sciences was created, such as the history of the CPSU, the political economy of socialism, scientific communism. These disciplines were considered to be privileged in all higher education institutions, scientific education in this field was considered to be the most prestigious, thousands of books, journals and articles were published every year on this theme, exceeding the number of publications in other sciences, either natural or less ideologised, for example such as psychology or sociology.

Propaganda gave a great deal of attention to creating the ideal journalistic image of the strict but just manager, concerned not only about production but also about the needs of the people, day and night, at the expense of his own health, untiringly thinking about the situation in the factory and about people's lives.

Finally, the form of the caring state and father-manager was celebrated in books and films. Moreover, now and then a really successful artistic product was created. For example, the film 'Predsedatel' with M. Ul'yanov in the leading role which is shown today as an outstanding film of the nation's cinema.

Paternalism in Consciousness

A result of the coercive-guardian activity of the state and of the propaganda machine was the inculcation in popular consciousness of strong paternalistic values: perception of the unequal status of leaders and ordinary members of society as normal; willingness to carry out only executive functions; refusal to innovate; the unacceptability of large differences in pay and in the level of well-being, and most important of all, the expectation of guardianship from above.

The weakening of state coercion, beginning from the 1960s, led to the strengthening of paternalistic policy both in the state as a whole and at the level of the enterprise. From the mid-1970s this policy assumed the form of social planning. The social development plan of the enterprise can be considered as the plan for the guardianship of the leader of the enterprise over the collective. It combined a collective agreement with a plan for the development of the personnel of the factory, covering all aspects of their work, health, welfare, housing and leisure activity.

The social development plan was a plan developed and approved by the administration of the enterprise as the basis of its own activity (the agreement with the labour collective never had more than a formal character). These plans were not an innovation of the enterprise administration, they were a part of state policy, they were financed out of the state budget, and the enterprise administration was responsible to state organs for their fulfilment.

False Paternalism

At the same time the paternalistic policy of the state and the enterprise alike was distinguished by its falsity. Very often fewer goods were received, and their quality was worse, than that which was proclaimed. The non-fulfilment of the social development plan was the norm, responsibility for which was far less than for failure to fulfil the production plans. The feeling became widespread that 'the bosses provide us less and pay less for it than was agreed'. The reasons put forward for this varied from 'the malicious intentions of the bosses against simple people' to 'objective difficulties which do not allow us to reach prosperity immediately'. However only in rare cases did this dissatisfaction take the form of open conflict.

Among the Kuzbass miners in the 1980s so-called 'sausage', 'tobacco' and 'soap' strikes happened fairly often. They had a local character – one or a few sections stopped, in rare cases the whole mine. This happened every year, in various places, and was related to the protracted absence of these products which were especially important for miners (sausage was the basis of the lunch which the miner took down the mine with him, soap was necessary after work to get cleaned up and wash away the coal dust, cigarettes were traditionally an important product whose absence is felt very acutely). There were other similar causes in addition – the absence of bread or oil from the shops, or very high prices being charged for them. But as a rule conflict was stopped, as shortage products 'as an exceptional measure' were supplied to the 'trouble-makers'.

DESTRUCTION OF THE CENTRALISED ECONOMY

The Disappearance of the Ministries

The dismantling of the centralised system of management became one further cause of the weakening of coercion in industry. Up to the end of the 1980s the fate not only of enterprises, but even of their separate subdivisions, was decided in the ministries in Moscow. The disintegration of the USSR also saw the collapse of the ministerial structure of management, which had completely controlled the situation in the enterprises, and without which the Director of an enterprise could not take a single significant step. The disintegration was so rapid that whole branches of industry suddenly found themselves without the traditional mechanism of management. For example, after the abolition of the Coal Ministry at the end of 1991 for several months there was no department in Moscow responsible for the management of the coal industry. It was only in the spring of 1993 that a responsible organisation, Rosugol', was established within the Russian Ministry of Fuel and Energy, but this organisation only really began to have an influence on the state of affairs in the regions in the second half of 1993. A similar situation arose in enterprises of the military-industrial complex in Russia. It is true that although the coal miners lost the ministerial structures they did not lose their customers, while military enterprises simultaneously lost their Moscow leadership and their military orders and corresponding finance and supplies.

Position of the Directorate

As a result of this the economic nomenklatura, formerly the most privileged part of the socialist nomenklatura, acquired an independence unprecedented up to then. It is difficult to say, and this is confirmed by the statements of the directors themselves, what this situation meant for them. On the one hand they had taken on an enormous responsibility for production, for the collective, while on the other hand they could do whatever they wanted, every form of control from above having disappeared simultaneously. But the position of the directors steadily improved so that they became one of the most powerful of the elite groups in society. The advantageous position of the directorate (now known as the economic nomenklatura) is based on the fact that, although they are the effective owners of the enterprises, juridically they remain employees of state enterprises which draw resources from the state budget, while having virtually no responsibility for their actions. It would be difficult to overestimate the advantageousness of this position, so the desire of the directorate to preserve such a situation for as long as possible is understandable.

In circumstances in which the means of repression were no longer available it became necessary to use the method of guardianship. Firstly, this preserved the dominant position of the administration in the enterprise. Secondly, workers were prepared to put themselves under such a guardianship. The paternalistic policy received a new impulse. But now not at the level of the state but at the level of the enterprise. In the past there were no fundamental differences between enterprises in the level of 'care for the collective'. The 'needs of the toilers' could not be ignored, but diligence was equally impossible – we know examples of the punishment of directors who had tried to build 'communism in one enterprise'.

Paternalism and the Progress of the Enterprise

In the new economic conditions which arose at the end of the 1980s and the beginning of the 1990s the situation changed radically. Differences began to emerge between enterprises which had not existed in the past. Above all these differences concerned the standard of living of the workers. For example, in one of the Kuzbass mines the total income of workers (including not only pay, but also deficit goods, share of profits, and later dividends on shares) was between one and a half and two and a half times higher than the analogous income of workers in other mines in the very same town. Now these differences have become extremely important. One has begun to develop, at the same time another struggles to maintain its normal level of production, while a third slowly declines in a process of economic and productive degradation.

The progress and the degradation of the enterprise is very closely related to the past strength of the paternalistic policy of the enterprise. Everybody ends up having to follow a paternalistic policy: both the old economic nomenklatura and the new entrepreneurs creating an 'absolutely market-oriented enterprise'. Attempts to ignore paternalism run up against opposition from various directions, of which opposition from the workers was hardly the strongest.

A clear example of the impossibility of abandoning paternalism is provided by the experience of the Kemerovo plastics factory Plastmass. This enterprise was a pioneer of privatisation in the Kuzbass chemical industry. The Deputy Director for Economics, who was quite young to hold the post and had higher education in economics, became the ideologist of privatisation. The privatisation of the enterprise was well thought out, the enterprise developed dynamically, first of all reducing the labour force, mobilised the potential of its scientific research institute, having established the competitiveness of its products. The sphere of managers and specialists was dominated by well educated employees, while the pay of ITR was two to three times that of the highest skilled workers. Despite this the pay of workers was significantly higher than that of workers in other chemical enterprises in the city.

One of the most impressive features was the ostentatious refusal of the management to indulge in paternalism in any of its forms. This was expressed in a kind of slogan: 'we will pay our workers enough for them to buy everything they need in the shops, without having to worry about prices'. But despite this the workers constantly expressed their dissatisfaction at the absence of the distribution of goods, envying workers in other enterprises who received various goods at subsidised prices, although their own pay was twice as high and they could buy exactly the same goods in commercial shops and still be better off. As a result, when a struggle for possession of the controlling block of shares broke out between the Director and the Chief Economist, the outcome was decided by the shareholders' meeting, at which the Director won a convincing victory, having put forward an openly paternalistic programme which proposed to buy and distribute goods, build housing and so on. In exchange for this the workers forgave him the fact that he had violated the constitution of the company in acquiring the controlling block of shares, having rejected the well thought out and considered programme presented by the Chief Economist, who had no social programme at all.

The expectations of workers of a just guardianship was strengthened and it was impossible not to take this into account for several reasons. First, the influence of workers on production has increased as a result of the collapse of the old state mechanism – through the election of managers and through the development of industrial democracy. Secondly, the workers have acquired the ability to exert a powerful influence on managers as a consequence of the disappearance of the threat of repression on the part of punitive and other state organs. Third, the directorate was not prepared to carry out an independent policy, power fell to them unexpectedly, and for some time the administration of enterprises was in a state of confusion. In this period it was vitally necessary for the directorate to maintain its position to avoid betraying the workers' expectations. It was precisely this situation that gave a new impulse to enterprise paternalism.

Initial Conditions

The complete mechanism of paternalistic management is revealed in those enterprises which carry out a strongly paternalistic policy. Above all, a series of initial conditions was necessary for a strong paternalistic policy. First, the enterprise must be in a strong economic position or be able to reach it in a short time. Second, the top leaders must enjoy a high degree of trust in the collective. Third, it was necessary to have reliable channels of communication in the collective between workers and managers and vice versa. Fourth, the enterprise must have a well-thought out development programme, guaranteeing the future development of the enterprise. Only under these conditions could the enterprise transfer to a situation of genuine paternalism.

The Distribution System

Above all paternalism consists in increasing the living standard of the workers by giving them more benefits, compared to other enterprises, in both monetary and more often, in non-monetary form. The personality of the leader at this point has a decisive significance. The first impulse comes precisely from him. His motives for suddenly abandoning the 'pseudo-paternalism of the period of late stagnation' may be various. In one case it may be the Director's consideration for the collective, who is connected to it by close links of team-work, who wants 'to help his people escape from destitution'. In another it may be an instrumental attitude of the Director to the collective, understanding that 'to use it as an instrument it must be maintained in good condition'. But independently of the motivation of the Director at the first stage he secures a real increase in the volume of benefits for the workers compared to other enterprises or analogous groups of workers.

Within the enterprise the management can twist the payment system 'in favour of the workers' or 'against the workers'. Obviously the creation of a system of payment 'in favour of the workers' allows them to earn more money, but this is always connected, directly or obliquely, with the loyalty of workers to management.

The other way of increasing the standard of living of the workers is the distribution of non-monetary goods. It is worth describing the system of distribution of these goods in some detail. Usually such a system has existed for several years, although constantly being modified.

The clearest example of a distributive system is the system of distribution of bartered goods in the mines. It began as a system of distribution of things among the shops through the trade union. Having sold coal for export the mine received imported goods to a value corresponding to the amount of coal sold. Then these goods are handed over to the collective for distribution or for sale at reduced prices. As a rule these were the most prestigious Western goods –

electronics, automobiles, fashion clothes, consumer durables. Within the collective there were constant attempts to find just principles of distribution. Every variant of distribution according to the traditional schema was tried out – from allocation to the best workers and social activists, to distribution by lots, without taking any account of the worker's labour contribution, qualifications and conscientiousness.

The system of distribution was made progressively more complex. The most popular became a system of accounting in conventional accounting units (usually accounts are kept in dollars) in personal employee accounts. In this system the dollars could only be used for buying those goods which the mine has acquired through its barter activities. Within this system it is possible to take into account the worker's labour contribution, qualifications and other particular characteristics, which made this system very similar to the regular system of monetary payments. A special infrastructure was established to implement this system – special departments for keeping accounts of the 'hard currency earnings', mine shops, with their staffs of assistants, where workers could realise their 'pseudo-dollars'.

The transformation of the distribution system was the outcome of a struggle for justice in the distribution of goods, but at every stage in the development of the system it remained an instrument of management in the hands of the administration. The administration controlled distribution firstly because it controlled the process of allocating goods to the distribution network, and secondly because as a result of distribution a considerable share fell to them. For example every enterprise chief has a so-called 'Director's Fund' – to which between 5 and 15 per cent of every shipment of deficit goods is transferred. Thirdly, it is not very difficult for the administration to control the process of collective elaboration of the principles of distribution of goods. Every manager already had a great deal of experience in manipulating public opinion in the pre-perestroika period. But in the period of election of directors and domestication of the Labour Collective Council (STK) many directors perfected their ability to conduct any kind of meeting or conference to achieve predetermined results.

These are the methods: the most important question to be resolved is that of the norms of representation – either the norm is large so that there are not many people and it is possible to exert influence on it, or it is small, in which case there is a large number of participants and the person who has the microphone under his control has the advantage, cutting off trouble-makers and conversely allowing those who are loyal to speak. Above all, the best technical procedure for selecting representatives of the collective is on the basis of shifts, which the chiefs of subdivisions can control without difficulty to ensure the selection of the 'necessary' people. Another way of manipulating a meeting is to spin out the meeting with discussion of secondary questions. Discussion might be dragged out for several hours, by which time people want to get the meeting over as quickly as possible and will adopt any proposal. There are other more refined ways of manipulating meetings and conferences. Thus very often unscrupulous and extortionate decisions, for example about the Director's Fund, are carried out on the basis of resolutions of a conference of the labour collective.

The Distribution System as an Instrument

The distribution system was an extremely effective instrument. Local strikes and conflicts have been crushed with the help of the skilful manipulation of the distribution of barter goods, buying off not only individual people, but also collectives, punishing them by reducing their rights to obtain goods. By receiving a higher income or shortage goods the collective became a hostage of the administration, for any attempt at protest was prevented by the fear that the administration would stop the activity which allowed the collective to get goods, hard currency and so on.

The situation in the Sverdlov mine in Kuzbass graphically illustrates this. A conflict arose in one section of the mine. Because of the geological conditions the drift had to be worked quickly. But the workers considered that the conditions proposed to the brigade were not advantageous and they deliberately dragged out the work in the hope that the management would not stand its ground and would accept their conditions. But instead of that the section was broken up, or to be precise a large part was transferred to another section, and workers from other sections were brought into this 'hot drift'. They had to finish exactly the same work, with the same conditions for payment, but they also had an unofficial promise from the Director that if they finished all the work on time they would have the right to buy a refrigerator at a subsidised price. The workers who had been removed were indignant, on those terms they would have done the work. But for the administration it was an important point of principle to punish the obstinate workers and to give an incentive to those who were obedient. Although the new workers in this section were condemned as strike-breakers, the effect was achieved: the work was carried out and the disobedient were punished.

Channels of Communication

Channels of communication between the administration and workers play a very important role in these matters. The most widespread is the practice of 'going to the people', and also the facilitation of access of workers to senior management.

In a silk kombinat the specialists and managers complain that it is impossible to meet with the Director of the enterprise to discuss any problems they might have. However this is the case with the leading specialists. At the same time the workers have almost unimpeded access to the Director to discuss their problems outside working hours and even during working time. Apart from this, the Director often visits the shops and chats to people in their workplaces. However the Director is no plaything in the hands of the workers. He only takes up those issues which he thinks are important.

More complex, but more reliable, is the organisation of the work of the representatives bodies of the enterprise. In this case they serve the function not only of providing information about the attitude of the workers, but also secure the participation of the workers in the decisions taken. This is apparent in the unique example of the work of the representative body of the mine Bratchenko. At the beginning, in 1987, after the adoption of the Law on State Enterprises, it was created as an STK. In 1989, when the mine became a leasehold enterprise, it was reconstituted as the Council of Leaseholders, and after the privatisation of the mine in 1991 it became the Shareholders' Council.

In the course of an interview with workers of the mine carried out in 1991 many different views of the activity of the Council were encountered. The majority of such evaluations were positive. In general no negative evaluations were given, and neutral ones only rarely.

In such a situation living connections with the workers allow the senior management to know what are the important problems facing people and to take appropriate decisions. Such channels are also important for reinforcing the trust of the collective in the senior management. In the Soviet economic system people were always alienated from management bodies and any attention paid by management to the workers is very highly regarded by the latter even to this day. Even the most clumsy attempts 'to go to the people' can prove successful, if in the course of them real problems are discussed or some kind of reliable information is conveyed. Regular meetings with ordinary workers – by being available to discuss personal matters, at the Council, or while visiting the workplace, create the image of management as 'ours'.

The Personality of the Leader

'Our boss' is not a type which emerges at once. In the centralised economic system the collective could not think of the boss as 'ours'. Otherwise he would stop being 'ours' in the system of management and would quickly be thrown out of it. The weakening of the centralised system led to the emergence of 'father-bosses'. To become such a person it was necessary first, even if only sometimes, to defend the collective against higher management, secondly to secure an increase, however small, in pay (in monetary or non-monetary form), and third, to have direct connections with the collective in some form.

To do this was very difficult and only a few bosses were able to acquire such an image among the workers. It has to be said that the reaction of the workers, who were experiencing real care for the first time was very positive. One could even say that the collective was in love with its boss. And, just as in the case of any love, the perception of the actions of the boss became almost universally uncritical. Those activities which in the past would have met with opposition were now perceived as something which goes without saying. And this is also a basis for the carrying through of radical reorganisation and innovation.

The presence of relations of trust between workers and management leads to the practical disappearance of the trade union organisation. And there is absolutely no question of the creation of new or independent trade unions. Paternalism as it were provides immunity against trade unions. Even if not simply individual leaders, but a whole cell of members of an independent trade union takes root in the collective, the mass of workers will not only ignore them but may even suppress their activity.

Just such a situation arose in the mine Bratchenko. In order to develop production the Director had to recruit a whole brigade from a neighbouring mine who had experience of working with the new equipment. Amongst them were leaders of the NPG, who had experience of working on strike committees. They tried to put forward demands related to health and safety measures, the conditions of transport to the face, but even these demands, which were on the whole just and not heavy for the administration, provoked a sharp reaction among the 'old' workers, telling the newcomers to shut up and not to damage relations with management. The result was that the management did not even need to react to these demands. The conflict was stopped by the workers themselves in its initial stage.

The Development Programme of the Enterprise

The development of the enterprise is the next step which makes it possible to stabilise the well-being of the enterprise and, most important, to make it possible to maintain it in the future. The development of the enterprise is not just a matter of its technical reconstruction, important as this is. But the organisational development of the enterprise is particularly important. As a rule this happens in the early stages of privatisation, with the purchase of the enterprise by the collective and its removal from the dictatorship of state management bodies. If the technical and organisational changes are radical and immediate, the economic mechanism and internal structural relations are only changed slowly and carefully. The introduction of any innovation in the sphere of payment systems or internal organisation is accompanied by a large number of consultations with various groups of workers. Sometimes such care and gradualness can give even rise to irritation at the absence of real changes within the enterprise. However such gradualness makes it possible to achieve very significant changes.

Sharp and significant changes are bound to damage the interests of some groups. In defending themselves such groups increase the level of conflict in the enterprise, trust disappears, and the basis for development is undermined. Gradual changes reduce the level of conflict, above all because people have time to get used to them, the changes are small, and because the most conflictual changes are rejected. As an example of such gradual change we can refer back to the development of the system of distribution, which was accomplished over a period of three to four years during which it was transformed from the system of allocation by lots, to the complex system using personal hard currency accounts.

Another feature of organisational development is the gradual diversification of production. On the whole the collective takes an unfavourable view of diversification. However an independent enterprise cannot risk its survival on a single product or a single technology. Thus the appearance of new enterprises, daughter firms, and auxiliary plants is inevitable. The process of their emergence is not transparent and is carried out by the management despite the views of the collective. Diversification is evidence that the management of the enterprise is getting used to the market and of the emergence of a new non-paternalistic management mechanism.

The mine Bratchenko has created several daughter enterprises. The first to be established was a brokers' firm, it created a commercial bank and almost simultaneously set up an insurance company. But this was the traditional way of setting up daughter firms. At the beginning of 1993 the sections concerned with the development of a new pit (a long way from the old coalfield) were separated into independent enterprises. Finally the mother firm and all the daughter enterprises created an investment company to construct the new mine complex and the necessary production infrastructure, in particular a railway to get the coal out of the new field.

The annoyance of the collective is related to the fact that the new spheres of activity are usually not those which are typical of the enterprise, giving rise to new and unaccustomed relations. Their advantage is not well understood, and their profitability is seen as a threat to the enterprise's own position. A typical attitude which is widespread is 'Why does a mine need a bank? So that we can close the mine, and miners will hand money out of the window?'

Preservation of the Collective

The last element of a powerful paternalistic policy is the preservation of the collective. Originally this has a hint of 'our goods are only for members of our collective'. This also appears in the system of distribution – only workers of the enterprise receive goods, and in the process of privatisation – workers have priority in the initial allocation of shares, and the closed shareholding company is seen as the most welcome variant of privatisation. Finally this can appear in a protectionist personnel policy of the enterprise when, for example, relatives of workers already in the enterprise receive preference in recruitment. The need to preserve the collective is an additional stimulus for the development of production because otherwise the renovation and optimisation of the structure would inevitably lead to reductions in employment.

Precisely such a situation arose in the factory Plastmass in the course of privatisation. Above we described the attempt radically to change relations within the enterprise to a market form. One of the first steps in this bold renovation was a reduction in the labour force of almost thirty percent. This reduction took the following form. First of all the workers of an experimental factory, which was a subdivision of the enterprise, but was in fact located in Novosibirsk oblast, were cut – or more precisely the factory was given its independence and continued to exist as an independent enterprise. But from the point of view of the factory's accounts the departure of the personnel of the Novosibirsk factory appeared as a reduction in employment. These distant workers accounted for about 60 per cent of the entire cut in the labour force. The remaining 40 per cent were 'their own'. These were in the first place discipline violators, absentees and habitual drunkards, but also, it seems, a small number of workers and engineers whom the management considered undesirable. So overall the level of redundancy was not very high. Moreover, those who were laid off received quite good redundancy payments, and were helped to find new jobs. But in public opinion these modest and by no means harsh redundancies were seen as a 'slaughter of the personnel'. The remaining workers were so frightened of the possibility of redundancy that against this background the administration managed to do something which in normal circumstances would have provoked a storm of indignation on the part of the workers: they repeatedly increased the pay of engineers and managers. After these two actions the workers were of one view: 'they twist us as they want, and we cannot raise any objections to them.'

The broadening of production on a new technological and productive basis creates large-scale redundancy of workers who are not suitable for work in the new conditions. It is therefore necessary to recruit new highly qualified workers, which leads to an increase in the number of workers again and all the workers, both old and new, become dependent on management, on the planning of the development of production, the number of workers, the amount of money allocated to pay, and so on.

'Incomplete' Paternalism

Very few enterprises are able to carry out a strong paternalist policy. The majority of enterprises fall into the category of those who are able to carry out a not very strong paternalist policy. It has already been said that a deliberate rejection of paternalism is very rare and insignificant. One can confidently assert that practically every Director would like to carry out a strongly paternalistic policy, but not all of them are able to go far. One may not have sufficient economic strength to assure the growth in the living standards of the workers, others are unable to build up the trust of the collective, a third may have no prospects for development and so on. Not being able to neglect the paternalistic mechanism completely the managers use the old 'pseudo-paternalist' mechanism, without abandoning the attempt to realise a strong paternalistic policy. Cases in which an enterprise has all the means to realise such a policy, but the management is not in a position to use the means which they have so that they lose such possibilities, are less widespread.

In one of the South Kuzbass mines the situation was as follows: the mine was privatised early, and had every opportunity to escape from the control of higher structures, and consequently to get access to export markets and so increase the standard of living of the workers. The mine enjoyed very favourable conditions, in the opinion of several specialists the best in Kuzbass for the extraction of coal and the development of production. Finally, the management enjoyed the trust of the collective, and for a time the management could have done anything it wanted, with the support of the workers guaranteed. But the indecisiveness of the management, and a subsequent struggle for power led to the loss of all these advantages and today the mine is to be found among those average enterprises which are not noted for anything in particular and which exist under the control of higher structures.

In such 'semi-paternalist' enterprises are to be found only separate elements of guardianship, above all the distribution system. In such a case there is no real separation of the enterprise from the state. On the contrary, the state is the guarantor not only of wages, but also of various non-monetary goods. State organs either supply the enterprise with deficit goods directly, or the state gives the management of the enterprise privileges for conducting commercial transactions which allow it to obtain the necessary goods.

The most important thing that distinguishes these enterprises from paternalistic enterprises is the absence of trust in the management and correspondingly the high level of conflict. But this in turn undermines the possibilities for the development of production, leading to the stagnation of production, even the possibility of its decline. As a result the basis of the welfare of the collective declines, the commercial activity of the management is strengthened, and on the other hand the demands of the workers and their distrust of the administration increase. Thus a new circuit of confrontation begins which worsens the situation even more.

The management of such enterprises is much less oriented to the collective. Care for the collective exists to the extent that it is necessary not only to retain power, but also to be able to claim symbolically to be 'a management which is meeting the social needs of its workers'. There is no special effort to provide information or build up trust. As a consequence a fairly strong oppositional mood develops which is expressed in the formation of independent trade unions or workers' organisations.

Decaying Paternalism

There are not many enterprises which are not even able to conduct a minimal paternalistic policy, although they are more than are able to practice strong paternalism. The main reasons for such inability is the very bad position of the enterprise – useless products, hopelessly outdated equipment, the absence of prospects, and so on. Sometimes the incompetence of the management contributes to such a bad situation. In such circumstances there is no question of improving welfare or of development prospects. The enterprise is totally and completely dependent on state financing, which as a rule is not very large and which barely allows the enterprise to stay afloat. The only tangible good which all the workers in such an enterprise receive is the right to plunder the enterprise's property and to violate discipline. Practically everything is misappropriated – money, equipment, supplies, the use of services for personal aims, and so on. The most important thing here is that matters should not lead to the complete collapse and stoppage of the enterprise, because if it ceased to exist the management would be held to account. Management plays the leading role, they 'take control' of the biggest and most profitable operations for their own benefit, sometimes drawing in a narrow group of trusted specialists and workers. For workers there remains only the direct theft and use of the resources of the enterprise for themselves, and the 'right to violate discipline' – the possibility of committing technological and disciplinary violations without any punishment.

In those cases in which the management of an enterprise finding itself in such conditions tries to maintain discipline to halt the decline of the enterprise, it provokes very strong conflicts. These conflicts take an uninstitutionalised form and as a rule come down to the issue of the re-election of the management. Moreover in the majority of cases the conflicts arise as a result of the clash of claims to the use of enterprise resources. The prospect for such enterprises is a slow death. Slow because even minimal state support can prolong the existence of an enterprise for years. And the maximal prolongation of the life of the enterprise is beneficial for a whole group of workers, independently of how much connection they already have with this enterprise or organisation.

THE LIMITS OF PATERNALISM

The End of Class Peace

A paternalistic policy, particularly in its strong forms, looks very attractive. The enterprise develops, the standard of living of the workers is high. However such a situation can only last for a certain amount of time. Gradually the tone of relationships in paternalistic enterprises changes, and above all there is a growth of conflict. It is the management which takes the initiative in aggravating the situation as it gradually begins to depart from the principles of collaboration with the collective and conducts the policy of an owner, interested in producing profits and in the economic efficiency of the enterprise. Such a policy often contradicts the interests of the workers, above all in the matter of increasing their standard of living. The workers have much less of an interest in the future development of the enterprise, particularly if the question is posed in the form of the alternative of investing in production or increasing wages. The other factor which gives rise to conflicts of interest is the question of redundancy. The more the administration switches to a market orientation, the more it gives in to the need to carry out such redundancies. And there is one more factor, not so obvious, but very important. During the period in which 'class peace' rules in the enterprise the administration grabs hold of all economic and juridical power in the enterprise. This is done with the knowledge of the collective, counting on the fact that the administration will carry out the will of the collective and is dependent on it. But at the point at which the administration departs from the principles of collaboration the workers find themselves pushed aside by management and fall into strong dependence on them.

This development takes place gradually. One can consider the first stage of this departure as activities which are foisted on the collective and restrict their rights so as to increase their dependence. Moreover this is done openly, with a willingness to deal with any who disagree. As an example of such an activity one can cite the introduction of new forms of employment contract, changes in the system of pay, and so on.

The Director of the mine Bratchenko after privatisation transferred the whole collective to an individual labour contract system with very harsh conditions. Among such conditions was the annual duration of the contract, which was the most painful feature for the workers. Practically all the workers were simultaneously placed in a situation of uncertainty – they did not know whether the contract would be extended the following year. Moreover it increased the feeling of dependence since according to the terms of the contract the obligations of the worker far outweighed his rights. In fact every worker from top to bottom found himself in a situation of personal dependence on a manager. The conditions for breaking off the contract were so vague that any misdemeanour could provide a pretext for cancelling the contract. The way in which the worker was appraised had decisive significance in this respect (for both workers and specialists this was done by the immediate superior). In the Director's own words, with the introduction of the contract system, he 'had raped the collective'.

The contract system gave rise to a large number of conflicts and increased tension. The Director saw all this but considered that it was normal. When he was asked about his evaluation of the contract system, having been told that the overwhelming majority of workers and specialists regarded this form of contract negatively, the Director replied 'And who regarded it positively?'. Having been told that only a small group of middle managers regarded it positively, he exclaimed with relief 'But I do not need any more than that!'. For the collective this was the first and biggest disappointment with their 'people's director'.

The cutting off of channels of inter-communication goes further. The management distances itself from the collective, the sphere of activity of the representative organ is narrowed, and it less and less frequently takes significant decisions, and more and more often is simply informed of decisions already taken, it is forbidden to consider a whole range of questions which the administration does not want considered.

The Director of the silk kombinat sharply reduced the access of workers to him after privatisation and his appointment as President of the new shareholding company. The Director of the factory Plastmass, preparing for the decisive showdown with his former Economics Director at the annual shareholders' meeting went to the shops, held meetings at which he showed a video about the 'villainous designs' of his opponent. The showdown happened. The Director stopped appearing in the shops, even when they were ready to strike, leaving his deputy to resolve the situation that had arisen.

Instrumental Relation to the Collective

In the relation between management and the collective one can trace more and more clearly a utilitarian or instrumental attitude. They use the collective and the enterprise as the means of achieving exclusively personal aims. Moreover they do this more and more overtly.

A typical situation arose in the Sverdlov mine. At the beginning of the 90s the Director of the mine began energetically to change the situation in the mine. He tried to reorganise the management and he began to reconstruct the traditional Personnel Department into a Personnel Management Department, recruiting for this purpose experienced sociologists and lawyers. He also got the leaders of the workers' movement on his side, having appointed one of them to head a special department to work out new payment norms and incentives. Together with this the tone of attitudes in the mine changed markedly. We have already given an example above of the punishment of a disobedient brigade which happened at this time. It is difficult to say whether the Director could have carried out the changes more logically and radically, but he was unwilling to change or to confront the most conservative part of middle management

The important thing is that after several unsuccessful attempts to develop the commercial activity of the mine he resigned his post and became the head of a large firm concerned with the export of coal. At the end, before he left, the Director faced many demands to stay, particularly from those whom he had supported and promoted to innovative subdivisions. Nonetheless the Director abandoned all his plans to take advantage of the opportunity to work in commerce, which gave him a pretty large income. Having received his starting capital and new opportunities from the collective, the Director stepped over the collective, over 'his responsibilities to people' and left.

Here one can see very clearly the instrumental attitude of the paternalist-manager to his collective. Of course not all directors abandon 'their' collective like this. But this does not mean that they have any the less of an instrumental attitude to the collective.

Strengthening the Administration

New tendencies are arising in the stronger enterprises – to slow or stop the growth in the standard of living of the workers and the processes already described above begin to develop, like those which have arisen in enterprises in which a relatively weak paternalistic policy has been carried out: mutual distrust, conflict and so on. True, here there is a significant difference – the administration has complete power. The power handed to the administration by the workers to carry out their will has been turned against them. Having exploited the trust of the collectives the directors are finally able to get control of the power which had fallen to them so unexpectedly. Now there is no point in protesting because this can immediately result in a reduction in earnings or a loss of work. There is no use in opposing this. There is no trade union organisation, and the workers have no experience of struggling for their rights.

The Preservation of Paternalism

However enterprise managers do not want to abandon guardianship completely. It is simply that paternalism will be used as the means to achieve a desired effect, even if management is prepared to use other methods of management. The basis of the preservation of paternalism remains the expectation of guardianship on the part of the workers. The character of this expectation may alter. For example, if earlier the expectation was related primarily to the quantity of goods received, the biggest expectation is now that management will take measures to preserve jobs. But just as before, these expectations are justified to the extent that the management needs workers. To the extent that this need disappears, the management will switch to the ruthless reduction of both the number of workers and the volume of production. After grabbing power in the enterprise the administration wants a test of strength, introducing unpopular changes, intensifying conflict, alienating itself somewhat from the collective.

One reason for the withdrawal of a paternalistic policy, as was shown by the events in Kuzbass in the summer of 1993, is the abolition or reduction of state support for enterprises. Immediately after the publication of the Presidential decree, notorious in the coal industry, on the freeing of coal prices, the mine directors put forward the argument that it was necessary to introduce compulsory vacations, without maintaining pay, for the majority of workers. The government replied with the proposal to retain subsidies for coal enterprises and gradually free coal prices over a long period. The Directors were not happy, but the directorate adopted this proposal, and in most cases the vacation was cancelled. In a few mines the workers were sent on compulsory vacation, but they were paid for it.

Management, having seized power, shows 'tolerance' to the collective for as long as the state continues to provide it with the means to do so.

Alternatives to Paternalism: the Authoritarian-Repressive Model

As replacements for paternalism one can consider two models: the coercive-repressive and the market. The first presupposes the creation of harsh, strong methods for the preservation of the power of management in the enterprise with the use of state bodies to defend their power.

The use of 'company police' is not excluded for maintaining power. Thus in the mine Bratchenko quite a large special subdivision was created to provide a round-the-clock guard for the mine and the adjoining territory. Moreover this internal police includes, in addition to security specialists provided with up-to-date equipment, former miners from this mine, who know the collective and the mine itself. Similar practices are becoming more and more popular. A special police subdivision protects the building of the South Kuzbass coal concern.

Another factor that allows one to refer to a return to the coercive-repressive model is the question of the revival of the 'Disciplinary Rules'. This document was applied in the coal industry and various other branches of the Soviet economy. In essence it is a supplement to the codex of the labour law, but very distinctive. This was an extremely harsh document. It strengthened the responsibilities of the workers and increased the rights of the managers, in comparison with other branches. Such strictness was explained by the higher degree of danger in coal enterprises. However in practice these rules made coal enterprises semi-military organisations, with much stricter discipline and responsibility, and their vague formulation provided a lot of scope for managerial arbitrariness. For example, the Rules declare the right of senior management 'in cases of special need to strengthen or weaken the punishment or penalty imposed by a lower-level manager on a worker'. After the 1989 miners' strike these rules were removed and the relations in the collective were regulated only by the general labour law. But almost from the moment of the withdrawal of this document voices constantly rang out from the ranks of the directorate declaring the need to re-establish the application of these Rules. In 1992 in the Supreme Soviet of Russia a new set of 'Disciplinary Rules' was introduced and approved on its first reading. It was planned to take the final decision on them at the end of 1993... And here is a quotation from the report in the Kuzbass regional newspaper: 'At the last meeting of managers – 'the coal generals' – last Friday the question of the need to strengthen the manageability of unprivatised enterprises in the branch was put.' (*Nasha Gazetta* 23.10.93).

Alternatives to Paternalism: the Market Model

The second model presupposes the introduction of market regulators, the use of economic technology, skilled labour power, the production of useful products and a strict economic regime. In these conditions contractual relations with workers can have a proper place, but these will already be relations between the buyers and sellers of labour power, and not the preservation of the 'united family'.

In 1993 an example of the new way of resolving problems appeared. The first was the creation of investment companies to build new coal mines and the second was the creation of commercial structures for the extraction and treatment of coal. Among the investment companies one should particularly note one created in the Bratchenko mine. Its main feature is the fact that it is underpinned by the capital of the mine and its daughter companies itself. The share of the state here is minimal. This company is carrying out successful projects to develop existing mines, to build new ones and develop their production infrastructures. In many ways this company provides the prototype for future complexes for the extraction and treatment of coal on a non-state basis.

The creation of commercial structures in the mines does not always proceed through the development of a firm which sells coal. There are various examples of commercial coal extraction enterprises. Above all is a joint enterprise with an English firm, producing equipment for the coal industry. The joint enterprise operates in the largest mine in south Kuzbass. The combines supplied from England allow the extraction of coal from seams where access is difficult. Another example is the creation of the mine Svobodnaya – this mine is today a private enterprise, developed only at the expense of its owner and loans.

Of course these examples do not indicate that their managers have abandoned paternalistic policies. On the contrary, today they try every means to be attractive for their workers. But these enterprises are much less oriented to the state, not because they do not want to receive subsidies, but because those who receive the subsidy today would have to share it with them. They have to find other mechanisms, other means of holding onto industrial power.

The Future of Paternalism

Managers are frightened by the novelty of the new mechanisms. Thus it is easier and preferable to preserve the paternalistic tradition. Seeing the concern of workers for paternalism, managers struggle to maintain state support for enterprises. For this purpose they use official and unofficial channels of influence on the state structures on which the preservation of state support depends, on public opinion, and lobbying. If all this does not help, they organise strikes in the course of which demands are put forward addressed to any and every higher body, right up to the President, but not affecting the internal relations of the enterprise.

Speaking about the role and place of paternalism in the changing industrial relations in the Russian economy one has to note two features – its wide distribution and its temporary character. Its wide distribution is explained by the wide distribution of paternalist values 'below', and the temporary character by the orientation of management to its own interests, all of which to a considerable extent contradict the interests of the majority of workers and the appearance among them of a market orientation – profits, economic efficiency, and so on.

The rejection of paternalistic values will be accompanied by painful processes. The realisation on the part of those at the bottom that they have been cheated and are without protection will be accompanied by emotional and perhaps aggressive outbursts of activity. Moreover it is very likely that the process of self-assertion of the new owners at the top will be accompanied by the use of harsh, powerful and inhumane methods in the traditions of the Soviet economy. The rapid abolition of paternalism may lead to rough events, strained attitudes, and the formation of mass independent trade unions. But it is more likely that it will be a gradual and long-drawn out process of the withering away of paternalistic values and gradual elimination of elements of the paternalistic mechanisms of management. Certainly various management models will be tried out: in some places the market model, in some places the repressive model. A great deal will depend on the political situation in the country or in the region. But in any case the tried and tested mechanisms of paternalistic management will continue to be used for a long time in the Russian economy.

5. Paternalism in Russian Enterprises: Our Understanding

*Samara Research Group**

It is impossible to understand the socio-economic changes taking place in Russian enterprises today without understanding the mechanisms of the inter-relationships which have been formed in the course of the entire seventy year history of Soviet society. The systems of management and of the distribution and exchange of information which have grown up within the enterprise continue to exist and define the background against which current innovations are unfolding. We will try to uncover one aspect of the life of contemporary Russian industry, which can be summed up in the concept of paternalism.

Why do we speak of paternalism? In our opinion this concept most fully and accurately characterises many features of the life of Russian enterprises: the strategy carried out by management, inter-relationships within the labour collective and the stereotypical expectations of workers.

In general outline we understand by paternalism relationships similar to those which existed in the patriarchal Russian community, in which relationships were constructed as though it were a large family. Such relationships are characterised by the primacy of the collective, a strict internal hierarchy (sometimes reinforced by charisma), non-monetary forms of relationship and so on. We use such a concept of paternalism to understand the characteristics of production relations. We do not see paternalism as a particular kind of management strategy, peculiar to the administrative traditions of Soviet managers, because we think that the concept of paternalism describes not only the sphere of management (for example, management policy or the strategy of the leadership of the enterprise), but also the sphere of interaction of all subjects of production (including the stereotypical perceptions of both the administration and of those under their command). It is, as it were, the natural environment of the life of the enterprise.

Without going into a deep theoretical discussion we will describe paternalism as a process and result of the interaction of two tendencies in the interrelations within the enterprise between workers and managers, which create a specific kind of atmosphere in the enterprise. On the one hand as a relation from the top down which is manifested in the forms of management: particular modes of influence, forms of implementing their decisions, as the conscious or unconscious policy (activity) of the leadership of the enterprise at various levels, paternalism 'from above'. On the other hand as a relation from the bottom up, which is manifested in the forms of subordination, perceptions of management decisions, expectations and demands of the activity of the administration, as perceptions (or expectations) by the subordinates of these or those actions of the various levels of management, paternalism 'from below'. We consider these two aspects as a unity, although these two tendencies – what is done and how it is transmitted 'from above', and how it is carried out and perceived 'below' – can be discordant, played in different keys.

There are interesting cases in which the administration intends one thing, but it is perceived completely differently, or completely contrarily, by the workers. Thus the Director of one factory bought a sausage plant with some hard currency, with the justification that although meat was produced by an auxiliary section of the factory there was not enough for all the workers. Now the factory's workers would have their own sausage and would greet his action with acclaim, because the hard currency had been used in the interests of the collective. However the workers were completely unimpressed by what they considered to be an unrealistic plan. This discord between the presentation and the perception gives rise to a whole matrix of various kinds of mutual perceptions. Only one of these perceptions will be inscribed in the framework of paternalism in its purest form, although one can obviously find features of paternalism in every type of mutual perception.

So by paternalism we understand a particular type of production relations which is marked by the following simple features:

1. Existence in the enterprise of a wide range of non-industrial activities.
2. Features of charismatic leadership
3. Strongly hierarchical management

4. Closed information
5. Egalitarian principles of wages and distribution
6. Non-monetary relations
7. Ideology of paternalism.

Below we will try to describe each of these features in more detail.

1. Non-Industrial Activity

Paternalism as a form of relation is inherent not only in the industrial sphere of Soviet and contemporary Russian society. It is a much wider concept embracing also the sphere of state policy, the social sphere, the sphere of human relationships – every sphere of social life in which the patriarchal, communal, stereotypical mentalities of soviet people are reproduced.

Paternalism at the level of the state is expressed both in the socio-economic policy carried out by the government and in the population's support, understanding and approval of such a policy, which corresponds to their expectations (which incidentally is evidence of the effectiveness of ideological activity).

One aspect of state management was its policy in relation to the enterprise. The essence of this policy lay in the fact that a substantial proportion of state functions for the social protection of the population were carried out through the enterprise.

The function of providing workers with rest and leisure facilities was met through departmental sanatoria, holiday camps, health resorts, rest homes, palaces of culture. The right to housing was met by departmental housing construction, so that the industrial giants were surrounded by massive housing complexes which dominated whole districts of the city, and the enterprise was also responsible for supplying these districts with heating, water, telephones and maintaining these facilities in working order.

State functions in the sphere of education and training in general were met though the system of departmental kindergartens, sponsored middle schools, factory professional-technical schools, technical-creative children's centres.

Health care was provided in polyclinics, sanatoria, profilaktori and clinics which were the responsibility of enterprises and departments.

Those enterprises which do not have their own social and welfare apparatus will often rent facilities on behalf of their workers, and this is even true of the new capitalist enterprises. For example, one of the new financial institutions is renting a health resort to provide holidays for its employees.

In identifying the activity of the enterprise in the non-industrial sphere as one of the features of paternalism we imply, first, the upkeep by the enterprise of the socio-cultural sphere which continues to function today, in spite of everything, sometimes even to the detriment of production in the strict sense, and the provision of cash subsidies for workers in the welfare sphere, second, the perception of the enterprise as responsible for the welfare of the workers and the desire to have goods and the patronage of the enterprise outside the sphere of production, particularly in recent years when the general instability in society forces people to look to their enterprise for support and any departure from a paternalistic policy in the extra-productive sphere is seen negatively.

Paternalism of the administration consists in the populist distribution of profits through which large sums are spent on buying consumer goods, maintaining the unprofitable welfare apparatus, building housing and maintaining surplus jobs.

The most senior managers often take a direct personal interest in the support and development of the welfare apparatus, even though it is often unprofitable for the enterprise. In one enterprise, for example, the Director personally proposed the purchase of a herd of pedigree cows to replace an existing herd which did not give milk of high enough quality to produce cheese. The money was found and the herd purchased. However the factory itself was in a deplorable condition and the money would have been much better spent to support production. Another example. The story of the sausage plant already mentioned had its sequel. Once they had bought the equipment to make the sausages (for hard currency), they found that they did not have enough meat, so the enterprise had to go to further expense and sign a contract for the supply of meat with a local collective farm. But then a further problem arose: they had no refrigerator in which to store the meat and the sausage, so the factory bought a refrigerated railway wagon. One can only guess what further expenses they will incur as a result of the idea of producing sausages.

With privatisation the law requires the enterprise to divest itself of some of its social apparatus, but many enterprises try to preserve their control of the social and welfare institutions, to maintain the privileges for their employees. There are plenty of examples which show the unwillingness of enterprises to part with these institutions.

Management and Industry in Russia

The provision of support for their own workers, the conduct of a strong social policy can work for various aims: to maintain the attractiveness of the enterprise in relation to others in the city, the use by the administration of the social apparatus for their own profit and so on. But whatever the aim this reinforces the image of the enterprise as benefactor, the ideological constructions of 'our own enterprise', 'the factory – my home', 'we are all one big family'.

The display of guardianship, of the care of the enterprise for its workers, particular in the sphere of distribution of social goods and benefits, is pretty well known and described. However paternalism assumes not only guardianship but also coercion. It would be interesting to trace the limits of permissible coercion. In some labour collectives a worker can be transferred from one job to another in the course of the working day (including transfer to different kinds of work – clearing up the premises, repair and so on), in others it only happens once a month and workers do not appreciate it if it is changed in the course of the week (on the norms of the permissible see the discussion of hierarchical management below).

Recently there has been a tendency to the reduction and separation of the social and welfare sphere from the enterprise. Thus the agricultural products of one of the factories are increasingly being sold outside at higher prices, and not through the factory's own outlets, people have to pay for the departmental medical service so that access to it now depends on having enough money and not on whether or not one works in the enterprise. With the tendency for the reduction in subsidies for social and welfare benefits for workers these will increasingly be available for money rather than as a privilege.

2. Features of Charismatic Management

Managerial charisma can similarly be regarded from two points of view: on the one hand the perception of the manager from below as a 'leader', on the other hand real acts which support this image of the Director. This in turn implies that the manager both 'consults with the people' and imposes punishments, exercises power 'with a strong hand'.

In one of our factories a telephone 'hot line' to the Director of the factory was set up and every worker could phone and report his complaints. At first the phone really glowed, then the hullabaloo died down and now it is hardly used at all, not because a lot of problems have been resolved, it is simply that people have had their emotional outbursts and quietened down. This project cannot possibly be considered as a serious attempt to generate a system of feed-back (it was no more than for show), but nevertheless it played its role – it indicated the democratism of the Director. Similar undertakings (such as the installation of a box for notes to the Director) served as a way of letting off steam, and it was especially interesting for the management to know what people were getting upset about. Sometimes workers would even get replies to their complaints and requests, but more to support the image of a just management than out of a real commitment to justice.

This kind of 'going to the people' is in our view a charade, not so much a consultation of the workers by the Director as an ideological act. On the basis of our observations even such a charade has become fairly rare. In the past, for example, the Director would sometimes come and chat with workers in the shops, but now he only speaks at conferences, shareholders' meetings and so on.

In interviews in which we asked people how they explained the particularly good situation of their enterprise they often replied: because we have got such a strong Director. The view is widespread among workers that it is thanks to the hard work of the Director (and even more flattering descriptions) that they receive cheese, meat and other benefits.

The construction of the form of management as one's own father, the Director as head of the household, does not necessarily presuppose a high degree of managerial authority. Even if the Director is not treated with respect, people still want to see him as head of the household; even if he is bad, his is still the father, and nothing can take away this stereotypical perception. The Director is the symbol of the enterprise. There is a very common view that whatever the Director wants will be.

The charisma of the leader does not imply love or adoration. The point is that, loved or unloved, exceptional functions are bestowed on him. His is the personality which plays the decisive role: he decides how the factory will be developed, in this way or that.

A striking example of such undivided mastery of the Director is in one of our factories where the Director illegally set the level of pay of workers sent on administrative vacation at double the amount calculated by the economists, without consulting anybody. And nobody raised any objection. Even if this was only a game for him, nevertheless it built up his image. However, the workers were not impressed by the fact that the Director had exceeded his powers so as to increase their pay. They saw the increase as a mere sop so that his authority among the workers was not increased.

Charisma does not necessarily presuppose that the Director has a high degree of authority, a universal recognition of his unlimited power to determine the fate of the factory. Some people may regard him completely uncharismatically, merely as the legitimate leader or even as a usurper. Thus the leader of an independent trade union, a fitter in one of our factories, does not like the Director but considers him as a partner in agreements concluded about this or that aspect of the relations between workers and the administration. He reasons: why change him – there is no sense, another person would hardly improve the position of the factory. Other people also do not like the Director, but try to expose various details of his personal life as part of a struggle against him. The Director for them is more than simply a functional position. It is not necessarily impossible to remove a charismatic leader, although the general view is that this is a matter for higher management, in the name of the factory as a whole.

The building of charisma (concrete acts to reinforce it) extends to the lowest levels of management. Thus the shop chiefs do not hesitate to represent a regular pay increase as their personal achievement – 'I beat it out of them'. One can also link this with the shop chief's traditional daily round of the sections. However there are also contrary examples, when the shop chief in a factory does not come down to the shop, and not all of the workers even know him, the figure of this shop chief not being surrounded with the aura of charisma (this was a former chief – merely a figure).

Excessively exaggerated admiration for the power of the leading person is one of the features of the psychology of Soviet workers and employees. The need for a 'strong hand', no matter whether it be just or unjust, to have an outstanding figure in command undertaking decisive actions, whether just or unjust. This is the expectation from below. Even if the workers decided to pursue a demand to the end (for example an increase in pay), they would have to take their demand to the leading person and if he refused it then that is all, unless one takes extreme measures (to strike, for example).

3. Strict Managerial Hierarchy

A strict managerial hierarchy is closely related to the charisma of the leader as a feature of paternalism in the enterprise.

The chief is not simply a post, functionally defined in the structure of production, but also 'our own father', who can punish (even if it is unjust) and to whom one must take one's complaints. Such an exaggerated understanding of the functions of management, an exaggerated understanding of the power of the post, is underpinned by ideological constructions.

The chief at any level can allow himself to shout at subordinates. The higher chief appears in the shop once a year according to his promise 'to twist their tails', 'to dish out a scolding' – 'I will check up in a week', and he does not appear again.

The shop chief is the head of the household and the shop is his patrimonial estate, he can manage it according to his discretion, he 'beats out the plan' with the foremen and they with the workers, and everybody does this under the rod, through storming. This type of leader reinforces his pre-eminent position 'with his voice', with sops and threats or sanctions.

Similar activities are on the one hand an element in the reinforcement of the image of the head of household, and on the other hand a display of the permissiveness of management. The sources of this phenomenon lie in the lack of rights of each lower level in relation to the functionally higher level, in the impossibility of any legal challenge to the decisions of the chief.

When a foreman hands out tasks and a worker asks 'what's the hurry', the foreman just says 'it has to be done!' without explaining why it has to be done ('I asked, so you do it'). The shop chief may use his position on the hierarchical ladder to 'ask' a worker to do something for him personally (for example, to repair his private car in the factory workshop) and he will not be refused.

It is important here that the authoritarian style of management is wider than the sphere of production alone, and extends to the non-productive sphere (which is related to the presence in the enterprise of a social and welfare apparatus). Abuse became the norm for such managers, it was considered proper. Thus the Director as a rule has his own fund which he can distribute however he likes and from which he encourages whomever he considers necessary.

This is also a psychological feature, expressed in the principle 'do not step forward' (and if you 'step forward', 'do not stand out').

This eminent position of the chief and submissive position of the subordinate is perceived as the norm. For example, it is permitted to disagree to an increase in the work norms, an increase in the intensity of labour. In some factories it is permitted to go to work on one's day off, for example it is simply announced that Saturday is a working day. Sending workers on compulsory (although paid) leave is also forced. And this is completely tolerated by the trade union and by the workers and by the administration (and is even considered as a blessing in conditions of a falling volume of production). We can also consider the sacking of workers, which in the overwhelming majority of cases is carried out to circumvent the requirement to pay severance pay to those who are made redundant by reason of staff cuts.

4.   Closed Information

The restriction of information about what goes on at the top, and its very limited distribution below, is closely linked to the two previous features of Russian paternalism. The workers, the foremen and even the shop chiefs hardly ever know the figures for the profitability of the enterprise, the distribution and expenditure of its money, the pay of the directorate, future redundancies and other information about the higher management of the factory.

The closure of information is one of the elements that supports the authority (charisma) of the leader. The less that people know, the more remote is the leader from their understanding.

The lack of information gives rise to rumours. There is dissatisfaction at such an information policy on the ground. In response to this there is a closure of information from below. Thus a worker will not say what he does to this or that part, it is his professional secret. He says only what it is to his benefit to say, and keeps quiet about the existence of the workers' special tricks. True, the foreman as a rule does not need this information because he is used to 'beating out' the work – he has enough levers, and is not interest in its finer points... At the same time the workers (and employees at the higher level) highly value those managers who possess that information 'from the bottom' and even have experience of work on the shop floor. It both inspires them (the shop chief knows their problems) and puts them on their guard (the chief might understand their machinations).

5.   Egalitarian Principles of Pay and Distribution

Egalitarian principles exist in various forms in the enterprise. The most common channels of equalisation are: 1) through the social and welfare funds; 2) through the distribution of pay; 3) through the distribution of work.

Examples: The egalitarian distribution of shares at the time of privatisation. The creation in the enterprise of funds to pay the shops which are at a standstill because there is no work. In one of our factories people were told in advance that the pay norms would not be increased on a profitable foreign order since the money was required to meet various shop needs, and also because it was unjust that you have an order but others do not.

In another factory metal is distributed in approximately equal portions to each shop, so that each will be able to work and earn money.

One should also note that even in those cases in which pay is not determined by egalitarian principles (for example between workers and the Director), nevertheless the expectation among the workers is that it will be closer, comparable to their pay, when the Director's pay is revealed (or in the extreme case should be closer).

6. Non-Monetary Relations

The role of money in the management of the productive life of the enterprise was in the past not very large. Because pay was equalised management had to use non-monetary stimuli.

Housing, cars, groceries (from auxiliary plants) could only be acquired through the factory. Production relations were built around the possibility of securing access to these goods. Thus non-monetary methods of management of the production process developed: 'spiritual grease', boards of honour, socialist competition.

Now money has begun to play a much greater, even preponderant, role: people go to work to get money. The non-monetary pragmatism of the workers is expressed more starkly. Thus non-monetary relations are in decline. Although even now they have some significance since funds still exist for the distribution of goods.

7. Ideological Expressions of Paternalism

One can add to the features of paternalism a particular atmosphere, a sense of collectivism, unity, of a common business, supported by the ideology of socialist society. We have already spoken of many of them. These ideas live on and are expressed in thoughts, feelings and deeds.

First, the idea of collectivism, expressed in mutual assistance between workers, their moral support for one another. The socialist interpretation of this idea is strikingly expressed in the principles of egalitarianism discussed above. Here the person stood for a part of the collective, not a separate worker.

The second feature of the ideology that we would note is the feeling of local patriotism, 'my factory', 'my workshop' – these are not only words reinforcing people's unity, but also words which urge people on to more intensive work, to displays of activism (in various kinds of meetings, in rationalisation proposals, in voluntary work and so on) expressed in the enthusiasm of workers to fulfil above-plan tasks, and in the administration's acquisition of money for the enterprise and its distribution among the employees.

* *The members of the Samara Research Group are Irina Kozina, Sergei Alasheev, Pavel Romanov, Irina Tartakovskaya, Lena Lapshova, Tanya Metalina, Igor Mansurov*

6. The Position of Women in Production

Lena Lapshova and Irina Tartakovskaya

It is difficult to write about the position of women in the system of production relations as they exist at the present time in industrial enterprises in Russia because it is not possible at the moment to present any kind of sharp and well-defined picture. There are several reasons for this. First, there is no movement for the rights of women specially concerned with these questions, nor even taking a genuine interest in them. This is related to the fact that the 'woman problem' itself is not present in social consciousness, and most of all in the consciousness of women themselves. Secondly, the socio-cultural peculiarity of Russia, only a few generations from being a mainly agrarian country, naturally implies the unequal position of women, which is perceived by both men and women as something which goes without saying. Because of this a large number of functional, sectional, educational and other differences are imposed on the differences between the sexes, concealing the true significance of women's problems. This is characteristic to the highest degree of precisely those branches of industrial production which are not specifically 'female' (as are for example, light industry, the sphere of services, and so on) but which imply the collaborative work of large numbers of men and women.

Thus the present article comprises a collection of fragments, put forward to illustrate various aspects of the position of women working in large enterprises, which were earlier part of the military-industrial complex, in which we have been carrying out our case study of 'the restructuring of management and industrial relations in Russia'.

GENERAL CHARACTERISTICS OF THE ENTERPRISE

The Production Association Rings is one of the largest ball-bearing factories in Russia. In 1991 it produced one fifth of all the bearings by quantity and 40 per cent by variety in the former USSR. Among the customers of the enterprise were not only engineering factories, producing things for peaceful use: agricultural machinery, consumer appliances, but also the military-industrial complex, to whom it supplied particularly precise bearings. In May 1993 Rings was privatised as a shareholding company of the open type.

The labour collective, according to the figures of 1st April 1993, comprises 25,937 people. This figure includes both workers in the industrial sectors and those employed in the sphere of social and welfare provision, utilities, services and so on, that is to say the non-industrial sectors (the latter amounting to 2,000 people).

SOME PAGES FROM HISTORY

The history of the factory dates from the Second World War, when in 1941 a Moscow ball-bearing factory was evacuated to the city of Kuibyshev (previously, and now, Samara). Around 3,000 workers and engineers were evacuated along with the equipment.

Women played a major role in the work of establishing production in the new location from the very beginning, replacing the men who had gone to the front on the machines. In the history of the factory the names of women appear among the first group of bearing makers in November 1941.

Back-breaking labour for eleven or twelve hours a day only earned people enough to avoid dying of starvation. It was forbidden to leave the factory. An order of 26th July 1940 forcibly attached workers to the enterprise.

The situation described in the book by E. Astakhov, *Zhinzn' prozhit'* (*A Life to Live*) (Samara, 1991) was typical of that time: in 1943 a show trial was held in the factory of a group of workers who had 'deserted' from the enterprise and tried to return to Moscow. They were all sentenced to long terms of imprisonment. The oldest of these women was thirty two.

With the end of the war the position of the workers remained as difficult as before. Pay by today's standards was miserly: with a machine-operator's month's pay one could buy only 'seven or eight loaves of bad bread' (Astakhov, p. 91) or two dozen pastries.

However the factory was not only the source of money, but also 'home' and 'benefactor', representing an all-inclusive system of subsistence, providing, albeit a minimum, of social welfare (flats and hostels, grocery rations and so on). To a considerable degree this system is still significant today, especially for women, although pay has become all the same the most important thing.

The serious shortage of labour in the post-war years gave rise to a new 'initiative', according to which female staff (time-keepers, copyists and others) were transformed into machine-operators. In those days it was considered fairly prestigious to work in this factory. Women with a relatively low level of education (primary or sixth to eighth grade) became machine-operators, taking over 'men's' jobs and earning as much as the men. Thus the factory gave women from the countryside a real chance to get on in the world, raising their social status, getting access to the social consumption fund and even building a real career. The majority of these women continued to work in the factory until the end of their working lives.

SOCIAL-DEMOGRAPHIC COMPOSITION OF THE EMPLOYEES.

If one looks at today's statistics what immediately strikes one is the fact that even today women make up a predominant part of the labour force. According to the figures for 1st April 1993 women comprised 57.3 per cent of the labour force, while men made up 42.7 per cent (14,855 and 11,082 people correspondingly).

The average age of employees was 47–49 years. Three quarters of the employees were workers, 13.8 per cent engineering and technical staff, 4.9 per cent worked in services, 3.2 per cent in MOP (Junior Service Personnel) and 2.2 per cent were apprentices.

Over recent years there has been a steady reduction in the numbers employed. This process is connected with the fall in the volume of production, along with the refusal of the management to continue to support an inflated establishment. Thus, while the collective of the association comprised about 35,000 people in 1984–5, today it has been cut by 10,000. The reduction in the number of employees has taken place relatively smoothly:

Table One: *Total Number of Employees*

1.1.90	29 959
1.1.91	28 784
1.1.92	27 942
1.4.93	25 937

The reduction in the number of employees was achieved through natural wastage: retirement, voluntary redundancy. Posts vacated for these reasons were not filled, and the wages attached to them were either withdrawn or redistributed among the remaining workers.

Over the past two decades the maximum labour turnover was reached in 1976, when it amounted to 14.9 per cent. The index then fell to 6.6 per cent in 1988, but more recently we can observe its renewed growth:

Table Two: *Labour Turnover*

1989	7.6%
1990	7.9%
1991	7.5%
1992	8.5%

According to the data for the first quarter of 1993 the number leaving exceeded the number taken on by 2.4 times, and for this reason the turnover amounted to 2.4 per cent, which was much more than the 1.4 per cent of the comparable period in 1992.

Altogether in January 1993 154 people were recruited, but 441 left. In February 221 were recruited and 428 left, in March 144 were recruited and 384 left.

According to information collected for the quarterly report of the Personnel Department, in 1993 the main reason for leaving voluntarily was dissatisfaction with the level of pay (23.9 per cent), followed by the failure to secure somewhere to live (15.4 per cent).

Today the low level of pay means that the enterprise is unpopular as a place to work. Certainly twenty years ago the factory was attractive because of its well-developed social and welfare apparatus and the possibility of receiving free housing. However at the end of the

1970s and the beginning of the 1980s the pace of housing construction slowed, and difficulties arose in the construction of hostels and kindergartens. Finally, between 1986 and 1988 the Association fell back to last place behind all the other local factories in the levels of pay of all categories of employees (the wage fund was then allocated by the Ministry). Nowadays the factory stands out from many enterprises in the city because of its low level of pay.

Table Three: Age of Rings workers at 1st April 1993

Age	number	%
Up to 30	4 347	16.7
30–39	6 171	23.9
40–49	6 472	25.0
50–59	6 330	24.4
60–	2 617	10.0
Total	25 937	100.0

The collective of Rings is getting old. The factory only needs highly qualified specialists which means that it recruits a minimal number of young people. The proportion of workers under thirty is only 16.7 per cent, about a quarter of the employees are in the age ranges 30–39 and 40–49, and a third of the collective are of pre-pension or pension age (see Table Three).

Recent years have seen an increase in the proportion of women workers. They are less inclined to change their place of work, because they find it more difficult to get another job. As a rule they are less well-qualified than men. Women are usually prepared to work for lower wages than men and, above all, they are very dependent on social benefits which are guaranteed by large state enterprises (including maternity leave, leave to look after sick children of school age, and so on). According to the figures for 1st March 1993, 945 people were on leave to look after children. Over the past three years there have also been radical changes in attitudes to apprenticeship: the proportion of women here has increased from 39.5 per cent to 54.3 per cent. Young women come to the factory more willingly than young men.

The rise in the proportion of women in the collective can be related to the lower turnover of female staff as well as to the changes that have taken place in recent years in the relationship between various categories of workers. A few years ago it was men who dominated basic production work. In the remaining spheres of work women were predominant. Recently there has been a steady fall in the proportion of basic production workers, who are paid on piece-rates, and a small rise in the proportion of workers on time wages, whose pay does not depend on the output of the shop (see Tables Four and Five). However in 1993 the proportion of women workers in basic production work also reached a half, amounting to 51 per cent.

To understand the reasons for the predominance of women in the factory more clearly it is necessary to look more closely at several general tendencies in the development of the labour force.

The average grade of workers is 4.2 (on a six point scale). Despite the steady growth in the level of qualifications in the factory as a whole, the majority of low qualified workers are women. In principle the qualifications of women are steadily increasing, so that the proportion of women in the skill grades three and four is increasing, and they are now in the majority here. However this takes place alongside the general tendency to the reduction in the number of jobs which require low grade workers. The proportion of women with high qualification levels, according to the figures of the Personnel Department, is as usual rather low. In the shops in which we conducted our case study we did not find any of them. There is very good reason to believe that the figures for women on the fifth and sixth grades really refer to employees working in the non-productive sphere, such as organisers of cultural and artistic activities, and so on.

Table Four: *Occupational distribution of employees in 1990 and 1993 (per cent)*

	1990	1993
Production Workers	37.3	34.4
Auxiliary Workers	40.4	41.5
ITR	13.0	13.8
Office Workers	4.2	4.9
MOP	3.0	3.2
Apprentices	2.1	2.2

Note: ITR are engineering-technical workers. Workers in auxiliary shops, such as preparatory or instrumental shops involved in basic production, are considered to be basic production workers. Auxiliary workers are those such as greasers, repair fitters, transport, ancillary workers and so on.

Table Five: Gender breakdown of occupational categories: 1990, 1993

| | 1990 | | | | 1993 | | | |
| | men | | women | | men | | women | |
	N	%	N	%	N	%	N	%
Production Workers	5 517	50.0	5 510	50.0	4 330	48.9	4 527	51.1
Auxiliary Workers	5 487	46.0	6 454	54.0	4 546	42.6	6 114	57.4
ITR	1 720	44.5	2 147	55.5	1 540	43.5	2 004	56.5
Office Workers	104	8.4	1 136	91.6	101	7.9	1 163	92.1
MOP	146	16.2	754	83.8	186	22.7	634	77.3
Apprentices	372	60.5	7 243	39.5	261	45.7	309	54.3
Total	13 346	45.1	16 244	54.9	10 964	42.6	14 751	57.4

Table Six: Distribution by skill grade, 1990 and 1993

| | 1990 | | 1993 | |
Grade	N	%	N	%
1	967	4.7	672	3.9
2	3 396	16.5	2 660	15.4
3	6 262	30.4	5 236	30.3
4	5 452	26.5	4 639	26.9
5	3 778	18.3	3 336	19.3
6	774	3.6	718	4.2
Total	20 599		17 261	

Table Seven: Distribution by sex and skill grade, 1990

| | men | | women | |
Grade	N	%	N	%
1	290	30.0	677	70.0
2	1 032	30.4	2 364	69.6
3	2 522	40.3	3 740	59.7
4	2 682	49.2	2 770	50.8
5	3 282	86.9	496	13.1
6	733	98.5	11	1.5
Total	10 541	51.1	10 058	48.9

Table Eight: *Distribution by sex and skill grade, 1993*

	Men		Women	
Grade	N	%	N	%
1	197	29.3	475	70.7
2	735	27.6	1 925	72.4
3	1 809	34.5	3 427	65.5
4	2 034	43.8	2 605	56.2
5	2 830	84.8	506	15.2
6	704	98.0	14	2.0
Total	8 309	48.1	8 952	51.9

The purpose of our research was not to resolve the global issues connected with the position of women in production, but much more to describe various aspects of this problem which we have uncovered in the course of our case-study and which, in our view, best reflect the general tendencies.

DISTRIBUTION OF THE LABOUR FORCE AMONG SUBDIVISIONS

In some of the shops the proportions of men and women are roughly equal, some are clearly 'women's' shops – for example the assembly shop in which the women are working predominantly at manual jobs – and there are 'men's' shops, in which the proportion of women is very small.

As an example of the organisation of the labour force in a mixed shop we can consider the rod machine shop (TsPA).

Five hundred and twenty seven people work in this shop, 170 of whom are women. The shop has a total of 255 production workers, of whom 71 are women, and 173 auxiliary workers (of whom 54 are women: storekeepers, cleaners, greasers, ancillary workers). The remaining categories of workers are ITR, altogether 56 people of whom 23 are women; office workers, all 15 of whom are women; and MOP (cloakroom attendants), all 6 of whom are women.

In the hierarchy of the shop the senior management posts are held exclusively by men. Of the seven sections, three have predominantly female workers and one is equally split, but there are only two women at the level of middle management: one senior foreman and one shift foreman.

Traditionally women work as time-keepers, economists, norm-setters, office workers in the administrative-economic departments, personnel inspectors. Half the technologists in the shop are women.

The women machine-operators in the shop do not have a high level of skill grading: the polishers, turners and greasers are on the second grade, stamp-operators on the third grade.

Women in the factory can find themselves in three basic situations: working on machines, carrying out work more or less comparable with that of men (working at specifically women's jobs such as assembly, but also at basic production jobs); taking on the role of auxiliary low-grade workers (greasers, ball-cleaners) or in MOP (cleaners, cloakroom attendants); or working as controllers. In our view all these categories of workers find themselves denied equal rights when compared with the positions in which men work. Let us look at these situations separately.

Women machine-operators do not generally work on the same machines as do men. Their machines require them constantly to repeat one and the same operation, the most monotonous work, 'which men cannot withstand'. Some women even work on manual machines (such as in the tenth department of the PA shop), which are actually rare in the Association. Such work, of course, is rather lighter than men's work from the purely physical point of view, but the rhythm is very stressful, not allowing the operator to leave the machine even for a short time.

In theory there is no division into men's and women's vacancies, except in cases where jobs are said to involve particularly heavy physical work, which women are unable to do. At present the following norms govern the maximum permissible loads which women can lift or shift by hand:

- lifting and shifting loads in rotation with other work (twice per hour) – 10 kilos.
- lifting and shifting loads regularly during a working shift – 7 kilos.
- the amount of active work carried out in the course of each hour of a working shift cannot exceed: with a working surface 1750 kilos, on the ground 875 kilos.

- the shifting of weights on trolleys or containers must not require a force of more than 10 kilos.

In practice these norms, of course, are often violated. Moreover the sexual division of labour has been firmly fixed over the years that the enterprise has existed.

As already noted, women are ready to work for lower rewards. Here, it goes without saying, objective factors also play a role – such as their qualifications.

Girls in Russian families are traditionally not taught to have anything to do with technology, 'with iron' – even if they grow up in a family of production workers. For young boys, by contrast, this is an important element in their education and prestige. Correspondingly, when it comes to choosing a specialism girls do not go to those schools in which workers are trained in up-to-date or complex specialisms. If they are trained it is in 'women's' industrial specialisms, and they are trained as assemblers, controllers or similar trades. As a rule they only end up working on machines 'off the street', without any kind of special preparation, and work on them mechanically, like robots, without any aspiration to change or improve their position.

Among the workers in the factory are some women who are machine-setters, but they only carry out the simple adjustment of the machines. As a rule, even experienced female machine-operators use the services of a male setter, although the male machine-operators do this work themselves.

A machine-operator who has worked for many years on a machine usually knows it very well and can transfer to the work of a fitter. Women do not have any incentive to try to master their machine to such a degree, partly because they have so few opportunities for promotion, so that they are rarely qualified to work either as fitters or as electricians.

PAY

Women's pay, even in those rare situations in which they do approximately the same work as men, is lower than that of the men. (In response to a complaint about low pay by a single woman machine-operator in the ball-making shop, her colleague asked with amazement and some indignation: 'What do you want – to earn the same as a man?' This demand seemed to her colleague to be extremely excessive, because between male and female operators there is certainly an objective difference: a woman cannot, for example, lift and put onto the machine very heavy abrasive disks, and as a result her grade is much lower).

Despite all this, women machine-operators all have a much more privileged position than other women workers in the factory. At any rate, their pay, although it is much lower than that of male machine-operators, is comparable with the pay of machine-setters – their comrades in the section (although such a position is seen by the shop leaders as temporary and unjust – the setters have much more complex work and they should receive more). The position of women who do the least skilled work in the sections, for example cleaning up the prepared balls after each operation, is much worse. Cleaning, greasing and so on of the automatic machines is purely manual work, dirty, not requiring any qualifications and badly paid. Moreover if before perestroika the gap between them and basic workers was not so large according to the financial calculations, now, on account of various 'twists' and coefficients it has become considerable, and their real pay has fallen.

The lowest pay of all is that of the MOP, the service personnel. Cloakroom attendants and cleaners in the PA shop, for example, receive almost five times less than basic production workers. As already noted, in this shop they are all women.

There is a similar situation with the pay of office workers: it is so low that men will not take these positions. Thus there are practically no male time-keepers, shop economists, ordinary workers in the Personnel Department, and so on (see Table Five).

The everyday duties of the office workers are monotonous and routine, and the work is very unproductive as a result of the absence of even the simplest calculating machines.

Despite all this the women office workers value their jobs not only because of the social guarantees that go with them, but also because the existence of free time during the working day allows them to go out shopping and sort out various problems of everyday living.

WORKING CONDITIONS

In practice women toil in just as harsh conditions as men. Although it is considered that women should absolutely not lift heavy weights, in fact they have to do this fairly often, since in reality in the process of production the need arises to do many things which are not anticipated technologically: for example, to lift metal onto one's machine on one's own, since the transport workers who should be doing this have long ago been cut back in all the shops, and not only in the 'men's' sections. In general it is typical that the influence of harmful working conditions on women is not formally taken into account in any way. For example, the controllers, who carry out the operational inspection, spend practically all of their working time in the shop. Despite this they do not count in that category of workers whose pay is increased by an additional coefficient as a result of the harmful conditions, although all the workers in this shop receive the coefficient as a result of the loud noise.

The problem of working conditions affects literally every category of women workers. Auxiliary work such as greasing or cleaning is always carried out by hand, so that the workers have to cope with the effect of harmful chemical substances and their fumes. Where they work in one place ventilation is sometimes provided, but to pay for this they have to put up with freezing cold and constant drafts. Women who work on the machines have to pay with their health for more or less higher earnings, since the machines have not been adapted in any way to take into account the specificities of the female organism. Thus, practically all the female turners working in the rod machine shop are on the special gynaecological register since they work in such unhealthy conditions. Despite this, there is no way in which they have been able to extract any privileges in compensation for so much serious physiological damage: for years women working in this section have been sending requests to the administration to reduce their pension age to fifty without any result.

They have also had to endure the worsening of all the daily inconveniences which arise as a result of specific features of the present period: the absence of soap, special shoes, special clothes, gloves (even in those situations in which gloves are provided, by no means all the workers receive them). In our conversations many women workers complained that their hands become absolutely numb from the metal.

Of the 10,713 women working in the factory 8,053 work in harmful conditions. In 1992 one in 9 of the 228 births in the factory were pathological. In 1992 45 women were operated on for benign tumours of the reproductive organs, and altogether there were 98 cases of women with benign tumours ('Podshipnikovets', 24, 08.04.93).

PSYCHOLOGICAL CLIMATE: RELATIONS BETWEEN MALE AND FEMALE WORKERS

Often in sections in which both men and women work they do not form a single collective: they drink tea, chat in the breaks, spend free time together separately. The different work which they do, as a rule, deepens the psychological segregation.

Thus, in the stainless section of the ball-making shop there are four women: one setter and three ball-cleaners, carrying out low-grade auxiliary work. The unequal position of the ball-cleaners is obvious. If the shop does not have enough work and the question of sending people on administrative vacation with purely symbolic pay arises, then the first candidates are precisely the ball-cleaners. While the machine-operators can refuse to go on vacation, the ball-cleaners cannot (this issue is considered by the brigade).

Representatives of the ball-cleaners – who are also members of the brigade – as a rule are not involved in the discussion of the KTU (coefficient of labour participation, which nominally determines the distribution of wages within the brigade). The unequal rights of women also appear in other ways – the condescending-scornful relation to them of male foremen, who nevertheless have pleasant relations with basic workers. One and the same request to the foreman, for example to take balls to the thermal department, which is usually done in this section by the foremen, may be satisfied or not depending on who made it – a male setter or a female ball-cleaner. The relationships between these categories of worker are very conflictual, they have a mass of related claims, since they depend on the quality of one another's work. This is also reflected in the life of the section. They never help a woman fetch a heavy bucket of water, moreover it even encroaches on the distribution of seasonal work, which is done by one of the brigadiers who is also trade union organiser of the independent trade union Solidarity, of which both setters and ball-cleaners are members.

ATTITUDES TO WOMEN ON THE PART OF MANAGEMENT

According to female workers from various sections, the shop management, as a rule, rarely investigates the problems that women have in production thoroughly, and frequently do not respond to complaints about working conditions, and so on.

Relations between male managers and their male subordinates are much more informal than those with women. Here is an interesting detail: when we carried out an interview with workers in the purely male section of automatic lathe operators of the rod machine shop, it turned out that they fairly often had the chance to associate with the shop chief: when he makes his round of the shop he regularly goes among them in the section, he answers questions about the state of affairs concerning production questions, sometimes gives some instructions (in Rings the majority of shop chiefs follow the whole career chain, beginning as a worker, and they know the details of the production process well). When we asked the female machine-operators of this same shop whether the shop chief was ever with them in the section, they were absolutely amazed: 'What on earth for! But what do we need him for?'

The controllers, as a rule, very often come up against great difficulties in resolving problems which lie in the competence of shop management, since they are not subordinate to the shop chief, so he does not see them as staff for whom he has some responsibility. Thus, for example, in one of the sections in which the technical controllers (OTK) worked, there was a breakage of the sewer which was not repaired for many weeks, so that the women controllers had to work in dreadful filth.

It is typical that a man is always preferred to a woman. Thus, for example, the chief of the ball-making shop in an interview said that at the present time women in the shop work only as cloakroom attendants, cleaners, greasers, ball-cleaners and in the OTK, although earlier they also worked on the machines. Now there is only one woman machine-operator left, but when she leaves the shop chief intends to take on a man in her place. This is a completely conscious policy, since it is inconvenient for them that they are not able to transfer women freely to other operations, which involve the lifting of heavy loads (the weight of a cassette with balls in various operations may vary from 2 to 20 kg).

All this, plus the additional burden of a whole avalanche of economic, everyday and family problems, beating down on women during their time in the factory with much greater force than on their sexual antagonists, leads to a specific psychological climate in women's production collectives. It was typical that all of the heads of subdivisions questioned by us, women as much as men, noted as one that although in women's sections there is higher discipline and carefulness, and incomparably fewer problems of drunkenness and absenteeism, they prefer to work with men. They refer to the difficulty of dealing with women as more emotional and unpredictable beings. Indeed women, through their position in the system of production, are in practice reduced to the role of 'tiny cogs', more inclined than men for this reason to demand for themselves 'a special approach', expecting to be treated not simply as a producer, but as a concrete personality. Because women have a more instrumental attitude and less commitment to the content of their work, they are less easy to manage than men since they do only what they have to do and are not inclined to show any initiative. Such a contrast on the one hand proves very irritating for managers, and on the other leads to humiliation, a pessimistic condition of the soul of women.

RELATIONS BETWEEN WOMEN

We have not observed anything like 'gender solidarity', which would unite women of various occupational categories. Although women have many common problems, they rarely get together to try to solve them. Between women workers and women ITR, women workers and women controllers, and even between women workers of different sections or occupations, very conflictual and unhealthy relations often arise, as indeed is also often true of relations between men, although when women do have friendly relations within a section they are usually closer to one another than men would be. Only women of one occupation and in a single section unite with one another. Women workers (of course women are just like men workers in this respect, without exception) often say that the (women) norm-setters, women employees of the economic department and related services do nothing and receive pretty high pay for this, which seems to them to be at the expense of the workers. Women white-collar workers for their part complain about the aggressive attitude of women workers, their rudeness and use of obscenities.

Certainly, women put into the unfemale conditions of heavy machine industry have always had a secondary role, and in these conditions they are rapidly marginalised. Bad language and even alcoholism are frequently found in the women's working environment. In several sections one finds women drunkards, who are well known by the whole shop. It is typical that male workers behave completely differently with women 'from the outside world' or even with the controllers, than with their fellow female workers in the section, seeing them as 'not real women', as 'unfeminine'. It is characteristic in this respect that many women who took the courageous step of joining the independent trade union 'Solidarity' give as one of the main motives for taking the decision the fact that the leaders of Solidarity took them seriously, a consideration which was expressed symbolically: 'They congratulated us on the eighth of March and gave us chocolates and kissed us.' Moreover their confidence in the honesty of the leadership of Solidarity and the human attention that they paid to their members outweighed the material benefits and privileges that they risked losing by joining the new trade union. Although the new trade union can offer only a very limited distribution of commodities, women are happy with the choice that they have made. However such episodes are exceptions to the rule.

WOMEN IN LABOUR CONFLICTS

All those aspects of the position and behaviour of women in production enumerated by us also define their behaviour in the course of labour conflicts. Because of women's more vulnerable position they are much more likely to be afraid of the consequences of engaging in open conflict, but at the same time, if a conflict breaks out, women are likely to be angrier than men, less ready to compromise, and more likely to want to see the strike through to the end. Moreover, because women have less experience of organisation and public activity than men, their strikes are more likely to be spontaneous and disorganised and more difficult to resolve.

As an example we can look at the strike in the shop of precise bearings (TsTP-1), which we studied in the course of our case-study.

Before describing the strike itself, it is necessary to describe the underlying cause of the events which took place and the reasons for the conflict arising. They are closely related to the system of pay and also to the specific features of the shop. About 870 people work in this shop, distributed in a series of production sections. The specific technological feature of the shop is defined by the fact that each of these sections has its own independent production tasks with its own production cycle: in one part upper and lower rings are prepared and in another part the bearings are assembled. There are no technological relations between the sections themselves.

The strike took place in the second section, which has about 120 people, but it did not affect all of the section, only the machine-operators, whose job was to grind and polish the rings, and the machine-setters (altogether about 50 people). The assemblers themselves, about 60 people, continued to work. (The rest were absent for various reasons.) It is interesting that this was one of the shops with plenty of work – making automobile bearings for VAZ. On assembly the workers are mainly women. Women are also still a majority among the machine-operators: they work on the grinding. The men in this shop are the polishers (only a few people) and machine-setters.

The cornerstone of the conflict was the system of payment in TsTP-1. The sections are paid by the final result and work on the brigade method, thus the allocation of work is confined within the brigade, and each worker's KTU is recorded every day. It is set by the brigadier or the so-called brigade council: the foreman and 2–3 workers. Usually the KTU is made up of units (the workers call these units 'sticks'), and the idea is that each one should have around 30 'sticks' for the month (depending on the number of working days). However it does not always work like that: one can receive a bigger KTU – two sticks if one covers for someone who is away. This may also be a consequence of the policy of the foreman: for example, the work of the polishers is very low skilled, the operation is not rated above third grade. In order to find some incentive to motivate the workers, in the expression of one of the foremen, they 'screw their KTU up tight' – they put it higher. The KTU may also be reduced as a punitive sanction, if the workers receive 'a bruise': in a neighbouring enterprise a blue triangle is put down as the sign against his name instead of a red one. This signifies a defect, a violation of safety precautions or, most often, a disciplinary violation: absenteeism, lateness, turning up to work drunk. Such a system of pay, as distinct from one based on individual allocation of work, contains a large element of indeterminacy: the worker does not know exactly how much he has earned. For example, if they screw the KTU of a polisher up tight and he receives 20,000 roubles, then the next month he will expect to be paid no less, independently of the circumstances.

Second moment: in TsTP-1 there is a very large number of products throughout the shop, and in the second department in particular they make about 400 types of rings, and this tendency has increased in recent months. The types of rings are significantly different in cost and, correspondingly, the KTU have different values, which the workers do not know.

Third moment: the structure of pay itself. Onto the basic pay is added a 30 per cent bonus and, most important, a 50 per cent inflation addition, introduced into the Association and called the 115th code. From meetings with workers it is clear that they do not like this system of pay since they do not relate the 115th code to what they have earned, they do not believe that it will be paid regularly and they call it 'the administration's pittance'. They would like the norms to be revised and this money included in the basic rate. In 1992 in TsTP-1 such a revision had been undertaken only once, which is clearly inadequate with today's pace of inflation.

Apart from this, the low basic pay has a very strong influence on the pay of the majority of people since a percentage of their pay is calculated not on average earnings, but as a percentage of the basic. The President of the trade union committee of shop TsTP-1 considered the problem of tariff revision as a very live issue and intended to insist on its inclusion in the collective agreement in 1993.

The next moment is caused by the organisation of production. Assembly workers in every shop, including number 2, assemble bearings from those rings which the machine-operators (in this section the machine-operators are also women, men only work as machine-setters) supply them. However the machine-operators must keep ahead of the work, so that every day the assemblers have a reserve of prepared rings and can therefore immediately begin work. Thus there are always some products 'made in advance', which are carried over to next month and are not included in this month's pay. This irritates the machine-operators. Generally such a system of pay often creates friction between those categories of workers who are dependent on one another: for example, if the machine-operators do not manage to make enough rings, or make a lot of faulty ones, they let down the assemblers, depriving them of their 'field of work'. Conversely, if balls do not arrive, the separator is broken, or simply some of the assemblers are ill, then the supply of prepared bearings is reduced, which are the only ones considered for calculating pay. Between the machine-operators and the assemblers conflicts therefore arise periodically, usually boiling down to verbal wrangles. The machine-operators in particular have been demanding a transfer to individual work allocation, so that their pay will depend on the specific work they have done and not on that of those on whom they depend.

Conflicts and tensions also arise between members of different sections, since many are convinced that their section in particular receives unjustly low pay. This also affects the relationships between other categories of workers, for example it was said of an electrician that 'he only screws in the lamp bulbs, and how much does he get, while I stand every day at my machine!'. However these conflicts usually do not go beyond the verbal level.

And, finally, the last factor, whose influence is difficult to trace directly, but in the opinion of many participants in the conflict was a latent factor in influencing their state of mind: the strike coincided with the sharp confrontation between Eltsin and the 7th Congress of People's Deputies, and this background of the general instability in the country and irreconcileability between the different power structures acted as an irritant in the consciousness of people, intensifying their dissatisfaction with life.

Let us now describe the immediate course of the strike. In the morning of 9 December, at the start of the shift, the foremen received the bookkeeper's accounting list for their shift, recording the total pay for November. The lists were then handed out, as always, not to every worker personally by hand, but to the brigadier (or another worker met by chance) for the whole brigade. Having received the lists the person can look not only at his own pay, but also at the earnings of strangers, which he communicates to his acquaintances. Then, again as always, there is an exchange of information between the brigades. As a result the machine-operators were interested in how much the assemblers received. This time the machine-operators and the assemblers earned about the same, amounting to around 5–6 thousand (that is only the tariff part, without bonus and code 115). Their pay seemed small, and its distribution unjust since the work of the assembler, although it is much more intense and monotonous is physically lighter – they sit at tables, dressed in white overalls (machine-operators wear blue) and so on. This whole process of gathering information took, according to the participants, about ten minutes. The workers began to gather in small groups, whispered together, and then the refrain was heard 'I am not going to work for that money!'. There were more women than men among the machine-operators, as already mentioned, but the behaviour of both sexes was in principle the same, except that the women were more angry and vociferous, but at the same time more nervous. Thus everyone stopped their machines and the workers sprawled around the section, the women huddling together in a group, while the men appeared more relaxed about the situation.

The shift foreman, having found out about the situation, informed the senior foreman. She (former President of the shop trade union committee, and a nervous bustling woman), without going out to make contact with the workers, phoned the shop chief. The shop chief, A.G. Shvedov, was in the section by 8.30. The workers surrounded him. The most widespread appeal was 'How can we live on this money?' (since all referred to the amount of basic pay, set out in the accounting list, without additions). Shvedov said that he would immediately summon the norm-setter and order her to sort things out, and wrote several names with the sum of their earnings (those who stood nearest to him), after which he suggested that they go back to work. However the workers refused. 'Only the administration can sort it out, and we demand that the Director should come to us.' Shvedov went up to his office, the workers went back to their section: the polishers to their room, the grinders to the table where they usually drink tea, and they sat around again. There were no significant developments for the rest of that day.

In the evening the secretary of the shop cell of the independent trade union Solidarity, who was working in the second department on assembly, phoned the home of the President of the cell N. F. Lakomi, who was on administrative vacation. The following morning Lakomi came to the section, met with workers, and proposed a meeting with the participation of representatives of the factory administration at three o'clock that afternoon. It is clear that he helped the workers to write a list of demands to the administration. (Lakomi himself denies this, asserting that the demands had already been written before he arrived. However Skvortsov, President of the shop committee of the offical trade union, having himself seen a hand-written copy of the document, says that the second half of it was written in Lakomi's writing. Lakomi's denial may be related to the fact that the strike was not carried out 'according to the rules' and, as Belenko, the leader of Solidarity, noted, from a juridical point of view it was defined as sabotage. Obviously they did not want to emphasise their participation in juridically improper activities.) In any case, he presented the demands to the shop chief himself. They included:

- increase in pay by 2.5 times
- introduction of individual payment
- removal of the foreman from membership of the brigade (at the time when the amount of work fell and they got rid of the auxiliary workers, the foreman took on their functions himself and was included in membership of the brigade, receiving an additional KTU on his basic pay. This was formalised in an appropriate protocol).
- demands about the work schedule of shop management. Several of its services, for example bookkeeping, began and ended work later than the workers' shift, which created considerable dissatisfaction among the workers.

Lakomyi dropped in again on the Director of Production Tsygankov, agreed about a meeting, and then went to the shop to see the President of Solidarity, Alexander Belenko. At three that afternoon a meeting was held in the assembly section in which the shop chief Shvedov, Director of Production Tsygankov, head of the factory Department of Labour and Wages, Kaplin, and also the President of the shop committee of the official trade union, V. B. Skvortsov, and Belenko, head of the independent trade union Solidarity, all participated. Between eighty and one hundred people took part in the meeting. Lakomyi went to the meeting. Here is a fragment of the recording, illustrating the course of this meeting, in which women took a particularly active part.

The first to speak was the Director of Production Tsygankov:

— I normally have regard for your demands, but I can see no reason to increase pay by 2.5 times. I cannot see any reason. If you received less than last month it means either that the rings were less valuable, or that you worked less. What can I say to you? Get back to work (strong uproar). Miracles just do not happen. Look at what is happening at the Congress (uproar). I cannot tell you that I will increase your pay.
A female worker: — But there has already been such a meeting, we warned that we will rise up!
Worker: — Earlier I was paid 500 roubles. Now, if you take account of present day prices, my pay is in the order of 70 roubles! Why do you not revise the norms?

Tsygankov: — The norms were revised not long ago, the rates were increased. Here I have an order about increasing pay by 50 per cent under code 115.

Female worker: — Those on salaries are now paid more than production workers! And auxiliary workers receive more. (uproar)

From the crowd: — Tell us then, 6,000 roubles – is that money or not?

— We meet with you periodically, but what is the point?

Lakomyi (showing the previous year's agreement): — the chief specialists cheated us! They promised individual accounting, and again they set 'sticks', labour days, as in the Stalinist kolkhozes. The average pay is 6,000, we shake with laughter!

Replies: — We still work, but there is no money at all!

— Do not switch on the machines in the shop.

— They receive millions at our expense.

Kaplin spoke, he could barely be heard above the massive uproar. Then the shop chief took the floor:

Shvedov: — We will not transfer fully to individual scales in the second department, but for the machine-operators we will try it as an experiment. My plan for December is already smaller than that for November, so that I cannot guarantee you more pay. I have only two types (of ring) for you. In general this is not a strike but sabotage, you may answer before the law. The plan has dropped by 22,000. Your bearings are not selling.

Replies: — What do we do now: listen and go away?

Lakomi: — Why not try introducing a percentage reduction on each bearing sold?

Tsygankov: — This is impossible, then we will become completely tangled up.

Lakomi: — Well in the shops this same bearing costs 100 roubles.

Skvortsov: — Let us set tough conditions: we can decide to pay according to the number of products sold. I understand that the cost includes the pay of the foreman, ASUP and so on. But then we must make an analysis of how much of their time they gave to the 14th department. Then it must be done for the eighth and for half of the second. Analyse who made how many rings, who assembled how many bearings.

Tsygankov: — Well, we have talked. But in the matter of pay – there is simply no money in the bank.

There was a buzz of indignation, but its volume was already less than before. Workers dispersed. Some gathered around Lakomi. One woman bitterly yelled to another who wanted to go back to work: 'Well just work! Work, who is going to stop you!'

In the end several demands of the workers were satisfied. For December the foremen of the female machine-operators introduced for each worker parallel individual duties, which were shown to the workers the day after the strike (and promised the following morning).

According to the foreman, the amounts earned on the basis of this individual accounting were even less than those paid under the collective system. In the morning an order was posted which had been hand-written by Tsygankov, announcing a 50 per cent increase in pay under code 115 (the workers, it is true, already knew about this before the strike). The work-regime of the shop management was modified in accordance with the demands of the workers. Of course these were only palliative measures, but the events showed the absence of any long-term perspective for this kind of spontaneous protest.

On the following day the second department returned to work.

The course of the conflict forces one to acknowledge that an extraordinarily large role in its emergence was played by motives of 'social justice' – the 'last straw' for workers was the information that the assemblers, those who in their view had the lightest work, received the same pay as they did. These motives practically always surface in similar conflicts: workers find that their pay is insufficient not in absolute terms, but in relation to other categories: administration, ITR, workers in other sections or other occupations. There are most often two such 'justice factors' named by the workers 'heavy physical work must be better paid' (type of judgement: 'he only screws in lamp bulbs', 'they sit there all day at tables, while I stand at a machine'; 'those on salaries receive more than us') and 'high qualified workers must be paid better' ('we receive less than auxiliary workers', 'I know my machine better than the foreman'). The second motive is met with more rarely but workers do often argue about their grading. In TsTP-1 the question of 'social justice' has become extremely acute, workers constantly compare their pay with other occupations, sections, shops, ITR.

The situation is also aggravated by the 'obscure' system of pay, still more confused because of the absence of individual accounting, which makes the amount of each worker's earnings truly unpredictable; and also the 'women's background' – two-thirds of the workers in the shop are women. Observation and interviews do not show any particular distinction between men's and women's behaviour in the course of the conflict, but the numerical predominance of women made it more spontaneous, when irritation obscured consciousness of their interests and the search for methods of defending them.

There was one more women's mini-strike in TsTP-1 which took place two months later for another reason. Seven workers of the third department of the shop struck for 3 days, from 1st to 3rd February. Their department was not fully occupied with work, so they were

compulsorily transferred to the fifth, where there was work. They refused and demanded that they be sent on administrative vacation (at
the time their pay amounted to 3,750 roubles), or, the administration
should decide to sack the pensioners (of whom there were five or six
in the third section) – 'then there will be work for us'. It is not so
simple to understand their motives, but possibly this was related to the
high intensity of work in the fifth department and the absence of
strong financial incentives to transfer. Juridically their refusal was absolutely illegal, and they received a reprimand. Five of them signed a
declaration resigning from the official trade union Avtosel'khozmash
and joining Solidarity, but then three of them were sacked. Those remaining obeyed the demand of the administration. It was typical that
this 'purely women's' strike was such not only in terms of the participants, but also in the fact that it was driven by anger, regardless of
expectations of success.

Generally, the Solidarity cell in TsTP-1 is the second in size after
the ball-making shop – 132 people with its own stamp and bank account. Many of them – 40 people – work in the second section (not
only on machines, but also on assembly). Apart from this, 60 people
in the shop do not belong to any trade union. The majority of members of Solidarity in this shop are women.

CAREERS

Can women make a career in an enterprise such as Rings? The equality between men and women that has been declared for many years
exists nowhere in practice.

All the top managers at shop and factory level are men. There is a
tradition that is unwritten, but strictly observed in all subdivisions, of
the priority of men in promotion. In fact the ceiling for a woman ITR
is the post of head of a bureau, head of a laboratory, or first category
designer. Even in 'women's' departments of the factory administration, such as social and welfare, economics, and personnel, the top
manager and his deputy are men. The only exceptions are the head of
financial management (today she is the only woman in a leading position in the factory administration, and the only woman in the factory
with her own office) and two deputies of the chief bookkeeper.

In the history of the factory there have been several women who
have reached top management posts, right up to shop chief. Thus, for

a period of twenty five years, beginning in 1949, N.V. Chuporova was at the head of the rod ball bearing shop containing 1000 workers. She worked until she retired and even had the honour of receiving Leonid Il'ich Brezhnev in her shop (then still simply one of the secretaries of the Central Committee, responsible for heavy industry). P.V. Savel'eva in 1950 held the post of Chief Engineer, uncharacteristically for a woman, and was then chief of the shop TsPP-1. E.K. Shiryaeva in the 1960s headed the repair-construction shop.

However all these episodes were accidental, atypical for the factory and related to particular circumstances (the severe shortage of men with technical education in the post-war years). Today one does not find women shop chiefs in the factory. The ceiling at the shop level is the post of shift or senior foreman (section head), or head of a second-level shop service: administrative-economic, office of technical control, timekeeping and so on.

This situation has a double explanation. Its roots are to be found in the socio-cultural traditions established in Russia. The reproduction of such a situation is also facilitated by the tradition of the 'male career', found in the majority of large enterprises.

As already noted, the professional career of practically every specialist begins on the machine. This unwritten norm has been maintained for many years. It is taken for granted that the best managers came from the depths of the factory, understanding the specific features of production in fine detail.

The result is that for a young woman arriving at the factory there are two perspectives for promotion: being active and improving her qualifications so as to become a foreman, or, having acquired the appropriate training (usually in evening classes provided by the factory) to move from a job on the shop floor to physically lighter work – office worker or engineer in one of the shop services. In the past the women shop chiefs reached their positions in just this way. However today our research, including a large number of interviews, shows that the majority of women do not want promotion to the services. As a rule they start and end their working lives on the shop floor. Their aspirations are limited to earning higher pay, and office workers and even engineers in the enterprise described earn less than basic production machine-operators, and the foremen receive less than the workers in their section. Thus in April 1993 the average monthly pay of production workers in the PA shop was 38,600 roubles, while auxiliary workers earned 19,792, managers and ITR earned 29,600, office workers earned 17,000, MOP earned 7,900 and apprentices earned 5,000.

The second type of career begins with graduation from a higher or secondary technical educational institution. The specialist is assigned to the job, or finds herself a job through informal channels: through the patronage of relatives or acquaintances in the factory.

Personal qualities and relationships certainly play a role in her further advance. And it is very difficult for a woman to 'make a career'. In the factory there is a system of reserves for promotion, in which the labour collective defines a possible candidate for appointment to a managerial vacancy in the given department or service. Thus, Personnel Management (a 'women's collective') put forward an experienced female colleague for the post of deputy chief of the department. However higher management has the last word on these matters, and a man who had worked previously in another service in the factory was appointed.

A similar situation arose in the system of technical control, in which only women work in ordinary posts and as foremen. Despite this the First Deputy General Director for Quality, all his deputies, and even the heads of several of the shop bureaux of technical control are men, although a man can only get into this post 'from the side', from other production structures, since, we note once more, in general they never work as ordinary controllers or as foremen controllers.

Thus a woman-ITR turning up at the factory immediately sees the 'ceiling' to her career possibilities, which is always strictly observed. Typically among the women workers and foremen in the service such a practice does not raise any protest: all our respondents spoke about it being natural that 'women cannot be bigger managers, they find themselves torn between family and work'. They do not themselves seek to change their job for a higher one and say that they would rather have a man as the boss than a woman. In our view, this is mainly related to the fact that those women-engineers who would like to make a career and to reach a more or less high post simply do not go to work in a factory, looking instead for work more suitable for women in scientific research and planning institutes. As one of the deputy shop chiefs put it 'I have worked here for more than thirty years, but do not remember any case of a woman with higher technical education coming to work in my shop'. Even those who have such education usually acquire it while they are already working in the factory, after which they are much more likely to transfer to physically light work rather than work with long-term prospects.

It is also typical that even in the case of those women who work in posts sufficiently senior for them to take part in meetings with the shop chief, their male colleagues, as a rule, do not take any notice of them: they smoke together, use unprintable language and so on. Most often their presence is simply not noticed.

One has to say that the factory creates a 'male' type of management, in which the male managers not only do not pay any attention to the specifically female characteristics of their subordinates, but also try not to admit women to management, taking all decisions without involving them and then informing their female colleagues. 'The bosses decide everything behind closed doors. They just tell us that the men have made the decision. The less we know the better.'

PSYCHOLOGICAL BACKGROUND

In the course of our many meetings with workers we were convinced every time that men reacted much more calmly to the economic difficulties they were living through, typically relating to them as to something temporary. By contrast, women felt very depressed. This is not least related to the real state of affairs in relation to the changes which are taking place in employment: in case of redundancy men, as a rule, have much higher qualifications, several specialities, and finally, simply greater physical strength, so that they can find new work much sooner. Women understand clearly what little chance they have if they are sacked, and therefore are ready to do jobs even if pay is low and working conditions are bad. 'Where will I go, if I am sacked' – we have often heard this pitiful reply given to us by women workers.

The majority of women we have met still feel that they are treated unjustly. As one of those with whom we met exclaimed in anger, 'Lord, what am I, will I still be a human being after this work?'. This sometimes leads to vague feelings of 'sexual antagonism', when women workers see that men are always in the most advantageous position.

Thus, our research allows us to conclude that the position in production of literally all categories of women is not favourable. They do not have the possibility of a successful career, they are exposed to many covert forms of discrimination, subjected to condescending attitudes and, finally, simply work in very harsh conditions harmful to their health. However all these specificities of their position are not accidental. On the contrary, they have deep roots in the socio-cultural particularities of our country, still recently a mainly agrarian sphere, being subjected to a rapid artificial urbanisation. Behind practically every aspect of the unequal rights of women is a completely real and objective situation: these really are the most low qualified, unambitious and sometimes also unpredictable workers, who are neither physically nor psychologically ready to work equally with men. It is typical that they make no claims to do this, considering such a state of affairs as completely natural.

But this situation is itself a result of the deep inequalities from which women suffer. In practice, in production there is a consolidation and deepening of the distribution of socio-cultural roles of both sexes which has developed historically, in which women play the secondary subordinate role. Women-workers (and of course not only workers) in Russia are still very far from understanding this situation and becoming conscious of their interests as a particular social group. In the absence of such a consciousness, a vague feeling of offence, of inferiority creates the emotional background for their activity which pushes them into conflicts in which at present they often do not play a constructive role, but only burn off accumulated negative energy (of course, this does not apply to women alone). However one can hope that the situation will not remain like this for ever. In any case, in the independent trade union Solidarity, organised by workers in defence of their rights, there are, apart from workers, altogether three foremen. All three are women.

Although our case study is based on one particular enterprise, comparing its results with those of analogous research carried out in the framework of our project on enterprises in other Russian regions (Moscow, Komi Republic, Kuzbass) confirms our conclusions. In part it deepens our conception of the factors which impede women's progress up the promotional ladder. Apart from those factors 'external' to women themselves that we have discussed in the article, 'internal' social-psychological factors play an important role in impeding their adequate self-identification. Thus women workers interviewed in a Moscow factory said that they would like to earn more, but under no circumstances would they want to earn more than their husbands. In a chemical factory in Kemerovo a woman, chief of the Financial Planning Department and a highly qualified specialist, refused a transfer to the higher post of Chief Economist, having said that 'she had already reached her ceiling as a woman'. Her ceiling in this case was evidently defined by her husband, who worked in the same enterprise, and who would be 'left behind' her on the career ladder if she accepted promotion.

The problems arising for women on the career ladder lead to the situation in which in contemporary industry there are several basic types of 'women's careers'.

1. 'The woman specialist'. In this case if the woman reveals herself to be a specialist of the highest level, the quality of whose work significantly exceeds that of her male colleagues, 'in the interests of business' she may be promoted, if she does not prevent this herself (as in the case of the woman in the Kemerovo chemical factory). Even more graphically illustrating this situation is the case of another Moscow plant in which a woman was made chief of a backward shop. When the position of the shop improved as a result of her efforts, the Director of the factory observed with relief at the production conference: 'Well, now everything is normal we must put a man in there. This is not women's work at all.'

2. 'The woman helper'. In a number of enterprises one can find a woman who is an informal leader, although she does not have a high official post, but has the complete trust of the top person in the enterprise and influence among the rest of the personnel. (Most frequently her official position is that of personal assistant (*referent*) or 'press secretary', but in one of the Kuzbass mines a post was specially created for her as 'Deputy Director for Strategy'). She is often on the second level, in the shadow of the leader, and often will accompany him for many years through the spiral of his career. Without her, consultation is unable to resolve any serious matter, particularly when it concerns personnel. Sometimes, as in the mine just mentioned, she will even carry out representative duties, speaking at various meetings beyond the limits of the enterprise. Moreover, as a rule, her position is not determined by the degree of her personal closeness to the leader, but by the level of her competence.

3. 'The marionette'. This type of career is a kind of inverse of the previous one. Formally the woman holds a more or less high position, but in fact she has nothing to do with making any important decisions (her duties in this case have to do just with 'female obligingness'). This situation is to be found in one of the Moscow plants, where the female head of the Finance Department, in her own words, 'spends her whole time signing bits of paper', the

sense of which she does not understand, so that she lives in fear that 'sometime she will be called to account for something', but she does not think to raise it with her boss. This kind of career sometimes allows a woman to rise to a fairly high position, but always linked to 'a game played according to someone else's rules'.

4. A 'career as a result of absence' gives a woman promotion to a management post in a situation in which the post itself is not prestigious and the enterprise finds itself in a difficult position. One can see such a case in a Moscow plant, where because of the low pay there is a very high rate of labour turnover, including engineering-technical workers, as a result of which women were made the chiefs of several shops (which never happened when the enterprise was prosperous). There is a similar picture in several shops in Rings, where women, in the absence of competition, are sometimes promoted to the posts of shift or senior foreman.

5. 'Lover of the manager' – this kind of career needs no comment. In the past it was very common in Komsomol structures, but is less obvious in industrial enterprises.

Naturally, the variants of women's careers in enterprises enumerated above are not exhaustive, but the existence and wide distribution of the patterns described is fairly typical, and each of them is distorted (except, perhaps, for the first, but it too presupposes that a woman cannot simply surpass a male claimant on her own). Very often such an unusual career leads to a violation of female psychology, to the loss of her natural style of behaviour: the woman is either completely masculinised (one can often observe this in industry in the case of female line managers), or, conversely, excessively accentuates the features of her sex, seeing the position of a woman specialist as some kind of special status, different from 'simply a specialist', demanding greater attention and toleration.

However much the most important problems facing women working in the majority of the enterprises in which we have carried out our research now are not so much problems with their careers as the fact that they do not have the power to maintain the position they already have. Thus in the factory Prokat in Samara women are one of the most vulnerable categories when it comes to redundancy, since according to a secret instruction they are to be sacked first. Cases of women being thrown out of social production or of compulsory reduction of their status (as, for example, in Prokat where they are demoted from machine-operators to assemblers) are becoming more frequent.

The difficult position of women in Russian industry is a major problem, because the absence in social consciousness of any consideration or even the most minimal understanding of the character of this problem means that of all the social problems which weigh so heavily on the path of Russian reform it is perhaps the most painful and difficult to resolve. Most of all for women.

7. Middle Management in Industrial Production in the Transition to the Market

Pavel Romanov

Middle management (also referred to as line management), in which we include shop chiefs and their deputies, and senior and shift foremen, traditionally play the key role in the reproduction of labour relations in industrial enterprises in Russia. To them falls the task of providing uninterrupted work at the level of the production unit (shift, shop, subdivision), at the prescribed level of efficiency and ensuring the necessary level of productive and executive discipline.

It goes without saying that the specific fulfilment of the functions at each level of the production hierarchy, the number of these functions and the scale of responsibility are not ossified and unchanging. Many factors contribute to their variability, among which are the size of the relevant subdivision (the number of workers), its internal structure, the character of the products which it makes, the technological processes used, and also the type of managerial strategy pursued and, recently, changes in the type of property.

In any case the functions and role of middle managers in the enterprise are determined by the specific position which they occupy in the production hierarchy – a position in which the administrator is subjected to very sharp pressure from above (factory administration) and from below (workers of the section or shift). Their intermediary role is expressed in part in the fact that on the one hand middle managers are the official, traditional and sometimes the only channel of representation of the interests of the direct workers, their subordinates, in the face of the factory administration, but on the other hand they are the channel of administrative activity, putting managerial decisions into practice.

In the outline presented below we try to present some generalisations on the basis of information gathered in the course of fieldwork, and various interpretations of the data. The first aim of the present text is to describe the basic features of the functioning of line management in the past (not only the distant past, it continues to be reproduced in many enterprises in Russia in which, for many reasons, changes are taking place slowly). The other aim is to record the process of change in the functions and scale of responsibility of line management, related to the global changes at the very heart of post-Soviet society – the introduction of the market and conversion, and to define the basic tendencies of these changes.

The features of the material presented and the possibilities of its analysis and interpretation are largely dictated by the methods of research, which was carried out simultaneously in 1992–3 in four regions of Russia and took the form of case studies in industrial enterprises.

I would like to express my particular gratitude for the inestimable help in the discussion of a whole complex of problems connected with the writing of this article to all my colleagues from Britain and Russia, and in particular to Simon Clarke, Peter Fairbrother, Irina Kozina, Sergei Alashaev, Irina Tartakovskaya, Pavel Krotov, Inna Donova and Galina Monousova.

LINE MANAGEMENT IN SOVIET PRODUCTION (BOUNDARIES OF A SOCIAL GROUP)

Characterising production relations at the middle level it is necessary to take into account the fact that this kind of management, relationships and the position of this category have been formed in the course of a long period of time. Their evolution has taken place under the influence of many subjective and objective factors, beginning with the attitude of the General Director to line management and his personal views about their role in production, and ending with the fluctuations, sometimes very significant, in the pay of ITR and specialists. However in our view, the basic mechanism which has created this situation is the Soviet economic system in the production sphere, established on the basis of the principles of the planned economy, centralisation, and the administrative-command type of economic management, as described in various artistic works of the late 1980s (see, for example, Alexander Bek, *Novoe Naznachenie*). Soviet line managers, being a part of this system, are the embodiment in absolute form of all its basic features and can serve as its illustration.

Before indicating the most significant features of line managers, which define them as managers, we will indicate one general and decisive aspect. It consists in the fact that one of the reasons for the low level of efficiency of the Soviet economy, at any rate for its stagnation, consists, in our opinion, in its excessive centralisation. The system of management in any particular enterprise was strictly regulated by formal and informal norms of the branch of production, of the superior Ministry and Department. From this point of view the position of administrative and higher employees was actually similar to that of middle managers in the enterprise, namely in their insecurity. Both these groups were hired employees, although in a situation in which the conditions of their hire were not clearly defined in advance. The state, as employer, established and changed the rules of its game very strictly, and sometimes the manager's very retention of his job depended on his fulfilment of them.

The fulfilment of these Rules required a certain effort. For the middle manager this implied in the first instance *the absence of any limits to the length of the working day*. The limits of the working day of the whole administrative apparatus, and of line management in particular, were usually dictated by the situation in production. In the case of an accident or any other irregular situation the chief of the shop or section was immediately telephoned, and on a 'busy' day never left the shop. In the case of the regular problems with the plan at the end of the month the shop chief and foreman had to have resort to incredible dodges – basically on the informal level, beginning by 'greasing' with alcohol and ending with reminders of previous misdemeanours, so as to force the workers to work overtime and work more intensively. At the same time the working day of the same shop chief had very conditional limits, for the extension of which no special payments above the norm were provided for.

Another no less typical feature of the working day of line managers was its filling with every kind of *paperwork*, required to complete large numbers of certificates and accounts. The over-organisation and bureaucratisation of the whole Soviet system led to the intensive circulation of paper in which reports, accounts and so on at the shop level had their own place.

As a result, the sword of Damocles of demotion as a consequence of the violation of any rule or misdemeanour hung over the head of

every representative of line management. Included in these misdemeanours were, for example, failure to fulfil the plan, disruption in
putting new equipment into commission, accidents. In this context we
remember the case which arose in 1989 involving the chief of the
tube-rolling shop, when during the night shift one of the workers in
the shop fell asleep in the part of the shop in which output was stored
and was crushed by a container of finished products. The subsequent
investigation resulted in the usual consequence – the shop chief was
demoted to senior foreman, the shift foreman to an ordinary worker.
Such injuries in production become a reason for the turnover of personnel. The reason for this is no more than mythical if one takes
account of the fact that in practice the majority of injuries are caused
by the obsolescence of the equipment and the feverish level of activity
in the shop which arises regularly towards the normal accounting date
for achieving the plan. Here we note that the present occupant of this
managerial post is the third in the last seven years. Thus we can define
another feature of the social group under discussion, *the instability of
their position.*

The formal rules, laid out in the widely distributed 'Foreman's
Handbooks', contain an extensive range of rights and responsibilities
of the foreman as a line manager. The responsibilities of the foreman
here usually come down to the need to secure the uninterrupted
working of the elementary production unit of the enterprise – the shift.
These are also related to the responsibility to maintain the equipment
in working order, organise their timely repair, supply the shift with
raw materials, parts and consumption materials, tools, special clothing
and so on. The foreman must regulate discipline, quality and safety
procedures. The enumeration of the rights and means of management,
however is also fairly extensive and includes such mechanisms as
temporary suspension from work, the imposition of fines, sacking and
loss of bonus. As incentives we can mention the Foreman's Fund and
a whole range of extra payments.

Direct conversations in the shops allow us to draw the conclusion
that the limits of the formal rules regulating the activity of the foreman are like the limits of the Soviet Constitution – the norms laid
down there basically exist only on paper, particularly in relation to the
realisation of the rights and means of management. For example the
forms of material incentive are limited to the derisory sums allocated
for the purpose. The use of punishment is limited by the length of the
bureaucratic procedures related to them.

The procedure for applying sanctions to workers is complicated. Now it is as follows: the chief of section writes a report, then sends it to the Director, agrees it with the trade union and the lawyer, and only then writes an order and submits it for confirmation. The chief of section may use this right once or twice, and then decides that it is a waste of his time. (Interview with Chief Engineer of Makeevka Mine in S.A. Belanovskii, *Industrial Interviews (Proizvodstvennye intervyu)*, Volume 3, Moscow, 1991, p. 107)

The problem of sacking those who are chronic violators of discipline became a real headache for shop chiefs and foremen. And the main reason for this was not the opposition of the bureaucratic mechanism of the trade union, but the chronic shortage of labour power, particularly of skilled workers. Being afraid of losing vital workers, the foreman was inclined rapidly to hide cases of drunkenness and absenteeism rather than to use a disciplinary order. We would designate this position of shop management as *the absence of real levers of power*. In such a position the manager was the object of a *double pressure* – from the side of the administration of the enterprise came the strict requirement to fulfil the plan and maintain discipline, without having been supplied with sufficient levers of management, while from the side of the ordinary workers, seeking to resolve their problems through a specific kind of blackmail, came the threat of leaving for another enterprise.

Despite the fact that until 1985 in Soviet society the real significance of money was reduced by the presence of more powerful social phenomena – informal relations, friendship, personal contacts, and so on, the level of pay existed as a more obvious qualitative indicator of the usefulness of this or that job. In this respect the divergence between the nominal position of the line manager in the management structure and the size of his pay was particularly notable. His pay was level with or less than that of a skilled worker. The Chief Engineer of Makeevka mine noted in 1978 that:

The section chief has no interest in the results of his work. If the plan is fulfilled the ITR receives a monthly bonus, but the worker receives it weekly. Thus it is possible to fulfil the plan for two weeks, but then not fulfil the monthly plan ... The workers get their bonus for two weeks, but the ITR get nothing. We are reaching a situation in which we have to keep workers' pay level with ours, otherwise we will be left without any personnel at all. (S.A. Belanovskii, op. cit., p. 107)

Speaking overall one can note that *the low level of pay* reflects negatively on the status of line managers and reduces their managerial powers.

However do shop managers carry out their functions, how was it possible to maintain production and manage the personnel? In our view it was the informal norms which arose in the course of the development of production relations that acquired decisive significance. We have already drawn attention to the 'greasing with alcohol' – the use of reserves of industrial alcohol to encourage intensive work at the end of the month ('... earlier, it used to be so that the workers would more easily agree to work overtime, the shop chief filled up from his reserve ...'). The foreman of one of the military-industrial enterprises in Samara (Clocks) spoke about the trusting relationships with the workers that he had established in the section:

> I know them all well, who has what problems. I have got one drilling machine operator here who did not come to work for a week – he drank a lot ... I went to him and had a chat – really, he had personal problems. In the end he also understood my position and he came to work. But we register absentees later, so it counts against them.

This kind of relationship forms a system of interdependence between managers and workers which, if he is able to create it, supports the insecure formal rights of the managers.

However in the majority of cases one cannot speak of line managers in the form in which they functioned in the Soviet period as a part of management. They were much more technical workers, who maintained the working capacities of such mechanisms as the section, shop, coal-face, but they were not at all managers of people. The administrative-command system of management put them in the position of transmitters of the decisions of higher structures, disciplined screws. This could not disregard the consciousness of the workers, who provided it with stability, which is reflected in one of the interviews:

> Questions of revisions of the norms, reduction of pay, and so on – all these overlook the consciousness of line managers. That is, of course they formally inform them, they sign the appropriate documents, but in reality they cannot imagine the consequences of the measures carried out. As a result they find themselves in a ridiculous position. They do not understand why, despite all their efforts, production collapses and why they are attacked from all sides.

MIDDLE MANAGEMENT AND WORKERS – PROBLEMS OF THEIR RELATIONSHIP

It is difficult to evaluate the relationship between middle management and workers on the shop-floor. The problem is not just that these relationships were, and are, far from being completely conflict free, as traditional Soviet sociology of labour tried to represent them, carefully trying to avoid paying any attention to this question. The basic difficulty is the ambiguous position of line managers, occupying a mediating position between the senior administration of the enterprise and ordinary workers. Line managers themselves (shift foremen) were and are barely conscious of this ambiguity themselves, it was not understood by senior management, but was of considerable interest to ordinary workers one of whom said:

> — What do you think of the foreman – is he one of you (workers), or one of them (management)?
> — We think that he is one of them, but the bosses, most frequently, think that he is one of us. But the foreman, most of the time, would like to be one of them (press operator).

Certainly in practice in the everyday life of the shop the foreman in particular most often has the role of executor of the decisions of higher management. His official duties were always concerned with the processes of managerial and technical innovation initiated from above. Not long ago they had to introduce the brigade form of organisation of labour, the foremen had to organise socialist competition and many other things related to the general idea of raising the productivity of labour.

On the part of the workers the shop management usually appears as the most accessible level of management for discussing problems. It needs to be emphasised that access to the shop administration was used precisely for discussion and the expression of the worker's feelings, and sometimes to send requests and complaints 'upstairs'. As a result of the centralisation of management a whole range of problems were submitted to shop management for resolution, as much in the shops of the biggest industrial enterprises as in small factories, over which the managers had very little control, so that expressing them had no more than a therapeutic value.

Is it possible to introduce changes in the norms? Why have they tried to cut the wage-rate? Why not improve working conditions? Line management cannot provide any answer to these questions. They had very limited access to the administration of the enterprise, the system of industrial trade unions only nominally represented the interests of the workers. As a result contradictions remained unresolved, and conflicts everywhere remained latent.

The latent uninstitutionalised character of industrial conflict is a typical feature of Soviet production relations. On very rare occasions conflict takes on a collective form, but most frequently it remains at the individual level, for example between the shift foreman and workers, or between workers and the shop chief. The size of the management structure is most important in this respect. The biggest pressure from below is usually experienced by those managers who in the given hierarchy have two features – first, that they can decide something, – second, that they are close to the workers.

Appeals to the foreman were always typical of those enterprises in which the shop was large, with a large number of workers. Such large shops are usually typical of military enterprises. The number of workers in Prokat, for example, amounts to 22,000, and the main shops have between 1,000 and 1,200 in each. The enterprise Clocks has 35,000 workers and correspondingly large shops.

A senior foreman at Prokat said, thinking of both shift and senior foremen:

> The majority of production problems are resolved at the level of the foreman. The workers very rarely turn to the shop chief or the trade union committee, and then it is not with problems related to production, but to do with their apartments, large purchases, plots for their dacha, garden plots, and so on.

The main burden of workers' questions about pay, the calculation of bonuses, and many other problems of shop-floor life falls on the shoulders of the foreman, despite the fact that his powers are comparatively limited. The organisation of labour in contemporary Russian industry underlies the fact that the foreman takes on not only managerial functions, but also responsibility for the psychological channelling of the negative emotions of the workers. The foreman short-circuited the majority of the claims and problems addressed to higher levels of the management.

As noted earlier, the role of the line manager is significantly different in enterprises of different sizes. These differences can easily be seen if we look at the position of the administration in small shops and compare it with their position in mass production shops and enterprises. For example, LenKon has fewer than 500 employees overall. In the press shop in this factory there are only 22 people, against 900 in the press shop in Prokat. In this shop there is no post of senior foreman, the shop administration comprises only the shop chief, technologist and one foreman. In the structure of the enterprise this shop is more like a specialist shop. As a result the duties of the foreman in this shop in many ways reproduce the responsibilities of the shop chief, who participates at the same time in carrying out productive tasks with the workers, on the one hand, and is linked to the factory administration, on the other. He secures work, distributes daily tasks, calculates pay, punishments and incentives, monitors technical safety, fire precautions and the quality of the product. The foreman here functions as an assistant, not having any levers of influence or specialised functions. Workers usually prefer to turn to the chief of shop with their problems than to the foreman.

We can see the same situation of line management in the Moscow enterprise Light. Ninety eight people work in shop 5, distributed in four sections. The management structure here is simple, with just a chief of shop and foremen distributed among the sections. Having handed to the foreman the responsibility for everyday control and the calculation of pay, the shop chief uses his power to control the everyday activity of the foremen. He re-checks the calculation of pay and strictly controls absenteeism, professional mobility and the movements of workers in the course of the working day.

It seems to us that the functions of the foreman, his status, his position, the character of his relations with workers and with the administration in the examples given correspond completely to those of the shift foreman in enterprises with large shops. Small shops have various characteristic features in their management structures. Among them one can include:

- absence in them of the post of senior foreman (even when they are on shift work or divided into sections).
- the shop chief concentrates in himself the powers of the whole of shop management, senior foreman and sometimes even foreman.
- the area of independence and responsibility of the foreman is significantly overseen and controlled by the shop chief. He does not have his own incentive fund, he does not distribute production tasks, the workers do not think much of him, and for the resolution of their problems go over his head to the shop chief. It

is interesting that the foreman is paid less than a worker, with his pay being on the same schedule.

MIDDLE MANAGERS – NEW CHARACTERISTICS

Undoubtedly we have found it extremely difficult to identify the tendencies and changes at the level of line management. Our observations show that changes of any kind take place extraordinarily slowly at this level, much more slowly than at the level of the enterprise as a whole or in its apparatus (in its structure, functions and strategy). The majority of middle managers do not identify any kind of change at all, not noticing the changes which have taken place, apparently because of their slow tempo. Despite this, the general development of the system of relations in enterprises also affects this level of the production hierarchy, as is shown by a whole series of tendencies outlined below, which have appeared differently in the different conditions of different enterprises.

Those tendencies that we observe today are not in most cases the realisation of a clear strategy resting on a definition of aims, models of the enterprise and its subdivisions such as they should exist, or at least should emerge as a result of the experience of reform and crisis. In any case, the results of our fieldwork, in our view, show that line managers tend to base their practice not on any kind of rational conception of management and the development of production, but under the pressure of events. Our opinion is that the dominant idea in this situation is that of maintaining the functioning of the productive apparatus, the need to 'deliver the plan' (today this is expressed as 'maintaining production'), to 'reduce power consumption', to 'raise the culture of production'... Today reality fully reflects the words of a worker expressed in 1990:

> Line managers – the overwhelming majority of them are people with an engineering education, and they approach all questions of the organisation of production purely from a technical point of view. Of the two basic factors of production activity – technical and organisational – only the first exists for them ... (Interview in S.A. Belanovskii, *Industrial Interviews (Proizvodstvennye intervyu)*, Volume 3, Moscow, 1991, p. 214)

At the same time external conditions, the pressure of events, create changes in the environment of line managers which force them to show some independence and enterprise and to act in a style that is new for them – as organisers. We will try to show that the administration of the enterprise, the 'high command' have taken some steps in that direction, feeling that in new conditions it has become impossible for production to function and to develop effectively without changes in the position of line management.

The direction of the changes in line management can really be best demonstrated through specific examples from the functioning of large industrial enterprises in the largest industrial regions of Russia. These examples, certainly, do not embrace the many possible variants of development. However in our opinion, they reflect the main features of management in contemporary industrial production in Russia.

PROKAT IN THE GRIP OF CRISIS

The Samara enterprise Prokat is one of the largest, if not the largest, producer of aluminium fabrications in the republics of the former Soviet Union. It produces a very wide range of products, including castings, foil, sheets, tubes, sections and many more. Among its finished products are also various consumer goods such as cooking utensils, covers for preserving, a wide range of domestic fittings, containers and sets of aluminium storage vessels for agricultural production. Prokat employs over twenty thousand people.

The structure of the enterprise is very heterogeneous, including a large number of shops with a wide range of purposes, including construction, not only related to production but also to civil construction, communal services, shops, socio-cultural objects (culture palace, holiday centres, a hospital, schools, a polyclinic, a huge stadium, an amusement park and so on). The factory maintains a fairly large agricultural industry, supplying its workers with butter, milk, fruit and vegetables. In fact the enterprise surrounds itself with a little empire, since the majority of the workers even live very close to it, in huge blocks of flats.

It has become more and more difficult for the enterprise to support such an economy. The fall in production led to a reduction in output of about 15 per cent by volume in 1989. The subsequent fall in production has been very large. This is expressed partly in the fact that in a whole series of shops there is not enough work for the full eight hour cycle, so that every day all the work is completed in 5–6 hours, and the rest of the time the shop is at a standstill. The biggest shop in the factory used to produce 1500 tons of rolled aluminium, but now production does not even reach 600 tons. The enterprise has frequently been forced to stop part of its production for a week at a time, sending the workers on unpaid leave because of the absence of raw materials and the collapse of orders.

The enterprise is equipped with basically obsolete technology and needs a large amount of money to invest in reconstruction, which it does not have. Even the most technologically up-to-date section is equipped with machinery imported from France and Germany which is ten to fifteen years out-of-date.

Such a large organism as Prokat was created over decades and until it came up against the economic problems typical of all industrial enterprises was one of the show-piece enterprises in the city and the country. It was a demonstration of the power and range of industrial development, an Achievement of the Genius of Soviet Engineering. We would add – not only engineering, but also management, since the successful functioning of such a complex system was impossible without the co-ordination of the work of its sections. The stability of its management and its generally quite good results, as recorded in many government documents, are also testimony to its successful activity. How could one of the flagships of the branch have bad results?

FORMATION OF THE MANAGEMENT STRUCTURE OF PROKAT

Indeed, the management of the enterprise was quite effective for many years. The reason for this in our view lies in the well-defined layout of the managerial pyramid, in which there was always room for brilliant and exceptional people who, as a rule, filled the top posts. Before looking at the specific features of this social group as managers in Prokat it is important to take into consideration the military-industrial character of the enterprise. This determined the strongly hierarchical structure of power and the authoritarian style of management in the enterprise. The level of discipline, the possibilities of suppressing internal dissent, and the style of relationships are strongly reminiscent of a military barracks. We can note, incidentally, that until recently the post of Director of a military-industrial enterprise was in time of war temporarily equated with the rank of General, and the enterprise would work under military regulations. The most important feature, however is that the administrative team, the character of management and the internal relationships are not at all firm and ossified, but are in a process of evolution which has become particularly obvious in recent times.

The formation of the factory's administrative apparatus has gone through various stages extending over a long period of time. The first stage includes the building of the factory and the mastering of its technology, equipment and production processes (1950s). Both the workers and the managers in this period were to a significant extent made up of marginal strata. Some of them, much the largest part, had never worked in metallurgy before. They were made up of demobilised soldiers, new recruits and migrants from the countryside. The others were specialists sent from other enterprises in the branch, often from other regions, and graduates of metallurgical higher education institutes.

This was a period in which it was easy to make a career, with the process of promoting the most proven employees to managerial work proceeding energetically. The available evidence shows that the skeleton and fundamental parts of the administration were made up of graduates of the Moscow Institute, fused with specialists from the Urals-Kamenets metallurgical factory (the home enterprise of the Director of the factory). Apart from this, the factory administration, in its concern to create a managerial structure, encouraged the professional development of the original builders, welders and riggers in every way possible, turning them into press-operators, founders and rollers. They achieved this by organising correspondence and evening courses in technical colleges and institutes.

The result was that in the course of the 1960s and 1970s the upward mobility of employees of the factory who had begun their careers in Prokat led to the creation of a fairly monolithic, tight-knit factory administrative team, linked together by the experience of working together for many years. Its essential feature was its orientation to expanding gross output, meeting its plan targets by any means.

Our respondents observe that this characteristic of the system of management was so strongly determined by the politico-economic relationships existing in the USSR that it was hardly affected at all by changes of Director (for example 'Were there any significant changes in the factory after the arrival of the new General Director?' 'I do not

think so. What could basically change? The plan has to be delivered.')
However it was precisely with the arrival of the new Director, about
whom we were asking, that Prokat decided to privatise itself, and it
was precisely the development of the market, of new tasks confront-
ing the management and demanding untraditional decisions that led to
several changes in the echelons of power within the factory.

The economic service of the factory acquired a considerable
weight, and new departments with a market orientation were created
(marketing, external economic relations, and so on). However we
should note that these changes unrolled slowly and on the basis of the
traditional system of management. The management strategy also pre-
serves the tendencies of the conservative structure which balances the
need for fundamental innovations and the aspiration to maintain the
existing situation. The role of the Director in all this was extraordinarily large, with an undefined range of responsibilities there was no
issue concerning the life of the factory that could be resolved without
his intervention. The Deputy Executive Director for Economics said
about this:

— Do I understand correctly that the administration of the enterprise is now
somewhat monolithic?
— In principle yes. You have to understand that the planned structure of Soviet
enterprises, with strict economic management from above, meant that patriarchal relationships developed in the factory.
Our Director is sixty five, the rest of the managers forty five to fifty. If one
manages to speak one-to-one with the General Director, then it is easy to resolve
any matter.

THE CRISIS OF THE MANAGEMENT SYSTEM

In relation to this it is not surprising that the situation in the management of the enterprise is such that any encroachment on the
prerogative of the 'administrative high command' to resolve *all* questions and to be involved in *everything* is perceived very negatively. In
this respect an episode with one of the shop chiefs, who proposed to
transform his section into a relatively independent enterprise, comes
to mind. A plan was presented in which the future profits and long-
term prospects were evaluated. This plan was met with an extremely
firm rejection. The General Director commented on this rejection
in his inimitable way 'I will not allow a Nagorno-Karabakh in my

enterprise!' Thus the system was stabilised, a centre of independence from higher authorities did not emerge, but was quashed.

However in the period of crisis through which we are living it becomes increasingly obvious that some things cannot be done through the traditional mechanisms of industrial management. In the first instance this is revealed in visits to shops, where one can discover representatives of customers in the office of the foreman or shop chief, correcting specific details with them at the time of dispatching the products. Many engineering workers in the shop, including line managers, carry out a wide range of jobs which were traditionally within the competence of the factory services.

— Are problems of the sale of commodities and the search for orders resolved centrally, or do you also participate in their resolution?
— Basically these problems are dealt with by the factory services, but they do not always succeed because of the breakdown in all the economic relationships. For this reason every shop has what we call a 'travelling brigade', which has links with our customers. To put it bluntly, their job is to 'beat out' payments from our customers. This group is basically made up of middle managers (foremen, deputy shop chiefs). But since our section at the moment has less work than others, the team in our shop is basically made up of workers from our section. Ten people are currently engaged in this work in our shop.

The system of management is particularly inflexible in handling the reduction of the number of workers in the enterprise, which is gathering pace. The principles according to which these reductions are being made are not the subject of this article, but it is an important fact that the decision about them was taken by the Director on the basis of proposals made by the Executive Director for Economics, but the information was provided by shop chiefs, on whose shoulders the responsibility for sacking specific people was placed, with the controlling figure being the number lined up for the sack. Here we should note that the administration of the shop did not participate at the stage of preparing this decision. However they, being the best informed about the position in the shop, frequently got into arguments with the 'high command', trying to resist the number of sackings (or even to substantiate a demand for an increase in numbers, which looks like total sedition). The chief of one of the shops complained in an interview in the factory newspaper:

According to the order we have to cut 50 people. This is a very large number for our collective. For this reason we had an unhappy discussion with the Chief

Engineer. I prepared carefully for it, took along the file of this year's orders. But the file did not help. As they explained to me, this is an order which simply has to be carried out.

Certainly if one analyses the fall in production as a whole in the factory one can see a very uneven picture, depending on the direction of the activity of the shops. While the shops engaged in basic production over 1992 and 1993 saw the volume of work cut on average in half, the repair and mechanical shops saw a fall of only 5–10 per cent, and some even increased the amount of work. This was connected, in the first place, with the increased need to maintain the ageing equipment. It is obvious that with such a large scale of production the economic services of the enterprise, working in the traditional style, cannot always develop an adequate redundancy policy.

It is not so much an awareness of the developing crisis of the managerial machine as an intuitive attempt to maintain itself that led the 'administrative high command' to begin to take real steps to strengthen middle management. These steps can be understood as various manoeuvres undertaken to preserve its support in a period of unpopular reform, but objectively the actions of the administration make possible the creation of a more complete managerial team in the form of line management.

STRENGTHENING THE POSITION OF LINE MANAGEMENT

At the present time the structure of management at Prokat is going through a transition from the traditional system of management of large enterprises of the military-industrial complex towards management by a shareholding company. Six hundred and twenty delegates were elected to the Shareholders' Council, including representatives of all the units which were the object of privatisation, including the social and welfare apparatus. The idea of the senior administration of Prokat was that these representatives should be made up of the heads of all the existing subdivisions and services. To do otherwise would be to introduce changes in the strict vertical structure of management established over many years, risking the introduction of uncontrolled elements into the system as a whole. We do not know what really happened as voting took place throughout the factory. We attended one shop election, at which the official candidates were thrown out and an alternative list elected, and we heard that the same happened in other shops. However the reported results of the election as a whole revealed no surprises, as it turned out that only about ten heads had not got through the vote. The view of the administration was that even this small number of unknown people was inexpedient, referring to the experience of one of the local banks, which had twelve people on the Shareholders' Council.

The basic reason for the changes in the position of line managers was the inclusion of the Prokat shop chiefs on the list of people who had the right to receive an additional privileged number of shares. On this list, alongside the shop chiefs, appeared the General Director of the factory, the President of the trade union committee, heads and their deputies of the factory departments (Chief Engineer, Economist, Bookkeeper, and so on). As a result of their privileged participation in the distribution of shares the shop chiefs joined the layer of administration as part of the group of the largest shareowners in the enterprise.

These measures, in our opinion, show that at the present time the management is conducting a gradual policy drive in the direction of establishing a particular position for the shop administration. In a series of interviews we observed the tendency to the development of a holding company in which the separate shops would emerge as separate firms. This cannot happen very quickly – at the moment none of the shop chiefs can even answer a question about the share of their subdivision in the profits of the factory as a whole.

STABILISATION OF THE TRANSFER OF PERSONNEL AT THE LEVEL OF MIDDLE MANAGEMENT

The redundancies being carried out in the enterprise have created a wave of anxiety about their future among the employees. However our conversations in Prokat and in other enterprises show that the basic emphasis in this process is laid on the production workers, and particularly the unqualified. The position of line managers looks fairly stable. An employee of the Personnel Department emphasised:

It is interesting that redundancy has affected managers at various levels the least of all. If we distinguish three levels of managers:

1) Heads of the factory administration
2) Heads of subdivisions and their deputies
3) Foremen and group chiefs

The first two categories have on the whole not suffered any redundancies. Only the third category has suffered redundancy, but throughout the period of redundancy only about ten of them have been sacked and two have left of their own accord. The rest have been redistributed through the factory. The majority of them have been transferred horizontally, without any loss of social status, only a very small number have been transferred to workers' positions.

We also know that the 'headquarters' administration also approaches changes in line management more carefully. Nowadays one hardly ever hears of unexpected changes in personnel among the leaders of the shops. Keeping almost all of its management team intact, Prokat, evidently, counts on their future support and is confident of their loyalty. One can even note an increasing share of administrative workers in the structure of the labour force, which is related to the reduction in the number of workers:

	1990	1992
Workers	81%	78%
Employees	19%	22%

Note: the term 'employees' includes not only managers but also specialists – technologists and engineers. However we should remember that it is precisely line managers who have not been affected by the cuts.

GROWTH IN THE STATUS OF SHOP MANAGEMENT AMONG THE WORKERS

Up to now, in pointing to the improvement in the position of line management, we have referred primarily to the shop chiefs, among whom such a change is most obvious. The position of the management team within the shop has not undergone any such additional reinforcement from the side of the shop of enterprise administration. However the position in the shop itself has changed decisively, which has created the preconditions for a strengthening of the position without any kind of external intervention.

This is most obvious in the shop itself, at the workplace on the machines and in the rest room of the shift foremen. For example, in one of the sections of the rod extruding shop the volume of production is only one third of that in the prosperous year of 1985. The volume has fallen gradually, and the number of workers has fallen correspondingly, so that only 52 of the 96 people still remain, 12 of whom have no work to do each day. Only one or two of the three presses work on each shift, although one is enough to cope with the full workload. Formerly the most highly qualified and best paid workers in the shop were the press operators. Now the position has changed dramatically. All those who are on piece-rates have lost out significantly in their pay since they are often without work.

As a result of the fall in production the highly qualified basic workers now have to work together with the auxiliary workers on loading and clearing up the premises, so that they lose pay. Often a worker arriving in the shop does not know whether or not he will have a full day's work that day. The distribution of work is carried out daily by the relevant foreman and the shop chief.

In the absence of the immutable pressure of the plan indicators there is no longer a shortage of basic workers, recruitment to the factory has ceased and, above all, there have been redundancies which lead the workers to fear for the security of their jobs. This, along with the reduction in the complexity of production for civilian orders as against the former military orders, allows one to speak of a fall in the status of the basic workers who were formerly the backbone of the factory collective.

> I got back from holiday and found that the wife of the shift foreman was working on my press, and since then I have been cleaning up the territory of the shop, which is very annoying. I tried to appeal to the senior foreman and to the deputy chief of shop, but they just said that if I did not like it I could leave. But where is there to go? Anyway it would be a pity to leave, the gang here work well.

To a certain extent the reduction in the role of the basic workers has happened against the background of an increase in the status of the foreman. At the present time, in our opinion, there have been changes in the status of the shop management in many enterprises, for the reasons indicated, the most important of which is the separation of the foremen from the labour collective and their acquisition of real signs of being managers. The workers on the shift can no longer reply rudely to the foreman, as they used to do, and are unable to refuse to carry out auxiliary work. It is not that tidying up has become attractive work for them, but that refusal to do it leads to their dismissal.

The procedure for dismissal has been considerably simplified in the past year, playing its own role in the strengthening of the status of line managers, including the foremen. Using this lever the shop administration can rapidly get rid of all those who breach discipline and brings the situation with absenteeism and drinking in the workplace under control, reacting immediately to such breaches of discipline.

We would not be right if we denied any role to the administrative 'headquarters' in the efforts to strengthen the shop structure. The increase in the pay of ITR, which has outstripped the increase in workers' pay, is such a measure. We were convinced that such a situation reflects the single-minded policy of the headquarters after a conversation with the President of one of the shop trade union committees:

> ... the machine operators are satisfied with their pay and do not want to progress upwards, because in the past engineering employees earned less than workers. Now they are trying to correct this position ...

According to the data that we have the level of pay of a foreman is now one and a half times that of a worker, and that of a shop chief two to two and half times a worker's pay.

PROKAT – AN EXCEPTION?

The tendencies appearing in Prokat, although they cannot be called a managerial revolution, create the foundation for the formation of a completely new type of manager, based on new principles. But Prokat is a particular enterprise: rich, with charismatic leaders, always holding a special place in the politics of the region. How typical are these tendencies in middle management for other factories, branches of production and regions?

It would be pointless to try to paint a complete picture of the evolutionary tendencies in management, and we will not try to do this. However a large number of interviews and observations provide a fairly large number of consistent facts on the basis of which we can identify a number of general tendencies in this direction.

For example, Rings is an engineering enterprise in Samara which is carrying out a reorganisation of shop level management without waiting for privatisation, combining shops into 'plants' according to their technological characteristics. These plants have their own management in which there is a clear tendency for an increase in the distance between the shop chiefs and the factory administration. At the present time the leaders of the shops prefer to resolve their problems themselves, with recourse to the help of the chiefs of the plants as intermediaries. Thus the integrative functions of the factory administration are partially weakening and there is a simultaneous growth in the number of functions to be fulfilled.

The plants that have been created even have some financial independence, for example the chief of the ball plant reduced wages on his own initiative in order to put the money towards other needs of the shop. Sometimes the administration itself willingly transfers functions to the plant management, particularly in connection with changes in wages, which were traditionally its prerogative:

> — Well, the Director of the factory was in Moscow and sent a telegram telling us to increase pay one and a half times, that is by 50 per cent, but the chiefs of shops and plants were given the power to increase the pay of those who turned out to be on low pay a bit more, and to increase the pay of those on high pay a bit less, they did not have to increase the pay of everyone equally, it was differentiated. So we only decided what percentage to give to this or that section.
> — And who decided that: the shop chief or the chief of the plant?
> — The shop chief decided ...

It is typical that in an emergency both workers and foremen at Rings turn to the factory administration and to the Director of the plant. They always refer to him as 'Director', leaving out the 'General', without any risk of confusion.

Another Volga enterprise, Clocks, producing a range of engineering products is in a severe crisis. It suffers more than other enterprises from the sharp reduction in military orders. Earnings are therefore low, so that highly qualified staff are leaving, adding to the number of those made redundant as a result of the impossibility of providing full employment. In such circumstances the enterprise administration is not relying on increasing its own managerial efficiency and its own resources, or on privatisation, but is gambling on getting support from the government. One of the most important factors preventing a complete breakdown in this situation has been the transfer to the shop management of the powers to seek and conclude agreements about the equipment and labour force of the shop. The shop chiefs, in our view, are not carrying out any kind of policy of their own on this basis. They are following the traditional routine of Soviet line managers, trying to maintain the production process in their own sections by any means. A large number of co-operatives operate intensively in the shops, renting space and equipment. But the shop management had first worked out the objective impact of the money earned on their production.

In Moscow, in the enterprise Light, the shop chiefs have been incorporated into the administrative high command in a completely formal way – the shareholding company proposes concluding contractual agreements with them similar in content to the contracts concluded with the administration of the enterprise. This involves not only a significant increase in status – the inclusion of shop chiefs in a single administrative stratum with the administrative high command, but also a significant increase in the level of their pay.

The Kemerovo enterprise Plastmas was one of the first in its region to be included in the process of privatisation. The management team, which stands at the helm of this chemical factory, brings together energetic people with a pro-Western orientation, whose first steps in the reform of the enterprise began with the removal of the existing pay imbalance between ITR and workers. All this work was carried out under the slogan 'specialists should earn as much as necessary'. At the present time the representatives of line management earn 2.6 times the worker's wage.

MIDDLE MANAGERS – THE PARTING OF THE WAYS

It is easy to imagine that the source of practically all the changes observed in line management is the leadership of the enterprise, the high command, whose own actions, apart from anything else, strengthen their support, preventing the possibility of opposition emerging. The directorate uses the possibilities acquired through privatisation and the Law on Enterprise to create a team of managers personally committed to it. They provide the hoped-for support for all the reforms carried out.

However all this relates to the full extent only to the chiefs of shops. The foremen and chiefs of section fall outside this process. In some cases, when there is a single-minded policy to increase the status of ITR by increasing their pay (as happened in Plastmas) line and section managers experience it for themselves. But in many cases their position has not changed in this way. It remains as before closely connected with the general atmosphere in the enterprise – if there is a general purge of jobs, and the workers are afraid of losing their jobs, then the possibilities of control on the shop floor are immeasurably greater than before. Through this the weight of the post of foreman increases, as he acquires the power to exert such control.

It would probably be incorrect to assert that the whole managerial structure of the shop is anywhere cohesive. Indeed at the present time there is a certain amount of disintegration going on. The shop chiefs, to the extent that they have acquired the features of real managers, are able to exert an independent influence on the situation and move further and further away from the lower positions on the hierarchical ladder such as foreman and chief of section.

One can see an example of such alienation in a fully antagonistic form in an enterprise in Syktyvkar. In the Pionerka factory we observed the unexpected phenomenon of cohesion connected with the breaking up of the collective interests of the shop foremen. A display of their independent position arose in connection with the production of a new line. The receipt of a military order required the reorganisation of the enterprise. Shop One was completely re-equipped to sew military uniforms, The creation of a labour force for the shop was achieved by transferring brigades from other shops under the leadership of their foremen, while the previous shop chief remained in post.

At first production led to a strong disproportion in the sewing of the various parts of the uniform (they produced far more trousers than jackets) and serious technological problems with the sewing (new material, very high specifications), as a result of which production fell sharply and the pay fell correspondingly, despite compensatory payments for the transition to a new type of production. As a result the shop chief reduced the foremen's bonuses. But the foremen immediately insisted that it was the shop chief who was responsible for the fall in production, because she was unable to co-ordinate the work of the brigades and could not supply the necessary quality of material – 'she went on pointless business trips to other enterprises without learning anything useful'. They went to the Chief Engineer and demanded the removal of the shop chief, a demand which was met. Thus the violation of the 'contractual pact' led to conflict, in which the higher level of management supported the rights of the foremen.

CAN THE CRISIS GIVE RISE TO CONFLICT?

Discussing the future of industrial enterprises in Russia one cannot avoid the question of whether the process of acquisition by line managers of real managerial features will increase the alienation of workers from the enterprise administration? Will this alienation, limiting the possibility for workers to represent their interests 'upstairs' (when there are no other possibilities), lead to open contradictions and conflict on the shop floor, and the generalisation of this conflict in a mass institutionalised form?

This is one of the most fundamental questions today, since social relations in industrial collectives, in which the organised mass of workers are concentrated, have decisive significance for the stability of the entire state system. As the events of 1989 showed, the strike movement of the miners in Vorkuta and Kuzbass had a serious, and still not properly researched, influence on the processes unfolding in Russia.

The end of 1993 and the beginning of 1994 were marked by the biggest crisis of industrial production in the whole period of reform. This crisis has hit not only industry but also the budget sphere – high schools, academic institutes, municipal enterprises, but its consequences are most appreciable in industry. In such a highly developed industrial region as Samara this crisis takes on its most sombre form. In a general way this regular crisis of money circulation, has caused a delay in payment of wages and salaries of 2–3 months. The increasingly strong monetary policy of the government led to a seizure of financial circulation which developed into the regular crisis of nonpayment, following that of 1991. The shortage of means of circulation, the impossibility of paying for purchases of raw materials and equipment – these problems became extremely widespread among enterprises.

Inside the enterprises these macro-economic phenomena led to a whole series of continuing consequences. In particular the exodus of workers is increasing – Clocks (over the past three months) has lost around 35 per cent of its production workers in a dual process, on the one hand, the intentional reduction of surplus labour, on the other hand, the voluntary departure of people who have given up hope of getting an acceptable wage. The same processes can be observed in Rings, while in Prokat the rate of growth of wages has fallen sharply, in the past having regularly followed the inflationary depreciation of the rouble.

The situation at the level of the shop floor hierarchy as a whole tends to alienate workers from co-operation with management. There actually never was any such possibility, but monetary relations and the process of eliminating surplus labour, which is the tool of middle management, has led to an intensification of the contradiction between these social groups. To the extent that this channel of representation of the workers' interests to the top of the administrative hierarchy is closed, and the process of creating independent trade unions has slowed down and their activity has reduced, the contradictions and conflicts which characterise the relations between managers and managed lose the last possibility of being resolved through mechanisms of negotiation and agreement between the interests of each side. Typically privatisation, against the background of which these contradictions are developing, does not provide any kind of corrective to them.

Looking at the present situation in enterprises it is difficult not to be reminded of Lenin's characterisation of a revolutionary situation – 'the top cannot, and the bottom will not ...'. However at the present time we run into a number of factors which do not fit into Lenin's schema. Institutionalised conflict is lessening, although the situation of workers gets worse day by day. We have heard various interpretations of this given in response to questions posed to managerial employees as well as to ordinary workers. The widespread judgement is of the following form:

> ... people are not prepared to take any decisive steps, because they realise the pointlessness of this. Look at the circle – everywhere it is the same: wages are not paid for months, but if they are paid the amount is simply ridiculous ... Nowadays we go to work and do not make any special effort, we work according to the formula 'you pretend to pay us, we pretend to work ... (09.03.94, sociologist Perm' Motor-Building Association)

Workers have not lost any channels through which they can represent their interests to senior management, since no such channels ever existed. Those processes of redistribution of power and responsibility which are going on within the management of the enterprise do not affect the institutionalisation of the interests of ordinary workers, they go on without any reference to them. As a result of the objective circumstances that we have discussed above, line managers take on the role of real managers and the workers' appeals to them can no longer play even the previous therapeutic effect, but this cannot be said to be a basis for conflict because of the insignificant role of such an effect in the past.

Trying to imagine the future course of events, we cannot answer the question about the future development of conflict in production collectives unambiguously. Calling the existing lull 'expectant' does not, in our view, unambiguously define this expectancy as a regrouping of forces before the storm. The traditions of hidden latent conflict are very deeply rooted in the consciousness of labour collectives. Most frequently in the past, and even more so today, conflict is resolved through the growth of alcoholism, neurosis, family conflicts and departure from the enterprise – individual forms. However the most important point is that today institutionalised conflict cannot resolve all the contradictions in industry. The crisis which envelops it simply cannot be resolved by such means. This point is so obvious that it is understood by both managers and workers.

Some resolution of the situation, certainly, might be expected from the development of the trade union movement. However independent trade unions at present are going through hard times. Having carried out their political mission – strengthening the pro-reform pro-government wing they, known for their pro-Eltsin sympathies, have moved into the shadows. In our view, the so-called 'official' trade unions demand a particular analysis, particularly at their lowest level. Among them one can observe some drift towards a more radical policy in relation to the administration, ready to defend the interests of the workers, and also the movement towards decentralisation.

How is one to answer the question we posed at the beginning of this section? Will the strengthening of the managerial position of line management lead towards the institutionalisation of conflict in the enterprise? In our view the likelihood of such a development is small. The Soviet political system as a whole and production relations in particular over the past 70 years managed to create a particular stereotypical form of conflict resolution in production. The top administration played the key role in this respect, using line management only as a connecting link. However the main sign of industrial conflict of the Soviet type, as it has existed until today, is its institutionalised and individual character.

The establishment of a more or less developed system of reconciliation of the interests of ordinary workers and those of the owners of the means of production, the administration of enterprises, is most urgent today. Despite the fact that the industrial crisis veils the existing contradictions, the establishment of such a system will be the guarantee of the stability of the social process.

SOME CONCLUSIONS

The activity of the top management in industrial enterprises, willingly or unwillingly, confirms the idea that the previous administrative-command principles of management of the large industrial monsters, such as continue to exist in such enterprises as Rings, Prokat and Clocks are ineffective in a market environment. In order to make these giants more manageable the administration has had to transfer some of its powers to line management (shop chiefs). This arises partly from the need to free the high command from the routine daily activity in support of production so that they can concentrate on their efforts to influence the government, organise privatisation, and to resolve global problems concerning the future of the enterprise. They have a more mercenary interest in the formation of a united management team, including shop chiefs, satisfied with their position in the enterprise, as an essential element in the preservation of the integrity of the enterprise.

Thus some of the functions of the senior administration (direct contacts with customers, negotiations with workers in the event of conflict, resolution of operational-organisational questions which go beyond the limits of competence of the shop) have been transferred to the level of middle groups (shop, plant). The shop leaders, beginning with the shift foremen up to shop and plant chief, have become more independent, and the level of their pay, which earlier was no more than the pay of a skilled worker, has correspondingly increased significantly.

There has not only been a vertical redistribution of functions but also an increase in the status of line managers. It would appear that this is conscious effort of the high command, directed at strengthening their influence and the manageability of the diverse production links. The means of increasing their status are varied – through an increase in pay, inclusion on the category of contracted specialists (just like the senior administration) and also as people having a significant share in the capital of the enterprise.

This process takes place against the background of a growing and almost universal exodus of workers, which happens as a result of the aspiration of the administration to get rid of its labour surplus. The value of a job and a stable income in these unstable times creates the preconditions for a strengthening of the position of line management as a whole, as when there is redistribution of work, when the list of those to be sacked is drawn up, and when there are very effective systems of punishment in the form of deprivation of bonus. Discipline in the shops has improved objectively, and this means that the lower levels of line management – shift foremen and section chiefs – have become more energetic. Apart from this, in the absence of any kind of organisation which defends the rights of workers, the immediate superior is virtually the only channel through which the worker can direct complaints and appeals.

There has been something of an erosion of the structure of shop management and the position of the shop chief has more and more moved away from those of section chief and foreman. The surplus of staff and changing social functions of the enterprise mean that the informal system of production management that has existed for a long time, in which non-material incentives and personal relationships had enormous significance, is playing a progressively smaller role and is moving closer to the formal system of duties and functions. The everyday practice of managers progressively frees itself from the informal levers of management, relying more and more on monetary incentives and punishments, with a much stronger preference for punishments than for incentives.

In all these tendencies we can see several lines of development of large industrial enterprises emerging at the present time. The essence of this (although not before privatisation!), is the division of the large enterprise into several independent production units combined under a holding company. In such a company it is inevitable that the role of middle management will increase – in practice they are no longer such, but become many independent agents of management – as will its status position.

Where for any reason privatisation has not taken place and will not take place, the position of line management inevitably is being strengthened and will strengthen in the future because it is determined by the objective requirements for the more effective organisation of the management of production.

8. We Didn't Make the Plan

Marina Kiblitskaya

The system of Soviet economic planning was based on the principle of command: the Ministry gave orders to the plant, the General Director then gave commands to his subordinates. As Dyker wrote, this system 'operates through the dimensions of hierarchy, subordination and obedience/disobedience, through vertical rather than horizontal links' (Dyker, 1981, p. 39). The whole system of 'Soviet planning' needs more focused discussion, but here we would like only to note that it was based mainly on the system of 'planning from the achieved level'. Because the whole system was highly centralised and the planning organs often could not get very detailed information about the enterprise, the only means of constructing plans was to look back to past performance and simply to make some addition to the achieved level in order to make plans for the future.

Under the Soviet system achieving the plan was overwhelmingly the most important objective of every enterprise. However although the plan was supposed to be rigidly laid down, and imposed on the enterprise with the force of law, in reality there were dozens of ways around the plan, from regular re-negotiation of plan targets to systematic concealment of failure. Nevertheless the failure to make the plan could have serious consequences, especially for the managers and other engineering-technical workers (ITR), whose bonuses, unlike those of the workers, depended directly on the fulfilment of the plan.

The Soviet system has now collapsed, but the legacy of the system remains at the level of the enterprise, which retains the principles of command and of planning from the achieved level in its internal operations. This chapter is based on research carried out over a period of eighteen months in one particular enterprise which carries out repairs to metro trains in a large Russian city. Although this enterprise transferred to leasehold in April 1990 it still retains the traditional forms of management, including the central importance of the plan. Moreover, because the system retains the very strong monopolistic features of the former Soviet system the break-down of one part of the chain means stoppages or problems for the rest of the chain. The present chapter investigates the causes and consequences of the dramatic failure to fulfil the plan in May 1993.

In the enterprise the plan is no longer handed down from the metro authorities, but is now constructed on the basis of negotiation with the main plant's client – still the metro authorities – and agreements with other clients. But the plan remains just as important, and just as much a constraint, because if the plant does not fulfil its contracts it will not get the money to pay for new equipment, meet the cost of wages and so on. So the whole system still operates in order to meet the plan. And if the plan is not fulfilled, there are a lot of problems inside the enterprise for all the employees and for the top managers, and outside the plant for the clients.

Within the plant the senior managers try to construct a scientifically approved plan for the enterprise, but because the real system of production operates in a really complicated way, it is almost impossible to predict the result. The weaknesses of the system of planning from the achieved level remain, because if there is no basis for increasing performance within the workshops, at the points of production, the system of planning by mechanical addition to the achieved levels will always fail. So the whole system of planning is incomplete. In reality there are a lot of factors which influence the fulfilment of the plan within the enterprise.

The plant for the repair of electric trains (REMET) was founded in 1940 and has been a leased enterprise since April 1990. It is now in the process of transforming itself into a shareholding company. The staff of 1233 employees is made up of 932 workers and 301 ITR. The enterprise is divided into two parts – one is at Popugai, near the centre of the city, the other is at Kukino in the suburbs. In the past, the plant belonged to the Ministry of Railways, and the Ministry planned the whole range of its production and the variety of its services. Now, there is a special Department of Planning within the enterprise, which has a very complicated system of planning.

Not so long ago high hopes were expressed of the potential of the system of leasehold for the resolution of the problems of the Russian economy. In an article published in 1991 the system was described thus:

> ... the main problem today is the search for methods of de-nationalising property. Currently the most effective way is leasing as an intermediate stage from state to collective property. The criteria distinguishing leasing from cost-

accounting ... are the ownership by the collective and workers of the means and output of production, ownership of the enterprise revenue, and an opportunity for the collective to run its own affairs. (Tchetvernina, 1991, pp. 216–7)

The transformation to a leasehold enterprise of the plant that I am studying certainly brought a number of advantages to the plant, including some of those identified by Tchetvernina. First, the plant was transformed from an unprofitable enterprise into a profitable one. Second, in the past the plant was subordinated to the Ministry of Railways and metro authorities, and came under great pressure from them in relation to output and other questions. In new circumstances the enterprise became more independent from such bureaucratic structures. The relationships with higher authorities now involve mainly negotiations about the prices of the units of production. The plant reached an agreement with the metro authorities to reconsider the prices for the carriages every three months. And they have to stick to this agreement, because if it is not kept (and it is usually the higher bodies who try to breach it, because they make a profit if they can delay price increases) the plant can secure the sanction of a fine, and can refuse to deliver the repaired carriages to the client. This means that the plant no longer suffers the pressure of orders from above.

I would say that the other advantages mentioned by Tchetvernina in her article are more questionable. She wrote:

... leasing changes the status of the collective and individuals by making them responsible for the enterprise's results. The advantages of collective self-management are clearly demonstrated when employees do not simply take part in decision-making but really manage the enterprise. (ibid., p. 217)

She also argued that

... leasing creates an effective system of labour incentives for the collective as a whole, as well as for its workers. That is because the collective is in charge not only of distributing wages but also of deciding how to use revenue, such as whether to expand production or build equipment to increase labour productivity, or build a sports complex. (ibid., p. 217)

This idealistic prediction is not borne out by my study, which concerns the difficulties which impede the fulfilment of the plan, problems with the incentive system and other problems.

It appeared that REMET was more or less able to meet its plan targets every month, when suddenly in May 1993 the whole industrial program of the enterprise appeared to collapse. One of the main workshops didn't fulfil the plan. The result was that the plant failed to supply the contracted repaired carriages to the metro, and for this reason incurred a penalty of about 110 million roubles. How did this happen? How did the events develop? How did a plant which was supposed to be increasing its production programme suddenly collapse, apparently without warning? These are the questions I will try to answer in this article.

If we look at the process of production as a whole in May, we can see that the whole plant worked as usual. As usual there was a shortage of material, a lack of workers and arrhythmic supplies of parts. As usual people went to work on Saturdays and worked in the evenings. But nevertheless nobody could remember such a serious failure in the past. Let us consider several numbers. The carriage repair workshop at Kukino was supposed to carry out maintenance repair work on eighteen carriages and capital repairs on one carriage each month. At the end of May only five of the carriages for maintenance repair were delivered. The carriage assembly workshop at Popugai, according to the plan, had to carry out maintenance repairs on eleven carriages and capital repairs on four, and in May fell short of the plan in respect of one capital repair only. As we can see, the most serious problem was in the carriage repair workshop at Kukino area. Figure One provides a general idea of plan fulfilment at Kukino area during 1993

Figure One: Fulfilment of the plan in 1993 in the Kukino area.

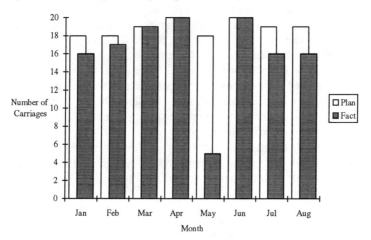

In order to analyse the situation we should try to investigate the whole range of reasons for the non-fulfilment of the plan. Let us start by considering some objective factors.

First of all, there was a shortage of supplies of materials and parts from different enterprises. In the past there was a centralised system of supplying materials within the metro system and a special store supplied about 40 per cent of the parts needed by the enterprise. With the transition towards a market economy this system broke down. And now the role of the Department of External Co-operation and the Department of Material Supply within the enterprise has increased. But the problem is that first of all the whole system of accounting and inspection of parts is not regulated. Second, the staff of this department are the same people as were there in the past and they have no special skills, they have not been taught such things as how to establish communication with new partners, they have no idea of how to work in the developing conditions of the market economy. The third reason is that the number of staff is the same, but the amount of work has increased. So sometimes they just psychologically and physically cannot organise this work in the best way. Besides, some of the partners who supply materials are in different parts of the former Soviet Union which are now sometimes situated in different countries, for example in Ukraine. If several years ago it was very easy to get parts from Ukraine, now it takes a long time, because there is a new customs service and before you can transfer parts from Ukraine to Russia it can take a month or more just to co-ordinate all the formalities. Because of this situation some departments within the plant faced the real threat of breakdown. That is why two people from the Department of External Co-operation went to Ukraine and carried out up to 50 bearings per person themselves in sacks. These were sufficient for two weeks, but then it was necessary to repeat the trip to Ukraine. This example shows us that in the conditions of collapse of the Soviet Union and the whole system of economic connections enterprises have invented a new system of 'carriers' (*perevozchiki*), i.e. people who try to resolve supply problems by carrying parts from one enterprise to another, from one part of the former Soviet Union to another. And this system coexists with the system of 'pushers' (*tolkachi*) –

... these are men who try to by-pass, or at least speed up the official supply system and obtain by semi-legal or even outrightly illegal means, the key supplies needed to ensure plan fulfilment. (Dyker, 1981, p. 64)

The supply position in May was really awful – there was no special caustic to wash bogies, there were no locomotive engines and other parts, but it is really difficult in analysing this situation to distinguish objective reasons for these problems, connected with the breakdown of the Soviet system, and the subjective reasons which, from my point of view, played an essential role. Thus one explanation for the supply failures could be the inefficiency of the Department of External Co-operation. The head of this Department had amply demonstrated his incompetence over the previous months, but because he was a good friend of the General Director nobody could do anything about the situation. He had been invited by the General Director from another enterprise, and in the Director's eyes he was a 'verified' person, on whom the Director could rely. In addition, he was in his early sixties, and therefore he was not considered as a serious pretender to the Director's post. Maybe as a technician or as a specialist in engineering sciences he was really good, but as the head of such a serious and important department he was really weak.

The other very important problem is the organisation of the rhythm of production. Because of the lack of parts it is very difficult to organise the production process. So the tradition of 'storming' at the end of the month very much continues to exist within the enterprise. Besides, interviews with workers and middle management showed us that parts are distributed in a very unequal way. Thus, the Popugai area has much better conditions because the main store is there, and there is a better system of communications between the workshops and the staff in the store. The Kukino area, because it is situated in another part of the city, has problems with supplies because people at Popugai have no motivation to supply the Kukino area. For this situation there is a Russian proverb: 'keep your own shirt close to your own body', which means in this circumstance that people in Popugai's workshop were closer than those from Kukino to the staff of the Popugai store, who distinguish between 'our people' from the Popugai plant and 'strangers' from the Kukino area. If people from Kukino go to the Popugai store to get some parts or material, in the words of one of the shop chiefs from Kukino: 'The Popugai staff will tell them to fuck off and they will get nothing'. So the Popugai area is in a privileged position. From the objective point of view there is no system of regulating the relationship between the parts of the plant and this creates real problems.

Now we would like to analyse another very serious objective factor which prevents the fulfilment of the plant – the shortage of workers. The production program of the plant is calculated by the Planning-Industrial Department in accordance with orders from the main client, the metro, and from other clients. In drawing up the plan this department takes into consideration the situation within each workshop: the number of workers, the productivity of each workshop and other indicators. But the main problem is that the Planning-Industrial Department draws up the whole industrial program on the assumption that the program will be carried out by the whole staff within the workshop. But what happens in reality? In reality there are a lot of vacancies. This situation is really interesting, because in the mass media there are a lot of reports about unemployment in Russia. Why in these conditions are there so many vacancies? In order to answer this question, we have to investigate more closely the real picture within the enterprise.

One of the main causes of such a situation is that the workers want to earn much more money. And it is possible for them to do this if they work not only for themselves, but also 'for that guy', i.e. for an absent person. The amount of money which the workers earn is calculated in accordance with the numbers laid down in the staff schedule, so there is an unwritten agreement between workers and middle management (foremen and the shop chief) that the shop will keep vacancies and the workers will work hard without any recruitment of new workers. This unwillingness of workers to allow recruitment is described by the Russian saying 'I will not eat it, but I will not give it to anyone else'.

The workers physically cannot fulfil the job with the reduced number of people, but nevertheless they object to the recruitment of new workers. The shop chiefs understand that if they recruit new workers to the plant, then the salary of the existing workers will be much lower (and consequently the labour motivation of the workers will be reduced). So the shop chiefs carry out a quite conscious policy of recruiting people to the workshop up to the limit of 70 per cent of the staff. As I mentioned above, the Planning-Industrial Department follows a quite different policy, they calculate the whole plan in accordance with the complete staff. Thus we can see that there is a real discrepancy in numbers between those who plan the industrial programme and those who carry it out. According to the data of the Planning-Industrial Department, it is possible to fulfil the whole production program for the month, indeed to repair 22–23 carriages per month if the sections are fully staffed. But as we can see (Figure Two) the number of workers within workshops is much less than is required. And this is one of the most important factors which constrains the fulfilment of the plan.

Figure Two: *The number of piece-work workers in the Kukino area, 1993*

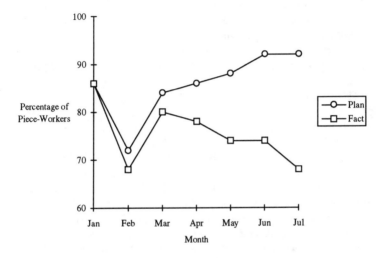

Another important objective reason for the failure to meet the plan is a lack of repair equipment. The plant is a monopolist. There is no similar plant in the city which carries out the same kind of repair, so metro carriages can be repaired only at this plant. But the demands are bigger than the plant can meet, so the carriages run for longer without maintenance each year. Because of the increasing runs, the parts are more worn out, and so the more parts need to be repaired. But the capacity of the special mechanical-repair workshop is limited, and the workers in this workshop can not provide the whole range of parts required. The repair equipment in the mechanical-repair workshop is very old and also can not cope with the whole volume of work. Thus, this is one more objective constraint on the ability of the plant to meet the plan.

In the ideal case the mechanical workshop would have a special circulating store, from which replacement parts could be drawn while the broken part is repaired. But the creation of such a store is a very difficult task and it can only be done in the future. It is not only in the mechanical workshop that there is no such 'normative stock', there is none anywhere in the enterprise. One might ask why the General Director does not buy new equipment or the whole range of parts required? And here we can see another constraint which has a major influence on the activity of the plant – financial constraints.

There is a limited amount of money in the plant for the General Director to spend on equipment at any particular time. But the problem is that almost all the equipment is now in such bad condition that it needs repair or replacement. It is impossible to replace all the equipment, although the equipment is being replaced step by step. The plant has got some new presses and lathes, but this is still a drop in the ocean.

The whole situation is aggravated by the bad organisation of the production process. There is a lack of responsibility at every level of the plant, which appears in a lot of examples of interaction between parts of the organisation. Here is one of them.

In February the Technical Inspection Department (OTK) raised a question about the automatic couplings. The head of this department warned the Deputy Director about the problems with automatic couplings in February: they are working at the limit of the permitted tolerance. She wrote a special message in the Deputy Director's Report Book. Her assistants warned the staff of the workshop in March and again in April that it is almost impossible to work with such automatic couplings. There was no reaction from either the Deputy Director or shop chief. Finally, the head of the technical inspection service, following her formal warning in February, decided to stop the production process and refused to accept the carriages with defective automatic couplings which did not correspond with the required standards. Because the service did not accept carriages the whole of production was stopped for a week. As a result six or seven carriages were not accepted by this service.

Undoubtedly, this delay influenced the productivity of the whole workshop. When this case was analysed at the production meeting devoted to the failure to meet the plan it turned out that the Deputy Director had simply ignored the warnings from the inspection service, and did nothing to improve the situation. However the head of the inspection department had also exceeded her rights: according to her job description she had no right to stop the whole production process without first warning the General Director of the enterprise. This example shows that people at different levels do not always fulfil precisely their own instructions and job descriptions, which can lead to big breakdowns of the whole plant.

People who are not very familiar with the Russian production process could easily be led to believe that the objective factors described above are more than sufficient to explain the failure of the plant to meet the plan in May. But those who know the Russian enterprise better know that all these factors explain nothing. All these factors have been more or less characteristic of Soviet production for decades. They influenced the production process in the previous months, just as much as in May, but nevertheless, the workshop fulfilled the plan or almost fulfilled the plan from January till April, as they had done month in month out over previous years. So, it is necessary to look more deeply, and to investigate the reasons which lie beneath the surface. So we would like to analyse other factors which had a very large influence within the enterprise.

FORMAL AND INFORMAL RELATIONS IN THE SOVIET ENTERPRISE

Production relations in most enterprises are characterised by the co-existence and co-operation side by side of formal and informal relations. Theoretically, the enterprise should produce its goods through the well-organised and institutionalised system of formal relations. In reality a lot of enterprise processes pass through a non-institutionalised system of informal relations. These kinds of relations penetrate the whole system of organisation, including:

- operations
- participants, including relations inside and outside the enterprise
- different levels of organisation
- the process of production
- the whole range of ways in which control is organised
- results

In general it is in practice the nature and extent of the informal system of production relations that largely determines the structure and functioning of the formal system, and it must also be recognised

that the informal system has its own dynamic. Because informal negotiations are not subject to official control and regulations it is
difficult to get information about such relationships, and it is really
hard to say to what extent such relations are based on informal agreements. But it is undoubtedly true that the informal system within
Russian production relations is extremely important.

One of the problems of getting valid information within the Russian enterprise is that at different levels of the enterprise the researcher
can find absolutely contradictory explanations of what has really happened and is happening within the enterprise. Sometimes these
contradictions concern very substantial questions. And sooner or later
the researcher could assume that people are telling lies. But there are
various different reasons why this might happen. One of the possible
answers could be that people at different levels of the enterprise possess different amounts of information. Those who are working on the
top levels of the enterprise very often have less information or distorted information about what is happening at the lower levels. That is
why inadequate information leads to insufficient and incomplete explanations. In addition, there is a desire 'to present the enterprise in
the best possible way to strangers'. This position is also deeply rooted
in Russian culture and we have a special proverb for this: 'do not
carry out rubbish from your house'.

From the researcher's point of view the most fruitful approach is to
hear as many explanations as possible with all their nonsense and ex-
aggerations and then try to construct your own opinion about what has
really happened. But it is also very useful to use a multiple-strategy, to
combine different methods in your research. For example, in one interview with a female foreman I was told that the workshop always
fulfilled the plan. At that moment I was at the beginning of my study,
but nevertheless, I already knew something about production, so I did
not believe this information, but in order to prove or disprove this information I spoke with different people and also I found the statistical
data, where it was quite clear that every month the workshop failed to
repair one or two carriages from the plan.

Why is the system of informal relations so important? One of the
main reasons, from our point of view, is the shortcomings of the formal system of production relations, and in this situation the informal
system is needed to supplement or even entirely replace the formal
system, whose restricted rules and instructions do not lead to satisfac-

tory results and do not reflect real relations of power, capability and influence.

The strength of the system of informal relations lies in the fact that it is firmly rooted in traditional values and practices and that the process is very flexible and speedy. And this leads to the alternative kind of explanations for the failure to meet the plan – explanations which refer to intrinsic features of the whole former 'Soviet system'. Under the Soviet system all subjects within different economic and social structures used informal methods which became established practice. The results of the case study show us that the informal system has a great importance within the production process in Russia. One of the aims of the case study was precisely to investigate the whole framework of industrial relations within the enterprise from the point of view of their formal and informal structure, organisation, operation and practices, as well as the economic circumstances to which they are subjected.

In looking more closely at the failure to fulfil the plan we find several examples in which the two systems are really complementary, and some in which the informal system completely replaces the formal system. To put it in the most general terms, the plan appeared to have been fulfilled month-in month-out by the operation of various informal relations, which made up for the deficiencies of the formal system. However as the situation inside and outside the enterprise got increasingly difficult the informal systems came under increasing pressure, until in May they reached breaking point.

In May a whole series of problems arose in these informal systems which, when they broke down, revealed the complete inadequacy of the formal system that was supposed to regulate production. Already in the discussion above we have seen the importance of informal relations in the operation of the system, supplies only being maintained by pushers and carriers, the informal relations between the incompetent supply chief and the General Director, the regular practice of storming, the informal system of distribution of supplies from the main store, the maintenance of a permanent labour shortage, the informality of the system of inspection. In the following sections we will investigate the crucial areas in which informal relations broke down catastrophically in May, and not by chance, as in the case of the factors already mentioned, but by conscious decisions of customers, workers and managers.

INFORMAL RELATIONS WITH CUSTOMERS

When we look at the official figures for the fulfilment of the plan it appears that on paper, apart from May, more or less all the planned carriages were repaired. But if we checked all these carriages at the end of the month we would see that almost every carriage still had defects and incomplete repairs. Yet all these carriages were accepted by the metro authorities. How could this happen? One of the explanations is that within each plant there is a system of informal relations surrounding such inspection. We are all people, we all have our weaknesses. So, the workers and the managers from the workshop established good relationships with the people from the metro inspection. The whole system works on the old principle – 'you do something for me – I'll do something for you.' That is why at the end of the month it is only the system of informal relationships that helps to get people to sign that this particular carriage has been accepted by the metro inspection's rolling stock service. Theoretically, it means that within the same day all these carriages should leave the gates of the enterprise and be delivered to their customers. But in reality, of course, all these carriages will continue to be repaired for at least ten to fifteen days.

Now let us consider what happened in May. Some of the customers – various metro depots – expressed their indignation at such a system. They expressed their opinions several times in the daily meetings of general managers of each unit with the head of the whole metro system. They rebelled against the old system, saying simply that they could no longer put up with such a long cycle of repair. They insisted that they pay for the job, for quality and for quick repairs. Instead of that they can not get their repaired trains back in time. They wanted a proper system of repair with concrete terms and conditions established. Their complaints created a great scandal and a lot of depot managers supported this complaint. The result was that the head of the whole metro issued a special order to the rolling stock service. This order laid down that any person who signed for an unrepaired carriage without authority would be sacked. Following this order everyone in the rolling stock service was very frightened, and they decided to carry out their work according to the rules, which meant that o nly those carriages which had been fully repaired were signed for by the SPS service. All the other carriages, which had some defects or problems, were not accepted. That is why this system of informal relationships broke down.

WHAT ABOUT THE WORKERS?

And what about the workers' role in all this? After all, they are the people who actually have to repair the carriages. They are the people who have to make superhuman efforts to complete jobs with inadequate supplies and inadequate equipment, working in bad conditions with bad organisation of production. They are the people who have to work in the evenings and at weekends to meet the plan at the end of the month. In the end it was the workers who did not make the plan because they were no longer willing to compensate for the defects of the system.

The most important reason for this is that within the plant there is a badly constructed incentive system, which does not focus directly on the producers. The system does not motivate the workers to fulfil the plan. The earnings of the administration of the workshop, as of all the managerial staff, depend on the productivity of the workshop and fulfilment of the plan. They have special bonuses of up to 50 per cent of their salary if the workshop or the plant meets the plan. As regards the workers – they have no such system of extra bonuses. Their bonus is related to each carriage that they repair. But the workers have little information about how the price of each carriage is calculated, and so how their earnings are calculated.

The workers' big dissatisfaction arises from the fact that those who do not fulfil the plan sometimes earn more than those who do fulfil it. The workers think that it makes no difference to their earnings whether or not they fulfil the plan, and so they have no incentive to do so. Thus, the system of worker's payment does not correspond with their aspirations. And there is a real contradiction in this sense between clerical workers, managers and the General Director, whose bonuses directly depend on the fulfilment of the plant, and the workers, who do not feel themselves sufficiently motivated to meet the plan. When I interviewed a shop chief about this matter, he said:

We have a piece-work system within the enterprise. For example, we should produce 20 carriages per month. We know the price of each unit of production (for example, one carriage). People, when they begin to fulfil the plan, know at the beginning how much they could get by fulfilling the whole plan of 20 carriages. And if they fulfil less, they will get less money. The workers' bonuses are included in every carriage they repair. If he repairs the carriage he will get a 75 per cent bonus. As regards the ITR, if the plan is met they get a 50 per cent bonus. But what happens is that the worker can not see his bonus. He may earn, say, 70 thousand roubles, but he doesn't realise that this automatically includes his bonus.

From this it is clear that the workers know the total wage that they receive, but they do not know how this breaks down into basic pay and bonuses. Below, we would like to present the opinion of one of the workers of this workshop about the fulfilling the plan and their 'clear' understanding of how the system of payment and bonuses is organised. Several people within one brigade were trying to understand how it happens that some of the brigades which failed to fulfil their plan earned more money than those who worked really hard in order to meet the plan. And in this situation they raised the question with the deputy shop chief:

We tried to find out how it has happened that electricians have received for the 16 carriages which they repaired more than we received for the 19 which we repaired. When the deputy shop chief passed through our section, we mentioned this point to him: it is not profitable for us to fulfil the plan at all, because there is no incentive. But he said that it is our responsibility to be ahead of the other brigade and to have two or three carriages repaired in advance. We tried to prove to him that he gets a bonus for meeting the plan, but we have none. Then he said to us that the price of every carriage includes the bonus too, and we just couldn't see it. If that is so, what percentage of our work is included in the bonus, and what idiot invented this system? It is automatically added to each carriage I repair and for me it is not clear at all whether it is good or not. No clearness, no stimulus. For a Russian man it was always clear if somebody told him something like: 'you get this money for this work, that money for that'. Here we have a totally different situation, and nothing is clear at all.

Thus, from our point of view, one of the most important factors underlying the failure in May consisted in the unwillingness of the workers to fulfil the plan. The workers' dissatisfaction with the bad incentive system, which gave them no incentive to make the plan, and which they had tried to change, led to an unwritten agreement between the workers in May in some sections that they would not fulfil the plan. For them it was one of the means of trying to draw attention to their problems. They had raised the question of the incentive system a long time ago, but nobody took any notice. They asked people at different levels of the enterprise about this unjust system, but got no answer. The First Deputy Director with responsibility for the Kukino area clarified his position towards the fulfilling of the plan later, in August 1993, when some of the workers raised this question again after one of the production meetings. Here is a short quotation from the diary of one of the workers:

> After the meeting we again went to the First Deputy Director and said to him that it is not profitable for us to fulfil the plan. We have no bonuses for fulfilling the plan. But people who do not fulfil the plan have the same payment as we do. Also clerical workers always have bonuses if the plant fulfils the plan. The First Deputy Director answered, 'If you are not mad about the plan, you should have nothing to do with this plant. There is no place for you here'. Then he told us to get out and hinted to us that he was spending 95 per cent of his time resolving our problems, but he has more serious production questions to resolve.

This quotation very clearly shows us the real attitudes of management towards the workers. The dictator's voice and tone still exist in the enterprise. But the problem is that times are changing, even if only slowly, and for workers it is not sufficient to hear orders only now. With the transition to the market economy some of them very quickly accepted the 'wind of the change' and now they are really trying to understand how the system operates, and how their labour efforts will be evaluated. And if they are really dissatisfied with the system which operates within the enterprise, sometimes it is in their hands to show the managers that they also can do something. Such a situation happened in May, when they were really dissatisfied with the whole system and part of the workers agreed that they wouldn't work too hard for no reward.

It is very interesting that the shop chief in this situation aligned himself with the workers. He tried to organise the whole production process, but there were so many barriers to this. In the middle of the month he organised some working Saturdays, but at the end of the month, when he received a strict order from the 'top' to work on Saturday and even on Sunday he refused to do it. He said in his interview:

> I realised that the workers are really exhausted, they are working like tired-out horses. And I didn't force them to work on Saturday. I thought that if it is not the fault of my workshop, but of a whole set of other circumstances, why should I do it?

ROLE OF PERSONALITY AND AUTHORITATIVE CONTROL

If we investigate the management structure at the Kukino area, we can see that the most authoritative figure within this area is the First Deputy Director, a man with a very strong character. In previous months the plan had been fulfilled mainly because of his great pressure on the people and his strict order 'to fulfil the plan'. In May he went on vacation and his responsibilities were taken up by his deputy. The deputy, although he had worked at the plant for a long time, is nevertheless considered by the specialists as completely incompetent in the organisation of production. So, another of the real reasons for failure was the absence of such an authoritative person from the plant. The deputy at that time was fully involved in the organisation of a small enterprise within the plant, and this was much more important for him than the organisation of production. Some of the managers complained that it was difficult ever to find him at his place of work – he was always absent.

Moreover, immediately after the failure to meet the plan in May there were rumours that the breakdown in the Kukino area was contrived by the Kukino management as a challenge to the governing body of the enterprise as a whole, to force it to pay attention to the Kukino area, which is too far from the top and whose problems are always resolved last.

WE MISSED THE PLAN! PURGING THE GUILTY

Everybody has always known that the whole system of production has always been irrational and inefficient and needed to be changed, and that economic crisis in the transition to a market economy makes such changes inevitable. Several people within managerial circles have long been saying that it is a bad system, that there is no clear organisation of production, but their voices were not considered.

It was clear from the middle of May that the plant would miss the plan by a long way (which was why I decided to carry out intensive fieldwork during this period), and at the end of May the full extent of the failure was apparent. But serious attention to this matter was only paid at the beginning of June, when the plant was faced with the problem of incurring enormous losses on its contracts.

An investigation was launched and a series of production meetings held to get to the bottom of it. But this was a typical Soviet investigation. The issue was not why did we not make the plan, but 'Who is guilty ?' and 'Who should be punished ?' These two questions become central at all the meetings devoted to analysing this breakdown, with only isolated calls to change the whole system rather than spending the whole time working out special punishments.

On the 7th of June, the Director organised a production meeting with the heads of departments and shop-chiefs to analyse the general situation. At this meeting many shop chiefs spoke, complaining about shortages of parts, about the failings of the Supply Department, and so on. The chief of the carriage-repair workshop demanded that the people, who, from his point of view, were responsible for this should be punished, including the head of the Department of Material Supplies. Eventually it was decided that in accordance with the regulations all engineering-technical personnel would be deprived of their bonuses. In addition it was decided over the next two days to prepare a special Order concerning the punishment of the people most responsible. The First Deputy Director for Production was urgently summoned back from his holiday to head the special group working out this Order.

In the morning of 9th of June, after the Order listing the proposed punishments had been prepared, the General Director organised a second production meeting, at which the calculations of bonuses for the various shops and sections for the month were announced, followed by a roll-call of the heads of departments, each of whom was quizzed by the General Director about shortages, with a cross-examination of those responsible for various failures of supply and production decisions.

A further production meeting was called that same afternoon, attended by about thirty managers, the main aim of which was to find 'scapegoats' for the failure to meet the plan and to decide their punishment. The meeting began with a reading out of the draft Order, which noted that the failure to meet the plan had cost the factory 110 million roubles, identified the main reasons for the failure, and proposed various punishments involving the deprivation of various managers of a proportion of their pay and bonuses. After the reading of the draft Order the Director asked for suggestions or opinions, and the meeting flared up. The whole atmosphere of this meeting was unpleasant and awful, and reminded one of a real 'bazaar' because everybody tried to 'throw the blame onto somebody else and justify himself'.

The sharpest argument was between the head of the Technical Control Department (OTK) and the Director. The former had been deprived of 20 per cent of her pay as a punishment, but she insisted that she had done nothing wrong and so did not deserve any punishment. The head of the OTK asked the Director a question:

> — Do I understand you correctly, that I have been punished for the fact that I stopped accepting carriages with defective automatic couplings, and that is what I am being punished for?
> Director: — No that is not right. For the organisation of quality. The question of quality is very complex and your fault is not that the automatic couplings are defective, but that in the organisation of work itself there must be a system of regular pressure from the management to maintain quality. In February you wrote an order to the Deputy Director, and he did nothing. But there are other people in the leadership. You know whom you should take these things to. You should write orders into the log repeatedly to say, repeatedly to record, repeatedly to resolve things and if everything is not sorted out you should come to the Director and tell him. It breaks my heart to say it, but you know that the result is that tomorrow the factory will come to a standstill. And this has consequences for everyone.

The head of the OTK put her question again:

> — I do not understand what I have been punished for, because I did not produce defective products or ruin the plan.
> Director: — We have explained it to you: because having seen a particular defect you did not register it correctly and did not resolve all the problems. You should have given an order to the Director or his First Deputy for Production or told them about the problem. There is a log for orders.

The head of OTK was becoming increasingly upset:

> — Paragraph 3.4 of my official instructions says that I am obliged not to release products which do not conform to the existing norms and to prevent the movement of defective products. How have I acted incorrectly? Where does the Order state what I have been punished for?
> Director: — Well, you violated point 3.1, which provides for a situation in which a fault is discovered. In that case you have to bring it to the knowledge of the Director of the factory.
> Head of OTK: — I was punished because since the 1st June the wheel shop has come to a standstill, but until then nobody gave a damn about anything, al-

though we have been writing orders since February and this problem was put forward then.

Director: — You stopped the shop. The metro did not stop anybody, and the factory is not allowed to stop. There is a shop chief, if he does not resolve the problem, it is necessary to go to higher authorities.

Head of OTK : — I have a question: why is everything confined to the questions about the automatic couplings? Why out of twelve carriages signed by the OTK – yes, we took responsibility for them ourselves, and signed them with bad automatic couplings, nobody stopped them. Why out of twelve carriages were only five accepted by the metro rolling stock service? What is the OTK punished for in this situation?

Director: — Not the OTK. I told you – the head of the OTK. I was not told about your problems, although I knew about this question at the end of May. Your should have signed this question into the log for the Director. You are being punished for not fulfilling point 3.1 of your official instructions.

They suppressed further discussion of this question and went on to elucidate others.

Then the question of the punishment of the Deputy Chief Technologist for the failure of the automatic couplings was discussed. People rose to his defence and said that he was to blame for nothing. The faulty part in the automatic couplings is not one of those which is renewed and it is not possible to resolve this problem all at once. The Deputy Chief Technologist spent all his time in the shop and the proposed 30 per cent reduction in pay did not seem just.

Then the question of the punishment of the Supply Department arose and its representative spoke:

— Apart from the reducing gears, all the problems of components in short supply itemised were resolved in one or two days. The chief of the carriage assembly shop comes to the Department five times a day and these were all resolved and, as you can see, the carriage assembly shop made the plan. And so you have to answer the question, why did the Kukino site fail to deliver such a huge quantity of carriages? Why are these questions now raised so sharply, why could this not be resolved at the time? Why did the shop chief himself not move quickly, phone? I heard nothing from him, not a single call for six months?

A cry came from the ranks:

— Because comrade Popov [First Deputy Director] was there, and he pushed them all, and he went off on holiday, he is still on holiday now, now they are making a mess of it here again.

Director: — Comrades, we are not in the market, I call you to order.

Then the proposal was put that the punishment of the Department of Material-Technical Supply should be kept to a maximum of ten percent, and not to punish its Deputy Chief at all.

Director: — Tell me, how is your conscience? What about the stocktaking? We have to do this sometime. Will Petrov [Chief of the Supply Department] work alone, or will you help him all the same? And work as agreed? So what are you proposing?
Head of OTK: — Can one ask a question?
— One can.

She repeats her earlier question:

— Why out of twelve carriages signed out by the OTK were only five carriages handed over?

The Director appeals to Ivanov, the Deputy Director for the Kukino site, who was in charge of the site in May.

— Anatolii Dmitrevich, please answer the question.
Ivanov: — Yes, I can. The carriages were not ready, they were not ready. I am also interested in the question: you had the right to stop production. But what right did you have to sign out 12 carriages with defective couplings?
Head of OTK: — It is very difficult to work with dishonourable people.
Ivanov: — I would have been able to turn out all 15 carriages, but the OPS knew what was going on, and they all had defective couplings.
Head of OTK: — This is a vile lie.

She is in tears, but continues to speak:

— I have no regrets about my pay, the thing is that the whole business is very unpleasant. I can even resign in favour of Anatolii Dmitrievich. But that is not the point. We are simply looking for a scapegoat and not for a reason. The reason is presented as something else: wanton practice, not the system. Everything rests on a personality and that personality is Petr Andreevich Popov. He is not at work and everything collapses. And as soon as he is not here they do not fulfil the plan, because there is no clear organisation of production. And now Anatolii Dmitrevich – a very dishonourable person – tries to pile it all on us. When we assumed responsibility and signed for 12 carriages, a total of five were handed over. We took on this responsibility, together with the Chief Technologist and Chief Engineer, but this was not the reason. Then he accuses me of having signed for them. Yes, because I understand and I spoke with Petr Andreevich about the fact that one cannot tear everything up all at once, because then we will not fulfil the plan at all. We need to get together again and think about how we will fulfil the plan in future, and not look for a scapegoat.

Director: — Is that your proposal?

Head of OTK: — I do not know. But I think that the question of the couplings has nothing to do with this investigation. And Ivanov is the only one who is at fault. At fault in the organisation of production. We must resolve the question of how we are going to fulfil the programme in future.

Then the Deputy Director for Economic Questions stood up and stated his opinion that nobody should be punished.

— I think that nobody should lose any pay. All the services worked in May as they had worked before, including the supply service. Everyone has been punished by the situation existing in the factory. There are imperfections in the situation itself which we must take into account. There has not been any wrecking. Maybe the service of the Chief Technologist and so on could have worked better. All the services mentioned in the order have already been punished by the situation existing in the factory.

I have spoken repeatedly about the fact that the existing regulations on the incentive system and the system of bonuses are inadequate because they do not take into consideration the particular features of each department and service. It is necessary to work out a differential approach to the different departments and services within the plant. But for this reason it is necessary to organise the whole system of accounting, for example for the Department of Material Supplies, and to calculate, how many parts were brought to the plant, how many were taken out and so on. But before such a system is organised it is absolutely useless to punish people, because this regulation has absolutely no connection with their labour efforts.

As regards the other departments, in accordance with the existing regulations we automatically punish people because the main workshops didn't fulfil the plan. But some departments, for example the book-keeping department, shouldn't suffer from this. If they had their own plan and they fulfilled it, they should not be punished. But the issue is the revision of the existing system. The new punishment doesn't correspond with the existing regulations. We cannot improve the regulations constantly by inventing such new orders. We should improve the whole system. The system of accounting first of all, because on that point the whole incentive system is based. That is for production.

And as to wrecking. Here it has turned out that there was a situation in which there were personalities, conflict situations, about which I did not even know [between OTK and production]. But we have already punished all the ITR for the existing situation [because they had already lost their bonuses for plan non-fulfilment M.K.]. But this order does not make any reference to the system and I think that this cannot go on month after month as a result of such an extraordinary situation.

One cannot put things right carrying on in this way all the time. It is necessary to improve the system. The system of accounting first of all, since the whole incentive system is based on that. This is my proposal and I am still more convinced of its rationality.

So my proposition is that the order should not be about cutting people's pay, but it should make maybe two or three specific points. For example, the Deputy Director for Production must prepare production, that means we must give precise dates for the perfection of the supply accounting, working out the normative bases. Concretely, not one programme is fulfilled. If he were made responsible for them regularly each month, then they would work more regularly.

Director: — Look, we have sacked one, two, three people in this service, and the situation does not change, the system is still there. The stocktaking has not been carried out. The order about carrying out a stocktaking has not been fulfilled, but nobody has been punished until this Order. So my opinion is that they have to be punished.

At this wider meeting management was divided about the question of punishment. Some of the members of management were for punishment, others for partial punishment, and a third group against any punishment, but for improving the whole system.

At the end of the meeting the question of punishment was put to the vote, with six of those present having a right to vote. There were four alternatives:

1. to punish corresponding to the proposals of the draft order, supported only by the Director.
2. to reduce the punishment for some individuals, supported by only one present.
3. to punish nobody, which got three votes.
4. to punish the Deputy Director for Production A.D. Ivanov, supported only by Ivanov himself.

Thus the majority took the decision to punish nobody. With this the meeting came to an end.

At the end of the meeting of management, the Director, who had tried to prevent me from attending such a 'scandalous' meeting, took me aside and said:

Marina Vyacheslavovna, now you have seen a little spectacle which I put on specially. I knew that my proposal would not carry, but I had to play it out.

So, in accordance with the existing regulations, all the engineering-technical staff lost their bonuses, but those shops in which the plan was fulfilled or slightly underfulfilled, received bonuses as follows:

	Plan	Fact	Bonus (%)
Popugai carriage assembly shop	15	15	16.34
Carriage repair shop at Kukino	19	5	none
Wheel shop	264	264	50
Wheel repair shop	205	182	50
Motor section	15	14	49.30
Electro-machine section	19	16	22.46
Bogie section Popugai and Kukino	15	14	none

In the most 'guilty' shop, because they had not fulfilled the plan and repaired only five carriages, there was no money to pay wages to the workers, so the shop chief went to the First Deputy Director and asked him for approximately 1.5 million roubles to pay the wages. He asked permission to pay a percentage for the carriages which were partly repaired, and as a result workers received 70 per cent of earnings for each carriage (15) which they had partly repaired. The average salary for the whole plant in May was 55 thousand roubles, the average salary in the carriage-repair workshop was 45 thousand roubles. The shop-chief earned 63 thousand roubles, but if we take into consideration the fact that he had in his hands a reserve fund, which is 3 per cent of the wage bill for the whole of the shop, he added 15 thousand roubles to his own salary, i.e. he had 78 thousand roubles. Thus, even if the bad organisation of production in the workshop was partly to blame for the failure to meet the plan, nevertheless the financial position of the shop-chief did not suffer.

WHAT HAS CHANGED IN THE WHOLE PLANT SINCE THE BREAKDOWN OF THE PLAN?

Nothing was changed. An Order was worked out which listed the duties of the main people responsible for the organisation of production, but this just duplicated their existing job descriptions, without any changes in the systems as a whole. The requests of the workers to improve the incentive system were ignored. The workers are still trying to improve the system, but without success. Nobody was punished.

From an interview with the shop chief which was conducted in August it was clear that nothing had changed at all:

> I asked them to punish the people responsible for the breakdown. The General Director put this question in the hands of the Board of Governors, but this proposal was rejected. Everybody wants to be very kind. Nobody was punished and nothing was changed. Now I again have nothing in the workshop. The heads were delivered only yesterday. Supply has gone to hell. If I were the Director, I would say: 'Lads, you worked like this, I propose this and this. I propose and insist that we punish those responsible. This is my responsibility. And as the person in authority, I order that this person and this person be punished' ... But now everything remains as it was in the past.

The General Director of the plant together with his First Deputy Director has invented a new structure for the enterprise. The new structure was worked out in great secret and only these two people were involved in it. As a result, several people who were directly involved in the breakdown were appointed to new and higher positions. The head of Material Supplies, in addition to his existing responsibilities, was offered a post as the head of a new small enterprise. Another person was appointed as head of carriage production. Just as in good old 'Communist' times, when a person fails to do a job at one level, the people at the top usually promote him. The same happened in our plant, when the person who was directly responsible for the breakdown of the programme was put in the new structure of the enterprise in a higher position and instead of control of only one part of the plant, is now responsible for two parts of the plant. This is the opinion of the one of the shop chiefs about this transformation:

> Now there is a restructuring going on. Ivanov has been put in charge of the whole of production. If it were up to me I would throw him out. But 'they' held him ... He is usually a very rare guest in the production area. It is difficult to catch him in the workshop, and nobody knows where he hangs out during the working day. He is zero in terms of production.

But there is a good reason why the General Director and First Deputy Director have kept this person. First, because he was quite flexible and quickly understood how he could benefit from the new conditions. He organised a small enterprise, which involved a restricted circle of people, including the General Director and First Deputy, who could get additional money for their own benefit.

Besides this, there are other explanations for such behaviour of the people at the top. From interviews with different people, I discovered that he has a relative who works as a guard within the enterprise. All materials and parts which are removed from the enterprise go through this person. So, he possesses all the information about the people who use their position for their own benefit. For example, the First Deputy Director built his own dacha (country home), and he needs to remove a lot of cheap material from the enterprise. In this circumstance, the same kind of relationships still exist – 'you do something for me – and I will do something for you'. That is why, because of his relative's information, Ivanov knows too much, and it is better to sustain a good relationship with him, because it is well known that if he dislikes somebody, he could make trouble.

The two Deputy Directors who offered some reasonably intelligent remedies were weakened and either some departments were taken away from them, or they were shifted to lower positions. They were simply left out of the new structure of the enterprise. One of them, who realised the game that was being played, said with bitterness:

> All the rules of the game are now constructed in a such way that it is possible to weaken me, but not for me to progress.

The main reason for this is the struggle for power of the General Director. He just wanted to weaken the potential pretenders to his post. With new conditions and with the transition to leasehold, the Director of the enterprise comes to possess a lot of power. He has much more power than, say, the metro authorities, and he doesn't want to lose this power under any circumstances, at least until he decides himself to give up his position and to move to a more profitable one.

The situation in the plant deteriorates day by day as debts mount. Like so much of Russian industry, the metro and its associated services is on the verge of collapse. But the General Director and some people very close to him are flourishing.

REFERENCES

Dyker, D., 'Planning and the Worker' in *The Soviet Worker*, Macmillan, London, 1981.

Tchetvernina, T., 'Labour incentives in alternative forms of production', in Guy Standing (ed.), *In Search of Flexibility: The New Soviet Labour Market*, ILO, Geneva, 1991.

9. Payment Systems and the Restructuring of Production Relations in Russia

Valentina Vedeneeva

The transition to a market economy in Russia is supposed to force enterprises to transform production relations by subjecting the enterprise to competitive pressure. The large enterprises which dominate the Russian economy are usually protected from the pressure of competition by their monopoly powers and political influence, but many small and medium sized enterprises have to innovate in order to survive. For this reason great hope has been lodged in the role of small and medium enterprises in the transition to capitalism.

Innovation involves the search for new markets, new investment opportunities, new products and new sources of supply, which has involved a considerable growth in the financial and commercial functions of enterprise management. But if enterprises are to compete in product markets in the longer term innovation also requires the reorganisation of production and the transformation of shop-floor relations in order to increase product quality and productivity.

The transformation of shop-floor relations in response to market pressures in turn requires the development of an effective system of penalties and rewards through which management can impose its authority on the shop-floor. Traditionally managerial authority was supposed to be imposed in the Soviet system by piece-rate systems of payment of wages and bonuses. Until the 1970s these systems were primarily individual, but from the late 1970s there was a rapid shift to collective piece-rates with the move to the brigade system.[1] However in practice there was a considerable gulf between the formal payment system and its practical implementation. In practice the system tended to be subverted by line managers who had to make substantial concessions to the workers under their command, individually and collectively, in order to retain their collaboration in the battle for the plan. In practice workers tended to receive the normal wage regardless of their individual productivity.

The outcome was that there was only a weak relationship between effort and reward. Managerial authority was maintained through an informal system of paternalistic bargaining in which there was a hierarchy of social groups, with individual incentives and penalties being provided on a personalised basis. This hierarchy provided a relatively stable structure through which to channel the effort to make the plan, but at the cost of any incentives for innovation.

The programme of perestroika was linked from the very beginning to proposals to improve production discipline and to replace the principles of 'levelling' by principles of 'social justice' in the system of wage payment, by which was meant increasing pay differentials in favour of skilled and technical workers, and directly linking effort to reward through individual incentives within economically rational payment systems. However such reforms were more easily proposed than implemented since they involved not simply a technical change in the payment system, but a fundamental change in the social organisation of production.[2]

In our experience there have until recently been few effective attempts to introduce new payment systems, and even now such attempts are confined to a relatively small number of the most 'dynamic' enterprises. The present case study relates to one such enterprise, Lenkon, which is a medium sized industrial enterprise producing simple industrial equipment, located in a large Russian city.

Lenkon was a pioneer of privatisation, which had broken away from a larger state enterprise to form a co-operative in 1989. By 1993 the labour force of almost 1,000 had been cut back to around 300, largely as a result of the fall in production linked to a decline in orders and the transfer of simpler production to a sister plant located in a rural area. Although enjoying an initial burst of prosperity as a pioneer, with the transition to a market economy in 1992 Lenkon faced increasingly stiff competition from lower wage producers elsewhere, while struggling to hold on to its labour force in the face of the higher wages paid by neighbouring enterprises. The management strategy in the face of this competition was to reorient production towards customised and medium series production, transferring mass production to the sister plant, and to attempt to achieve productivity gains by upgrading the labour force and improving incentives.

The introduction of a new payment system played an important part in this project. Piece-rates had long been identified as being inconsistent with the achievement of high standards of quality, and so the management decided to move to a system of time wages. However the new payment system was moulded not only by management's strategic ambitions, but also by more mundane constraints of the continuing shortage of skilled labour. In practice the shift to time wages was associated with a loss of managerial control, the new system was judged a disaster and was rapidly abandoned.

THE TRADITIONAL PAYMENT SYSTEM IN LENKON

Until the 1st October 1992 workers at LenKon were paid according to the traditional piece-rate system. Workers were allocated to one of six grades, defined according to centrally determined scales, depending on their qualifications. In practice, according to the present head of the Personnel Department, workers were overgraded in order to push up their earnings a bit. Every month each shop received a defined sum of money to be spent on wages which, as a rule, was the same every month (subject to the shop having fulfilled the plan). Formally the Labour Collective Council (STK) of the shop, a body elected from all the workers of the shop, was responsible for defining the level of earnings of the workers, while the brigade council met monthly and defined the Coefficient of Labour Participation (KTU) of each worker, which provided an index which determined his or her individual pay.[3]

In practice things worked rather differently: the KTU was generally worked out by the brigadier, and often 'it was not those who made the biggest contribution to production who received the highest pay'. The process of defining the level of earnings, according to one of the shop chiefs, was pretty unhealthy: the money was divided 'with rows', the question of pay was resolved 'with shouts, fights and blood'. Since differential payments gave rise to so much conflict within the shop and the brigade the tendency within the Soviet system was strongly towards wage equalisation. Wages could be supplemented with small additional bonuses paid out by the foremen.

The foremen were the tsars of the shops, because they had plenty of opportunities both to influence the size of the earnings of each worker – thanks to their having the Foreman's Fund at their disposal – and for abuses, particularly by means of artificially inflating the pay-roll, signing up 'dead souls' and so on.

The foreman also had considerable power to influence a worker's earnings through his or her control over the allocation of work. Although workers were in theory paid according to their grades, in practice the foreman paid little attention to gradings in the allocation of work, and workers were paid according to the norm for the job, whatever their individual grading. According to one of the brigadiers:

> The technologist or foreman gives the worker the blueprints and sketches and applies the norm. And whoever I give it to, will do the job. I do not look at his grade. If he does the work, he is paid for it. If someone is on the third grade and he does the work of a sixth grade worker he is paid more.

The size of the earnings of workers was also influenced by such factors as the introduction of new technology, the installation of new improved equipment, the improvement of the organisation of work, the rise in the volume of production (up to the spring of 1992), and an increase in the price of the product.

The different size of wage funds available to different shops meant that there were significant pay differences between shops, even for comparable work. The press-stamp section was traditionally considered the most 'prosperous', and was thought of as the 'core' shop in LenKon, together with the section which produced the most expensive units, those produced in medium runs.

PRIVATISATION AND WORKER SHAREOWNERSHIP

On 1ˢᵗ October 1990 LenKon became a 'people's shareholding enterprise'. However the payment system was essentially unchanged. Although the STKs remained until the end of 1991 they had lost their power, although formally they retained their function of distributing pay at the level of the shop. However the initial strategy of LenKon management was to harness the workers' energy not through the payment system, but through the new commitment born of the novelty of shareownership.

Unlike most co-operative and private enterprises LenKon workers did not receive high wages, indeed their pay was below that of comparable state enterprises, and this was a cause of some dissatisfaction.

However many of the workers felt that their situation as employees of Lenkon gave them greater 'security', and felt that their pay was 'more guaranteed'. 'In comparison with my acquaintances at other enterprises I feel more confident' – said one worker in the spring of 1992 – 'I have more confidence in tomorrow'. It seems that one of the factors in this confidence was the feeling, new to Russian workers, of one's own participation in the future of the enterprise, not in words but in deeds, a feeling derived from shareownership.

Initially all the employees of the factory, including workers, engineers, specialists and managers, had an equal opportunity to buy shares, and practically all the workers became shareowners. They could each buy up to fifty shares at privileged prices (they had to pay 200 roubles for shares of a nominal value of 1,000 roubles), besides which they could take credit from the factory (at first at 15 per cent a year, then, a year later, at 25 per cent, then at 40 per cent). The percent of dividends paid out at first was low, however the fact of ownership of shares had a large moral significance. 'Shares – this is the desire to make oneself safe', said a worker, 'for me it is important to feel secure'. In 1991 the dividends were increased and paid quarterly, amounting to more than 200 per cent for the year, which could amount to a significant bonus.

Since almost all the workers had shares, the fact of ownership of shares did not yet have a very significant influence on the distribution of income. The workers did not express any dissatisfaction that any of their fellow workers owned more shares, and friction between workers did not arise. The foremen claim that with the creation of the shareholding company the workers began to work better: in the opinion of one foreman the worker-shareholders 'worked more diligently'.

The initial euphoria of privatisation did not last for long, and a concentration of shareownership soon took place as many workers sold their shares. There were many reasons for this: barter became more active in 1991, and barter goods could be traded for shares. Goods in short supply, including domestic appliances, became more expensive, so people needed cash. Others could not pay off their credit from the factory, especially as the rate of interest on credit rose. Some people simply did not have enough money for drinking, and sold their shares to buy a few bottles.

At the same time the dividend was cut, and quarterly payments suspended, which meant, in a time of inflation, that the shares showed very little return. In the spring of 1992 the workers still held several hundred shares, with most of them having between 20 and 40 shares, while a few had up to a maximum of 80, but since then there has been a rapid concentration of shareownership.

Many workers are convinced that management has conducted a deliberate policy of forcing the workers to sell their shares. For example, one worker told us that the administration deliberately delayed increasing pay in the face of escalating inflation in the spring of 1992 in order to force the workers to get rid of their shares (although LenKon also had good reason to hold down wages in the face of a collapse in sales). A middle manager told us that at about the same time the administration offered the workers the opportunity to use their shares to buy a consignment of bartered consumer appliances.

By the spring of 1993 20 per cent of the shareholders held 80 per cent of the shares. Although a handful of workers were large shareholders, most of the shares were in the hands of middle and senior management. With this concentration of shareownership the level of dividend pay-outs was substantially increased again, to a rate of 250 per cent per quarter.' Since the majority of workers now only have a few shares, many of them argue that instead of a quarterly dividend payment, the management should pay out part of the profits due to the workers in the form of wages, monthly. At the meeting of shareholders in February 1993 they put forward such a proposal, but it was naturally rejected by the management of LenKon. These aspirations of the workers are also supported by some of the section chiefs, who consider it normal that the profits should go into a general fund for wages, 'in this way pay will be increased for everyone, then there will be no distinction between shareholders and non-shareholders'.

Privatisation has not been a failure — the LenKon workers retain a high degree of trust and confidence in their senior management. However the concentration of shareownership has eroded the impact of privatisation as an effective lever of restructuring, since the majority of workers no longer derive any benefits from increases in profitability, as divisions between shareowners and non-owners create a basis for potential conflict. With the weakening of the incentive of shareownership, management has turned its attention to the pay system.

THE INTRODUCTION OF TIME WAGES

Privatisation had already been associated with a widening of pay differentials even with the traditional piece-rate system, as pay was tied more closely to results, a move which was generally popular with the workers. For example, workers welcomed additional payment for working overtime or at weekends, in place of the old system in which they were blackmailed into doing such work without reward by the application of informal pressures.

In April 1992 the average earnings at LenKon amounted to between three and three and a half thousand roubles, with the difference between the minimum and the maximum workers' pay amounting to approximately one thousand roubles, a differential of about 30 per cent, which was greater than it had ever been before. 'My earnings depend on my work, the more that I do, the more I receive' said one of the workers in an interview. He even claimed that 'an interest in working better has emerged'. However any progress down this route was cut off by the collapse of production which faced LenKon as sales fell with the transition to a market economy from January 1992.

In May 1992 output was cut from 2.5 thousand to 1.5 thousand units a month, primarily as a result of the fall in demand, which management claimed was caused as much by the inability of customers to pay as by the increased prices for the products. The management tried everything they could think of in the attempt to maintain production. Thus, for example, a so-called 'formula' was announced to the workers, according to which everyone who secures an order for the factory receives 0.1 per cent of the total value of the order (once it is paid for!). Nevertheless the fall in production continued and the most highly skilled workers began leaving LenKon.

In this situation the immediate priority of management was to maintain a minimal level of employment and a sufficient level of wages to hold on to the workers who formed the 'backbone' of the labour force. Between 20 and 30 per cent of the employees of the enterprise were made redundant. These were primarily workers with a poor disciplinary record, working pensioners, unskilled workers, technicians and clerical workers, with a large proportion of those laid off being women. At the same time the working week was reduced to four days, while ways of increasing pay were worked out.

The problem with the existing payment system was that wages fell in line with the decline in production, and as wages fell the best workers were the first to leave. The only solution was to abandon the piece-rate system and shift to a system of time wages. As the shop chief said:

This was a necessary measure. If we had kept the system of piece-rates, it would have been necessary to cut not 30 per cent but 60 per cent of the labour force.

In September 1992 management increased pay to an average 9.5 thousand roubles (with a minimum of 3,000 and a maximum of 15–20,000).

TIME WAGES AND THE NEW PAYMENT SYSTEM

Although the basic reason for the shift to time wages was the urgent need to hold on to the core workers, the transition also fitted in with the new management production strategy, which was based on the transfer from mass production to small batch production, including custom production. This necessitated a much greater emphasis on quality, which was considered to be inconsistent with a piece-rate system in which payment depended only on output, with no incentive to meet quality standards. The essence of the new strategy, according to the Vice President for Economics, was 'to become leaders in a narrow field, in which we can be better than the others'. The initial belief was that time wages, with appropriate bonuses, would enable management to overcome the problem of quality.

The new system of time payment was introduced in the basic production sections from the 1st October 1992. Shop chiefs welcomed the innovation for making it possible to maintain the pay of workers who had had to be assigned to low grade work.

Many workers have been assigned to work which is not their normal job: tidying up the territory of the factory and shops. The important thing is that people should receive pay in order to work. But under the piece-rate system it would not turn out like that, since there is a price for every job. The workers would not receive as much as they receive under time payment.

The change to time wages was linked to a new system of grading and bonus payments which had potentially far-reaching implications. The aim was to assert managerial authority by imposing a formal rationalisation of the payments system, to overcome the social pressures to levelling and wage equalisation and the exercise of personal discretion which were characteristic of the traditional informal relations of the shop floor.

THE GRADING SYSTEM

The administration worked out a new internal tariff scale, which replaced the traditional six grades by five, with a base rate of 35 roubles per hour and coefficients defined, depending on the grade of the worker. The minimum coefficient (for Grade One auxiliary workers) was 0.6; the highest coefficient (for Grade Five instrumental fitters) was 1.93. The re-grading, in the words of a shop chief, had the aim 'of resolving the problem of payment in order to relate it more closely to the results of work'. However the process was somewhat ad hoc, and was not rigorously formalised. Each shop was assigned a quota of each grade, and grades were awarded to workers, within the limits of the quotas, by the collective decision of a group comprising the shop chief, foremen, brigadiers and some workers. However these grades were not entered into the workers' work books, which contain a permanent record of their work history.

The informal character of awarding grades made it possible to overcome various obstacles which arose at shop level, and so to subvert the supposed attempt to formalise the system from above. For example, it was officially forbidden for workers to 'skip' grades, but in practice such accelerated upgrading took place. Similarly, in one of the shops the quota of fifth grade workers was exhausted although two more workers had, according to their shop chief, a full right to the highest grade. These workers were officially assigned to the fourth grade, but on the basis of a verbal agreement with the shop chief they are paid as fifth grade workers, with the money coming from the Foreman's Fund, although with no guarantees but the shop chief's honour. This means that if a new shop chief were to arrive the situation would erupt into open conflict between these workers and the new shop chief.

BONUSES

In addition to their hourly wages the workers are paid bonuses which amount to a maximum of 30 per cent of the wage fund, comprising a bonus of up to 12.5 per cent for the quality of their work, 12.5 per cent for meeting the deadline for completing work, and 5 per cent for maintaining the 'culture of production' (keeping their work place in good condition, maintaining their tools and equipment, and so on).

The decision about the size of the bonus is taken by the shop chief, sometimes together with the foreman.

The workers' bonus payments are perceived as a distinctive 'stick', that is a means 'to keep them on a lead', to make them more dependent on management, since the shop chief has the right to reduce the size of bonus payments. The transition to time payment has had a major impact on the status of the foremen, since it has considerably reduced the scale and scope of their authority. 'The foreman is just one of the workers, who has definite powers which he must use for the benefit of the work', whereas the head of the shop or section in practice has acquired the full powers of an owner. However many possibilities for manipulating money remain. Thus, according to one of the foreman, 'we do not formally document the material incentives paid on top of the bonus'.

In addition to the regular bonuses which are paid from the wage fund, the Foreman's Fund provides the resources with which foremen can pay discretionary bonuses. The Foreman's Fund is made up of 50 per cent of sums accruing against hospital certificates and holiday pay, and in addition money not spent on wages if the plan has been fulfilled with a smaller number of workers. The money in the Foreman's Fund is dispersed in the traditional way.

> If a chap works with spirit, with initiative, interests himself in not wasting time, and in the results of his work, he receives an addition to his pay from the Foreman's Fund. In this way we encourage those who are willing to work if necessary in the evening or on Saturdays.

KLASSNOST

The most innovative feature of the new system of pay at LenKon is the introduction of 'klassnost'. This system was introduced as a 'means of evaluating the present and future service of an employee in the eyes of the shareholding company' and is awarded individually to workers and employees. When it was introduced in the autumn of 1992 a Class One employee received a bonus of 3,000 roubles, with 1,500 roubles awarded for Class Two. In order to receive Class Two it is necessary to have worked at LenKon for not less than two years (in practice it is three years), and for Class One not less than five years. 'In order to receive klassnost', considers the head of the Personnel Department, 'it is necessary to prove that you are worthy of it'. In a sense klassnost is a replacement for the former honorific awards to favoured workers, although the net of klassnost is spread more widely: approximately 50 per cent of the workers received klassnost. The award of klassnost was not a matter decided once and for all: workers may be either lowered a class, or deprived of klassnost altogether – for example for disciplinary violations or an unconscientious attitude to work.

Again the implementation of the system immediately involves the bending of the rules which tends to subvert its purpose. In the opinion of the head of personnel a highly qualified specialist can receive klassnost earlier than the date formally laid down – 'even a few months' after coming to work. Many workers believe that it is possible to get such favourable treatment, but only 'through patronage'. One of the shop chiefs confirmed this belief, considering that for a worker to be awarded klassnost early the shop chief himself would have to apply to the top management of LenKon on his or her behalf, so that everything depends on good will.

The impact of klassnost is also undermined by the traditional exercise of personal discretion at shop floor level. 'Every foreman, every brigadier, wants to have a lot of people with klassnost, so that the workers will be motivated'. Many old employees have not received klassnost as a result of a record of drunkenness or absenteeism. However as a foreman put it, 'they are not hurt' in their pay packets. In his words, 'there is a foreman's or shop fund – call it what you will. And if he shows himself to be a good worker, we give him a supplement'.

'There are comrades whom we have deprived of klassnost' says another foreman 'for disciplinary reasons, absenteeism, appearing to be drunk. We accept that he is a good specialist, but his discipline is bad, and we deprived him of the first class. And we divided this 3,000 roubles into two halves and gave it to two other comrades, and they then had second class and received 1.5 thousand. We still have candidates to receive klassnost, but they do not give us any more. But we do not offend them. We have a fund in the section – we spin, we extricate ourselves. What is it called? That is a commercial secret.'

THE WORKERS' RESPONSE

As far as the workers are concerned the main significance of the new payment system is the centralisation of managerial power, which reduces the ability of workers to influence their levels of pay, a feeling echoed by line managers who have lost some of their discretionary powers. For example, the new grading system means that pay is determined by the grade of the worker, not that of the job, so that workers assigned to higher grade work feel that they are underpaid.

The bonus system, which has shifted power from the brigade to the shop level, has led to widespread expressions of dissatisfaction with the decisions of the shop chief, workers regularly declaring his or her decisions to be unjust. This dissatisfaction has not yet led to open conflict, but it is widely voiced, and it appears in the expressed desire of workers to revive the system of STK and KTU, since they consider that they have the right to participate in the determination of wages on the level of their brigade and section.

Workers were equally dissatisfied with the system of klassnost. On the one hand, workers felt that the criteria for the award of klassnost were not sufficiently clear. On the other hand, they were unhappy with the differentiation between workers having and those not having klassnost, a distinction which many felt was artificial. This is not simply a matter of money, but also the management makes no secret of the fact that in the event of further cuts those without klassnost will be the first in line for the sack.

The introduction of klassnost is felt by many workers to be a violation of the principles of social justice, even to those who have klassnost. As a rule they only express their complaints to the head of section, who has no authority in the matter of klassnost, because these bonuses are not paid by the factory, but by the shareholding company, and so are a matter not for line management but for the Shareholders' Council and the Directors. Many workers demand the abolition of klassnost, with the money being divided among all the workers. However the management of LenKon attaches a great deal of significance to this institution.

'What has been the benefit of klassnost? For example, these people agree to work beyond the end of the shift, or to come in on their day off, without anything being said, without any objections and without additional pay' says the head of the Personnel Department. He argues that 'the introduction of klassnost has proved itself, although I would have called it something else: klassnost – this is an index of loyalty to the firm.'

The most important overt conflict created by the new payment system arose as a result of the destruction of the old status hierarchy as the introduction of time wages led to a reduction in the differentiation of pay between workers in different production sections. The workers in the most highly paid section lost their privileges with the transfer to time wages, and reacted forcefully to what they considered to represent a halving of their existing wage level, from the equivalent of a basic hourly pay of 70 roubles to the hourly rate of 35 roubles proposed by the administration.

The workers wrote a collective letter to the administration of the factory, in which they demanded an increase in the minimum hourly rate to 70 roubles. After the management of LenKon refused to meet the workers' demand, they then threatened to strike. However the workers did not go further to implement their threat of a strike. On the one hand, they risked dismissal since the Constitution of the share-holding company includes a clause declaring that workers do not have the right to strike. On the other hand, the administration made conciliatory gestures, sending a representative to the meeting of the workers of the section and conceding an increase in the hourly rate to 40 roubles. It was our impression from conversations with the workers involved that at present they were not ready to insist on the maximum fulfilment of their demands. The important thing for them was to see that the management was ready to take steps – even if small ones – to meet them. The concession of the administration had more of a moral significance, but the workers evaluated it very positively: 'we expressed our opinion, and although it was only valued at five roubles, at least it was heard' one of the participants in the conflict noted.

THE FAILURE OF THE REFORM AND THE RETURN OF PIECE-RATES

The replacement of the piece-rate system by time wages was successful in raising wages and retaining labour in the face of the fall in production and short-time working. However in terms of the wider objectives of the management it proved counter-productive, not so much because of the overt conflict to which it gave rise, but because of the failure of the new system of pay to improve production discipline, either in terms of productivity or in terms of quality.

Workers agree that the immediate result of the abolition of piece-rates was that they lost any interest in the results of their work, and sharply reduced the intensity of their labour. 'Now we are on time wages, what's the hurry?' say the workers. With production down this did not matter so much, until there was a need to accelerate the pace to meet an order. As a shop chief put it:

When a person works badly, he gets as much as if he works well. But then a rush job arrives and it is necessary to work more intensively, a person now has to hurry, which was not necessary earlier. But now they have got used to working quietly.

The reduction of the intensity of work then disrupted the rhythm of production, leading to friction between the different production sections – which are links in one technological chain, exacerbating conflict between shops and sections.

As one of the foremen put it:

Time wages drove us mad, it was a bit of a mistake ... the workers arrived, knocked out eight hours work to get their basic pay, but most of them were not interested in the bonuses. In the past if a worker earned a rouble, he received a rouble. But now he has made a rouble, but earns about 200 roubles for the shift. Sometimes he can sit down, just sit around. And the work – it is really knocked out. If the foreman will stand for it, they will do anything.

According to the foreman about 50 per cent of the workers in the section are like this. Shop and section chiefs also felt that time wages removed their incentive to search for additional orders, which could provide work for their sections.

CONCLUSION

The failure of the attempted wage reform at Lenkon reiterates the experience of previous such reforms within the Soviet system, which have attempted to devise 'technical' solutions for what is in fact a more fundamental problem, that of imposing an effective managerial authority on the shop floor. Within the Soviet system managerial power was exercised through a system of 'authoritarian paternalism', based on extensive informal bargaining. If workers failed to meet their plan targets, they could face serious sanctions, but within those limits they enjoyed a very considerable negative power on the shop floor.

The collapse of the Soviet system has by no means removed this perennial problem. Indeed it has only exacerbated it by weakening or removing the repressive apparatuses which provided external guarantees of managerial authority, without providing any but the most privileged enterprises with the means to provide workers with positive incentives. As far as workers are concerned the transition to the market economy involves more than trading one form of subordination for another. Workers do not, in general, aspire to take control of production themselves, nor, in general, do they resent successful managers being well paid, but they do expect to be rewarded for their own efforts, and they expect their managers so to organise supplies, production and sales as to ensure that the resources are available to pay them properly. Lenkon introduced its reform in the face of falling production and sales, so that it was not in a position to pay sufficiently large bonuses to make it worth the workers' while putting in more than the minimal effort. This meant that line managers had to continue to try to use the traditional methods of inducing workers to work, while removing many of the means which they had formerly had at their disposal. The problem with the reform at LenKon, as with that of the Soviet system as a whole, was that it undermined the old system, without providing an effective new system to put in its place.

The failure of the reform, and its subversion by line managers, should have made clear to senior management the extent to which the effective conduct of production depended on the ability of line managers, from shop chief to foreman, to use their discretionary powers to persuade workers to meet the monthly plan. Although the traditional system of piece-rates appeared to be based on positive incentives to work, in practice it was based on a whole array of positive and negative incentives, backed up by the plan as the target which had to be achieved without question. The reform failed primarily because, on the one hand, it removed the unquestioned adherence to the plan, and on the other hand, because it reduced the discretionary armoury in the hands of line managers.

However the management of LenKon persisted in the attempt to find a solution to the problems of production discipline through an appropriate formally rational payment system. In February 1993, in the wake of the problems raised by the shift to time wages, a new sector for labour and wages was created within the Personnel Department, headed by a specialist brought in for the purpose of developing yet another payment system.

The administration now claims that the system of time wages was only a temporary solution to the specific problem of retaining labour, a tactical step which had led to serious negative results, in the form both of substantial over-expenditure on wages, and of a reduction in the incentive to work. In the view of the new wages specialist the previous problems at LenKon had not been piece-rate payment as such, but that there had been no proper evaluation of norms and appropriate levels of payment, a fault which he considers to be the responsibility of the management of the shareholding company. As a result he has now begun a systematic job evaluation to provide the basis for a new piece-rate system.

However the new job evaluation is not as impressive in practice as it sounds. Every worker is required to fill in a time-sheet, itemising the work done on every shift, which is then countersigned by the shop chief. Since production remains at a low level, and the intensity of work remains very uneven, while there is no monitoring of the accuracy with which sheets are completed, this can hardly be considered to be a serious exercise in work study!

On our last visit to LenKon hundreds of completed time-sheets were accumulating in piles, while nobody had any idea what to do with them. Production was being maintained on a hand-to-mouth basis, with increasingly gloomy long-term prospects. LenKon has not overcome its basic problem of finding new markets, and the senior management is looking to a foreign buyer in the hope of salvation. It is highly unlikely that any foreign buyer will be interested in Lenkon's production facilities, all the indications being that it will be bought for its site, to provide warehousing and office facilities.

NOTES

1   On the brigade system see Darrell Slider, 'The Brigade System in Soviet Industry', *Soviet Studies*, 39, 3, 1987, and Leonid Gordon, Galina Monousova and Alla Nazimova, 'Novye formy brigadnoi organizatsii truda', *Rabochii klass i sovremennyi mir*, 1, 1987.

2   For a radical critique of 'socialist' wages policy see Leonid Gordon, 'Sotsial'naia politika v sfere oplaty truda', *Sotsiologicheskie issledovaniya*, 4, 1987. See Don Filtzer, *Soviet Workers and De-Stalinisation*, Cambridge: Cambridge University Press, 1992, Chapter Four on the failure of the Khrushchev wage reform; Bob Arnot, *Controlling Soviet Labour*, Harmondsworth: Macmillan, 1988 for a discussion of the failure of Brezhnevite experiments in this direction; and Don Filtzer, *Soviet Workers and Perestroika*, Cambridge: Cambridge University Press, 1994, Chapter Two on the failure of the 1986 wage reform.

3   On the traditional payment system see Alastair McAuley, *Economic Welfare in the Soviet Union*, Madison, University of Wisconsin Press, 1979.

4   This is calculated on the nominal valuation of the shares, so is not as large as it sounds when inflation is taken into account. However it is very large compared to the rate earned by workers on their savings, and can still amount to a lot of money for those with large shareholdings.

Index